by Bill Chiaravalle and Barbara Findlay Schenck

BICENTENNIAL
1807
WILEY
2007
BICENTENNIAL

Wiley Publishing, Inc.

Branding For Dummies®

Published by
Wiley Publishing, Inc.
111 River St.
Hoboken, NJ 07030-5774
www.wiley.com

Copyright © 2007 by Wiley Publishing, Inc., Indianapolis, Indiana

Published simultaneously in Canada

For general information on our other products and services, please contact our Customer Care Department within the U.S. at 877-762-2974, outside the U.S. at 317-572-3993, or fax 317-572-4002.

For technical support, please visit www.wiley.com/techsupport.

Wiley also publishes its books in a variety of electronic formats. Some content that appears in print may not be available in electronic books.

Library of Congress Control Number: 2006934821

ISBN-13: 978-0-471-77159-3

ISBN-10: 0-471-77159-7

Manufactured in the United States of America

10 9 8 7 6 5 4

1O/RV/QS/QX/IN

WILEY

About the Authors

Bill Chiaravalle knows brands and how to build them. His experience includes a decade-long stint as Design and Creative Director at the world-renowned brand strategy and design firm Landor Associates, where he worked on the branding programs for American Express, AT&T, Bacardi, Bell Atlantic, Danone, Delta Airlines, FedEx, Gatorade, Hyatt, IBM, Microsoft, NEC, P&G, Smucker's, Sunkist, Sutter Home, and many others.

Since founding his own firm, Brand Navigation, in 1999, Bill's role as Principal and Creative Director has been to assist clients large and small in the development of strategic positions and creative visions and expressions for their brands. A short list of clients Brand Navigation has worked with include Microsoft, Intel, *The Miami Herald,* Thomas Nelson Publishers, Krusteaz, Canterbury Cuisine, John C. Maxwell, and Bubbies of San Francisco.

Bill was born in San Francisco and received his training at the Academy of Art University in San Francisco. He has been honored with numerous branding, design, and industry awards. Away from brands, he enjoys spending time with his wife and four children, biking, swimming, fine dining, and jazz music. He lives in Sisters, Oregon. To visit his company online, go to www.brand navigation.com.

Barbara Findlay Schenck knows marketing and why brands are so important. She's a business strategist with more than 20 years of experience helping companies and organizations shape their brands, messages, and marketing plans. She's worked internationally in community development, served as a college admissions director and writing instructor in Hawaii, and cofounded an advertising agency in Oregon that ranked as one of the Northwest's Top 15 at the time of its sale in 1995. Since then, she's written *Small Business Marketing For Dummies, Business Plans Kit For Dummies,* 2nd Edition, and numerous branding and marketing courses, presentations, and plans.

When not thinking about marketing issues, she's likely traveling, golfing, enjoying the Northwest with her husband, Peter, or trekking to the San Francisco area to visit their son, Matthew. You can contact her via e-mail at BFSchenck@aol.com.

Authors' Acknowledgments

Where to begin?

We start by giving heartfelt thanks to the long list of businesses and organizations that have entrusted their brands and business hopes to each of us over the years. Here's to your continued success!

We also give huge thanks to Wiley Publishing, Inc. for allowing us this once-in-a-lifetime opportunity to explain branding in the famous format of the world's most famous book brand. Acquisitions Director Joyce Pepple, Acquisitions Editor Mike Lewis, Senior Project Editor Chrissy Guthrie, and Senior Copy Editor Elizabeth Rea made the making of this book a pure pleasure and won our highest regard and appreciation.

Special thanks also go to Bill Berenson, owner of Brand Architects, who applied his widely regarded expertise and wisdom during the technical review of this book. We're fortunate for his talent.

Additionally, we each have personal lists of thanks.

From Bill: In addition to developing brands for over 20 years, I've been involved in the design of more than a thousand book covers in my lifetime. But I'd never considered writing one — until Barbara Schenck approached me. Thank you Barbara and Peter, you have been kind advocates for almost a decade. Thanks also to my staff at Brand Navigation: Ben, DeAnna, Russ, Steve, Terra, Mark, and Brittany. Without you, designing brands wouldn't be near as much fun.

Special thanks to my children, Heidi, Wil, Michael, and Laura, who love me regardless of my obsession with brands.

And, most of all, to my beautiful wife, who is not only my business partner but my friend and the love of my life. You complete me.

From Barbara: Deep thanks to Bill for agreeing to coauthor this book and for adding so significantly to its value. And immeasurable gratitude to those who make all the joys and successes in my life possible: My husband, Peter, my son, Matthew, my three sisters, and my parents.

Finally, thanks to you for selecting this book as your brand building guide. As you enter or travel farther into the world of branding, please take all our best wishes with you!

Publisher's Acknowledgments

We're proud of this book; please send us your comments through our Dummies online registration form located at www.dummies.com/register/.

Some of the people who helped bring this book to market include the following:

Acquisitions, Editorial, and Media Development

Senior Project Editor: Christina Guthrie

Acquisitions Editor: Michael Lewis

Senior Copy Editor: Elizabeth Rea

Technical Editor: William Berenson

Editorial Manager: Christine Meloy Beck

Media Development Manager: Laura VanWinkle

Editorial Assistants: Erin Calligan, David Lutton

Cartoons: Rich Tennant (www.the5thwave.com)

Composition Services

Project Coordinator: Erin Smith

Layout and Graphics: Lavonne Cook, Brooke Graczyk, Denny Hager, Joyce Haughey, Stephanie D. Jumper, Barbara Moore, Heather Ryan

Anniversary Logo Design: Richard Pacifico

Proofreaders: Melanie Hoffman, Jessica Kramer, Nancy L. Reinhardt

Indexer: Galen Schroeder

Special Help

Marc Mikulich, Rev Mengle, Kirk Bateman

Publishing and Editorial for Consumer Dummies

Diane Graves Steele, Vice President and Publisher, Consumer Dummies

Joyce Pepple, Acquisitions Director, Consumer Dummies

Kristin A. Cocks, Product Development Director, Consumer Dummies

Michael Spring, Vice President and Publisher, Travel

Kelly Regan, Editorial Director, Travel

Publishing for Technology Dummies

Andy Cummings, Vice President and Publisher, Dummies Technology/General User

Composition Services

Gerry Fahey, Vice President of Production Services

Debbie Stailey, Director of Composition Services

Contents at a Glance

Table of Contents

Introduction

· ·

Congratulations! You're about to take control of your brand.

If you're thinking, "I don't even have a brand," then this book is definitely for you. It's also for anyone who wants to build a better brand, repair a broken brand, extend the power of a brand, or start from scratch and create a brand-new brand.

Branding has always been a red-hot topic (pardon the pun, pardner), but that's even more the case in today's competitive business world. When consumers hear your organization's name, memories pop up that influence what they think and how they buy. Those memories are the basis of your brand. If you have a name people know, then you have the basis of a brand. This book is all about making sure that the brand you have is the brand you want.

Branding is the single biggest buzzword in marketing today for good reason: Brands pave the way for marketing success. Count on this book to demystify the topic and lead you to a better, stronger brand so that you can compete successfully in the big, branded world around you.

About This Book

When the publisher of one of the world's most recognized book brands asked us to write a yellow-and-black book on branding, we knew we were looking at a tall order and some pretty sky-high standards to live up to. We gulped. And then we jumped at the chance.

Branding For Dummies is the first jargon-free, plain English, do-it-yourself guide to branding we've seen, and we've looked high and low. True to the *For Dummies* philosophy, it deciphers the foreign language of branding with a lighthearted tone and easy-in, easy-out facts and tips. And it does all that with a dose of humor, lots of examples, and a promise to enlighten anyone interested in the topic without confounding or confusing the conversation.

Here's our pledge: You don't need an MBA or even a marketing or business background to make sense of this book. All you need is an interest in the topic of branding — a curiosity about what it is and how to do it. We take care of the rest.

You probably already know that branding works. This book shows you how to make it work for you.

Conventions Used in This Book

This book includes a few style conventions aimed at keeping the information easy to read and understand. First, a few words on the language we use:

- When we say *brand,* we aren't talking about side-of-the-steer ranch brands. We're talking about brands for businesses, organizations, concepts, campaigns, and even individuals.

- Throughout this book we talk about *brands* and *branding programs.* To synchronize our thinking with yours from the get-go, *brand* refers to the set of characteristics that arise in a customer's mind when that person hears your name or sees your logo; *branding program* refers to the process you follow to develop a clear brand image in your customer's mind. In other words, the brand is the destination you aim to arrive at; the branding program is how you get there.

- To describe those who comprise your target market, we use the words "customer" and "consumer." They're the people you're seeking to influence with your branding program. For some readers, the audience is comprised of retail clients. Others target online visitors, business clients, wholesalers, or a combination of buyers. Those working to brand nonprofit organizations or fundraising or political campaigns may target voters, donors, subscribers, or members. Entrepreneurs gearing up to start new businesses are probably seeking to build brands in the minds of cutting-edge employees, venture capitalists, and early-adopter customers. In this book, we use the words "customer" and "consumer" to cover all bases.

To keep this book easy to scan and read (and to meet *For Dummies* branding standards!), we incorporate the following style conventions:

- Anytime we introduce a new term you need to know, we *italicize* it.

- We **bold** key words and phrases in bulleted lists as well as the action parts of numbered lists.

- Web site addresses appear in `monofont` to help you isolate the URL quickly and easily from surrounding text.

What You're Not to Read

If you have the time and inclination, by all means, read every precious word in this book. We'd love nothing more!

However, if you're a "Just the facts, ma'am" kind of person, you can skip the gray-shaded sidebars, which contain information that complements but isn't essential to your understanding of the surrounding chapter content. The sidebars are full of interesting approaches and examples that can help round out your branding knowledge, but you can get by just fine without them.

Foolish Assumptions

First things first: Anyone smart enough to want to know more about branding is no fool. Thanks for entrusting us with your interest. We've done back flips to make sure that this book includes everything you need to know about branding, all presented in plain English with easy-to-understand translations for every technical term.

In writing this book, we made a few assumptions about you and the many others we hope will use this book.

✔ You're not a marketing professional — or if you are, you're looking for a branding refresher course that starts at ground level and builds topic knowledge from there. To make this book useful to every reader, we gear our explanations and advice to those who are charting new territory by entering the branding arena.

✔ You're interested in building or strengthening a brand — for your company, for a nonprofit organization, for your new business, for a campaign (fundraising, political, social, you name it . . .), or for yourself by making your name into a local personality or a small-scale celebrity. Regardless of your branding objective, we're guessing that you're not expecting to become the next Nike or Apple, but we think it's a safe bet that you'd like to acquire some of their branding strength. Who wouldn't!

✔ You're willing to invest effort to achieve the returns that result from a good branding program. To help, we include worksheets, charts, and sets of how-to instructions to guide the research, planning, positioning, design, implementation, and management involved in fueling your success with the power of a great brand.

How This Book Is Organized

Each of the six parts of this book deals with a different phase of the branding process: Getting familiar with the language and lay of the land, building your brand from the ground up, launching your brand, putting your brand to work, protecting your brand, and managing your brand with a little advice.

Part I: Everything You Ever Wanted to Know About Branding

Building a brand is a lot like building a house. You need to begin with a strong foundation, and that's what Part I delivers. Chapter 1 provides an overview of how brands work and what it takes to build one. With Chapter 2, you move into branding action, figuring out what kind of brand you want to build, how your brand fits within your organization, when to start branding (the short answer is, right now!), and what steps to follow. Chapter 3 helps you launch your branding program by setting your branding goals, defining your brand identity, earmarking the necessary funds, and assembling the team that will turn your brand idea into reality.

Part II: Building a Brand, Step-by-Step

This part is your brand construction guide. It starts with Chapter 4, which walks with you through the essential research phase of finding out who buys your product and why, what competition you're up against, how your offering is different and better, and what distinguishing characteristics you should be branding. Chapter 5 capitalizes on your research by helping you fill a unique position in the marketplace — and in your consumers' minds. In Chapter 6, you get the formula for creating your brand definition and business promise, and Chapter 7 helps you brainstorm, choose, adopt, and protect the name for your brand. Finally, we wind this part up with an all-important chapter (Chapter 8) that features Bill's proven advice on developing your logo and tagline — the face and slogan for your brand.

Part III: Launching Your New Brand

This part is all about putting your branding strategy to work. Here's where you get our best consulting advice. In Chapter 9, we help you craft, test, and launch your brand marketing plan. Chapter 10 is all about spreading your brand message through a public relations program, and Chapter 11 fuels your program with ads that work, packaging that competes, and promotions that drive results. Finally, Chapter 12 helps you move your brand online, with tips on everything from building your Web site, integrating your image online and offline, driving traffic to your site, and creating online relationships through permission mailings and the marketing muscle of blogs and podcasts.

Part IV: The Care and Feeding of Your Brand

This part helps you reap the value of your brand. Chapter 13 tells you how to build brand support from the inside-out, first by becoming your brand's key evangelist and then by creating a team of brand champions who take your brand story on the road to business partners and customers. Chapter 14 offers the formula for keeping your brand true to its purpose and promise. Chapter 15 helps you put a price on your brand and then leverage that value through brand equity protection and development. Chapter 16 is a must-read for anyone considering the opportunities (and seeking to avoid the land mines) of subbranding, brand extensions, and brand partnerships. Chapter 17 winds this part up with advice on how to monitor the strength of your brand, how to fix a broken brand, and how to manage the brand revitalization or rebranding process.

Part V: Protecting Your Brand

This part contains only two chapters, but you can't afford to skip either one. Chapter 18 is all about protecting the legal right to your brand. Chapter 19 is all about defending your brand from attacks, whether from innocent, zealous designers who want to put their own marks on your image, from managers with lofty but misguided ideas about brand-tainting "opportunities," or from natural or other disasters that shake the foundation of your brand and your business.

Part VI: The Part of Tens

This final part sends you off with three ten-part lists of advice. Chapter 20 features ten laws of branding, Chapter 21 helps you avoid ten big branding mistakes, and Chapter 22 presents snapshots of ten of the world's most valuable brands.

And don't miss the Appendix, which lists great branding resources to turn to for additional information.

Icons Used in This Book

This book wouldn't live up to the *For Dummies* promise without the symbols that sit in the outer margin alerting you to valuable information and advice. Watch for these icons:

The bull's-eye marks tried-and-true approaches that will save you time, money, and trouble as build your branding program.

It's one thing to read advice and steps to follow. It's a whole other thing to read a true story of how an actual business tackled an issue topic successfully. This icon flags great branding examples and lessons we've learned from firsthand experience.

When there's a danger to avoid or just a bad idea to steer clear of, this icon sits in the margin like a flashing yellow light.

This icon points out branding's golden rules. Watch for them throughout the book.

Where to Go from Here

True to the *For Dummies* format, you can start this book on any page. Every portion of the book is a self-standing component, which means that you don't have to read sequentially from cover-to-cover to make sense of the content.

If you're new to the field of branding, Chapter 1 is a great place to start; you get a good overview of the contents of the entire book as well as a crash-course on the whole topic, language, and process of branding. If you're in a hurry because you're facing a crucial branding issue or wrestling with a branding problem, turn to the table of contents or index to guide you straight to the advice you need. If you already have a branding program but want to polish the luster of your brand or even do some rapid brand repair, skip to Part IV.

In other words, use this book from start-to-finish or cherry-pick the contents. So long as you end up with a clear brand identity that you project consistently in your market, your approach will have worked. So turn the page — get started!

Part I
Everything You Ever Wanted to Know About Branding

The 5th Wave   By Rich Tennant

In this part . . .

If all the talk in the business world about branding leaves you feeling like you're tuned in to some very foreign language, the chapters in this part will serve as a welcome translation guide. They present clear-cut definitions for all the terms that arise in branding conversations, and they take a look at why brands are so powerful, when and how to create a brand, what it takes to manage and protect a brand, and how to incorporate branding into your business strategy.

If you're in business, branding is a key to your marketing success. This part gets you headed in the right direction.

Chapter 1

Branding ABCs

Maybe you're launching a new company or a new product, and you want to establish a strong brand from the get-go. Or maybe you've been in business for a while, and you're getting ready to do some brand repair, brand extensions, or rebranding.

Perhaps you've just joined the marketing team for an established business, and you want to come up to speed — in a hurry — on the whole topic of branding and how to do it best. Or, you may be among the many marketers who aren't quite sure whether or not you even *have* a brand, but you're pretty sure you need one, and you want to know which steps to take in order to end up with the brand you set out to build.

No matter your starting point, if branding action is on your agenda, this chapter gets you going in the right direction. It provides an overview of the reasons that brands matter, why you need one, and how building a brand delivers value that far exceeds the time and effort you invest.

What Are Brands, Anyway?

Brands are promises that consumers believe in. Chapter 2 provides a complete definition of brands and branding, but if you remember nothing more than this three-word description — *brands are promises* — you're well on your way to branding success.

As you venture into the world of branding, keep these truths in mind:

✔ **You establish your brand by building trust in a one-of-a-kind promise about who you are, what you stand for, and what unique and meaningful benefits you deliver.**

✔ **You build your brand by living up to your promise every single time people come into contact with your name, your message, or your business.** It makes no difference whether that contact comes through advertising, publicity, word of mouth, the buying experience, customer service, billings, returns, or ongoing communication.

✔ **You strengthen your brand by constantly reinforcing your brand promise.** If encounters with your brand are inconsistent or not in line with what people expected they could count on, you essentially break your promise, breaking your brand and risking your reputation and business as a result.

Building brands takes focus, passion, persistence, and diligence. Plus brand building requires effort and money. The payoff, and it's a big one, is that strong brands build business and equity for their owners. The following sections shed light on what brands do and why they're such a big deal.

What brands do

Brands create consumer trust and emotional attachments. As a result, they foster relationships between consumers and products that withstand pricing wars, transcend offers from new competitors, and even overcome rare lapses in product or service excellence.

Great brands aren't just known and trusted. They're loved.

For examples of brands that enjoy strong bonds with customers, the next time you're stuck in traffic, look at the logos posted in the windows of the cars around you. Each time you see a logo decal, try to think of that brand's chief competitor. Then ask yourself "What's the chance that a buyer of the competing brand would 'wear' the brand's logo with such pride?" Only brands that strike deep emotional chords with customers make their way into hearts, minds, and car windows! Chapters 13 and 14 provide a playbook on how to develop a contingent of brand enthusiasts inside and outside your organization.

As you develop your brand and it gains strength and loyalty in your market area, look forward to reaping the following benefits.

Perception is everything

Many people think that the logo is the brand, but, in fact, the logo is just one representation of the brand. Your brand isn't how you look or what you say or even what you sell. Your brand is what people believe you stand for. For example:

✔ Starbucks sells coffee. It stands for daily inspiration.

✔ Apple sells computers. It stands for thinking differently.

✔ Disney sells animated and amusement park family entertainment. It stands for making dreams come true.

Your brand lives in consumer minds, so branding is the process of developing consumer beliefs and perceptions that are accurate and in alignment with what you want your brand to be.

Brands make selling easier

Brands are a big business today because they make selling easier in person and online. People prefer to buy from companies they feel they know and can trust, and brands put forth that assurance.

Whether you're selling products to consumers, investment opportunities to stockholders, job opportunities to applicants, or ideas to constituents, a brand paves the way for success by establishing awareness of your unique and meaningful promise before you ever present your sales proposition.

When people are aware of your brand, they're aware of the positive characteristics you stand for. Long before they get ready to make a purchase, they feel they know who you are and what unique value they can count on you to deliver. As a result, when it comes time to make a sale, brand owners can concentrate on the wants and needs of the consumer rather than take up valuable consumer time trying to explain themselves and their unique attributes.

Without a brand, you have to build a case for why you deserve the consumer's business every single time you get ready to make a sale. While brand owners are closing the deal, those without strong brands are still introducing themselves.

Imagine you're setting out to buy a new laptop computer and you see one emblazoned with a known logo — the face of a known brand. It's likely that your next step is to dive into a discussion with the salesperson of how much memory the particular model you're viewing contains, how the machine can be customized to your needs, what software is included, and other details that will move you to the purchase decision. On the other hand, if you see a no-name model — even at a dramatically lower price — you're likely to first try to assess the quality of the manufacturer. You may ask the salesperson where the computer was made, how long the manufacturer's been in business, whether the manufacturer is reliable, whether other customers have been satisfied, and many other mind-calming questions about consumer satisfaction levels, warranties, and return programs that you wouldn't raise when dealing with the known entity of an established brand.

Selling a no-name item takes time and patience. It's a costly route to a sale in a retail setting, and it's nearly impossible online, where there's no one standing by to offer explanations, inspire confidence, counter resistance, or break down barriers for your consumers.

Brands trump commodities

In the marketplace, you have either a one-of-a-kind brand or a one-is-as-good-as-any-other commodity. When it comes to creating a marketing success story, there's no question that brands fare better because

- ✔ **Brands are products defined by and chosen for their unique distinguishing attributes.** People buy brands because they relate to and trust their distinctions and promises. Consumers are willing to spend extra time and money in order to obtain the brands they believe in.

- ✔ **Commodities are products that are easy to substitute and hard to differentiate.** Commodities are purchased simply because they serve a purpose. Oil, coffee beans, wheat flour, and milk are all commodities. Consumers buy commodities because they meet minimum standards and are available when and where they're needed and at the lowest price.

Brands build equity

Brands that are preferred and valued by consumers deliver a long list of business benefits that translate to higher sales, higher profit margins, and higher owner value. Consider these brand advantages as proof:

- ✔ Consumers are willing to pay more to buy brands because they believe that the brands deliver outstanding and desirable benefits.

- ✔ Consumers stay loyal to brands, buying them more often, in greater volume, and without the need for promotional incentives.

- ✔ Retailers provide brands greater store visibility because they know that brands drive sales and result in higher store revenues.

- ✔ Brand owners don't need to launch new offerings from scratch. They can grow their businesses by leveraging their brands into product and line extensions.

✔ Brand owners find it easier to attract and retain good employees because applicants believe in the quality of the workplace based on advance knowledge of the caliber of the brand.

✔ Brand owners run more efficient operations because they align all decisions with the mission, vision, and values that underpin the brand promise.

✔ Brand owners benefit from increased market share, increased investor support, and increased company value.

Why brands are a big deal

The list of reasons the word "branding" arises so often in today's business conversations is long and growing. With more new businesses and products than ever before, and with a competitive arena that — thanks to the Internet — now stretches all the way around the world, brands are more necessary than they've ever been before. Here are a few of the reasons why:

✔ **Brands unlock profitability.** Today's marketplace is full of more products than ever before, and, overwhelmed by the selection, people choose and pay premium prices only for products they've heard of, trust, and believe deliver higher value than the others. If consumers think all products in a category are virtually the same and no offering is better or distinctly different from the others, they simply grab whichever one is available at the lowest price. That's a profit-squeezing reality that brand marketers gratefully avoid.

✔ **Brands prompt consumer selection.** For the first time in shopping history, consumers can shop and buy without any geographic limitation. The Internet and other at-home shopping options allow far-reaching access to any product, anywhere. With a few clicks or keystrokes, consumers find and select products with names they know and promises they trust. In this boundless marketplace, brands rule and no-name products barely survive.

✔ **Brands build name awareness.** For good reason, new businesses and products increasingly go by invented names instead of by known words. For one thing, more than three million U.S. trademarks are already registered, so any marketer who wants to protect a new name practically needs to create a never-before seen word in order to succeed. For another, 99 percent of all words in the English dictionary are already reserved as Internet addresses and are therefore unavailable to new marketers. As a result, most new offerings are launched under invented names, and invented names require strong and diligent branding in order to achieve consumer awareness, recall, and meaning. (Chapter 7 is full of advice for naming your brand.)

✓ **Brands increase the odds of business survival.** New businesses and new products are being launched at an unprecedented pace. According to the UPC Database, nearly 100,000 new bar-coded products were introduced in 2005 alone. Only those that ride into the market on the strength of an established brand or those that are capable of building a brand name in a hurry can seize consumer awareness, understanding, and preference fast enough to survive.

Brands have been around for centuries, as the sidebar "The red-hot history of branding" explains. But they've never been more important — or more essential to business success — than they are today.

Seeing the Big Branding Picture

Your brand is an image that makes its way into consumers' minds to influence how they think and buy. It's based on the promise people believe about you and the reputation they link with your name as the result of all the times and ways they've come into contact with you, your name, your logo, or any aspect of your brand.

The red-hot history of branding

In spite of the fact that "branding" is the biggest buzzword in today's business world, most consumers still link the concept back to the Old West, where brand symbols were burned onto the hides of steers and stallions in order to identify livestock that may have ventured off the ranch or away from the herd.

In fact, the history of branding goes even farther back in time.

In the medieval age, the marks of makers were seared onto everything from loaves of bread to gold and silver products in order to identify their origins and integrity. Even ancient pottery bears marks that resemble brands, causing archaeologists to believe that the concept of branding goes back as far as 5,000 years.

In the 1800s, in addition to serving as identification, brands began to take on a new and important marketing role. It was during those days that manufacturing breakthroughs led to mass production,

and with mass production came an unprecedented glut of products that vastly exceeded the needs of any one local market area.

Manufacturers who were used to personally presenting, explaining, and selling their goods to friends and neighbors were suddenly shipping their products off to fend for themselves in distant locations. Realizing that their goods were leaving home accompanied by little more than their product labels, manufacturers began efforts to build their names into brands that stood for quality, distinction, and honesty.

In short order, the concepts of publicity and advertising gained momentum as 19th-century manufacturers worked to build name awareness, product interest, trust, and purchase motivation.

Two centuries later, the purpose of branding remains the same: To build, maintain, and protect a positive image, high awareness, and product preference in consumers' minds.

What's involved?

Chapter 2 walks you through the steps involved to build a brand from the essence of an idea to the esteem of a known and trusted offering. For a glimpse of what's involved and how branding is a never-ending cycle, look at Figure 1-1.

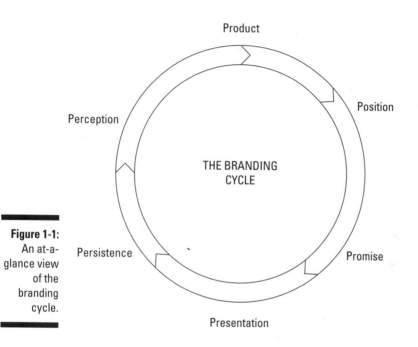

Figure 1-1:
An at-a-glance view of the branding cycle.

Branding is a circular process that involves these actions:

1. **Product definition:** You can brand products, services, businesses, even people or personalities. But you can't start the branding process without first knowing what it is you're trying to brand and whether your brand will be a one-and-only or one of several in your organization. Chapters 2 and 16 provide assistance with this beginning step.

2. **Positioning:** Each brand needs to fill a unique, meaningful, and available spot in the marketplace and in the consumer's mind. To determine your product's point of difference and the unique position it (and only it) fills in the market, see Chapters 4 and 5.

3. **Promise:** The promise you make and keep is the backbone of your brand and the basis of your reputation. Chapter 6 helps you put your promise into words.

4. **Presentation:** How you present your brand can make or break your ability to develop consumer interest and credibility in your offering. Start with a great name and logo (see Chapters 7 and 8), and then launch your marketplace communications with professionally produced and compelling packaging and communications. The chapters in Part III tell when, where, and how to proceed as you send your brand message into the marketplace.

5. **Persistence:** This is the point in the branding cycle where too many brands lose steam. After brands are launched, brand owners often get tired of their own looks and messages and begin to improvise with new looks, new messages, and even new brand personalities and promises. Just when consistency is most necessary in order to gain clarity and confidence in the marketplace, brands that lack persistence go off track. To save your brand from this pitfall, turn to Chapters 8 and 19 for help writing and enforcing brand presentation and management rules.

6. **Perception analysis:** In a consumer's mind — which is where brands live and thrive — a brand is a set of beliefs about what a company offers, promises, and stands for. Great brands continually monitor brand perceptions to see that they're in alignment with the brand owner's aspirations and in synch with consumer wants and needs. (Chapter 17 provides questionnaires and advice for conducting this assessment.)

Based on the results of perception analysis, brand owners begin their loop around the branding cycle again, this time adjusting their products, fine-tuning their positioning statements, strengthening their promises, updating their presentations, rewriting their brand management rules, and once again monitoring perceptions in order to guide ongoing brand realignments and revitalizations.

Who's involved?

Brands grow from the top down and from the inside out. What that means is that your brand needs commitment from the highest levels of leadership *and* support from employees in every department and at every point on the organizational chart.

Assembling your branding team

Whether you have a 1-person team or a 1,000-person team, every single person in your organization has to be involved in building and maintaining your brand. In order of who you bring on board first, here's who to involve:

1. **Organization leaders:** Don't try to build a brand without the leadership, buy-in, and active participation of those whose names appear at the very top of your organizational chart. Great brands are expressions of the vision, mission, and core values established by leaders, and therefore leaders need to head up the branding effort.

2. **Marketing and brand management team:** This group takes on the day-to-day responsibility for advancing, maintaining, protecting, and fine-tuning the brand. As you name your team, name one person to serve as your brand manager and chief brand protector. Be sure that this person is a senior-level executive who has the authority and commands the respect necessary to oversee what, in time, will become your organization's most valuable asset — your brand.

3. **An organization-wide team of brand champions:** Every person in your organization serves as an expression and an ambassador of your brand. If one person fails to uphold your brand promise — at any point from an initial inquiry to a post-purchase product or service concern — the strength of your brand is weakened. That's why great brands begin with internal launches that achieve team understanding and support (see Chapter 9). They also include ongoing brand orientations and training sessions to ensure flawless brand experiences (see Chapters 13 and 14).

Enlisting professional help

Brand development requires professional expertise and effort from those within and outside your organization. One person — or even one outside firm — can't do it all. Pick and choose from the following professional resources:

- ✔ **Brand consultants:** These are firms that specialize in the soup-to-nuts creation, building, and management of brands. They're experienced in everything from positioning to naming and trademarking to logo development to launching brands internally and externally. If your organization is seeking to build a brand that reaches into large markets or competitive fields, the expertise of a brand consultant can be worth the expense many times over.

- ✔ **Public relations specialists:** New brands are newsworthy if they're presented with the right news hooks and angles. An experienced public relations professional can help you get your story into circulation. Depending on the size and ongoing nature of your needs, a public relations freelancer may be able to handle your task as a one-time assignment. But if brand publicity is an ongoing objective, a public relations firm with greater staff and media resources may be the way to go. (Flip to Chapter 10 for more on public relations.)

- ✔ **Logo designers:** If you need help only with logo development or refinement, hire a graphic designer with a great logo portfolio. Ask to see samples to be sure that the caliber of design matches up with your expectations. Then use the advice in Chapter 8 as you manage the logo-development process.

- ✔ **Advertising agencies:** Some ad agencies specialize in brand development. Others focus on creation of print, broadcast, or interactive advertising. Yet others are known for outstanding packaging development, and even for their public relations departments. Whatever your needs, be aware that professionally produced communications can make a big difference in the strength of the brand image you transmit.

Chapter 11 offers guidance as you determine your needs, locate the right resources, conduct interviews, manage the selection process, and work with the professionals you hire.

When interviewing professionals, ask to see case studies to determine whether those you're considering have the experience you seek. Many companies present themselves as brand developers when, in fact, they handle only one aspect of the branding process, such as logo development or brand advertising.

Gulp! How much does it cost?

Brand development budgets run the gamut depending on whether you're building a brand that will face only moderate competition in a small geographic region or a brand that aims to elbow out major competitors in the global marketplace.

A glance at branding budgets

Table 1-1 shows a lineup of the major tasks involved in brand development along with the range of price tags involved. Brace yourself: The high-end figures are apt to cause heart palpitations.

Table 1-1	Professional Brand Development Fees	
Task	*Low-End Fee*	*High-End Fee*
Name development	$10,000	$75,000
Brandmark (logo) creation	$3,500	$150,000
Core brand presentations (Web site and collateral materials)	$10,000	$250,000+
Advertising	$10,000	Millions annually
Signage, vehicles, packaging	$20,000	$250,000+ annually

As Table 1-1 verifies, there's a huge range between the low-end costs involved to build a professional brand that competes on a local or regional basis and the high-end costs involved in building a powerful brand that can flex its muscle nationally or internationally.

As you reach for your calculator to start tallying up the costs to your business, avoid the temptation to strike out certain line items that you think you can handle on your own without incurring outside costs. Businesses that start with do-it-yourself logos and presentation materials achieve false savings. They economize on the front end, for sure, but they also cost themselves the benefit of a strong, competitive, professional first impression.

If your goal is to build a brand that you can grow, leverage, and even sell in the future, invest the money required to get off to a good start. By the time you amortize your start-up expenses, the cost will be minimal in comparison to the value received.

In lieu of big bucks . . .

In case you're clinging to your billfold or balance sheet, shaking your head, and wondering how you can build a brand on your kind of budget, remember this truth: A well-defined and consistently delivered brand strategy can level the playing field.

If you don't have the budget to develop the most powerful brand identity, triple or quadruple your efforts to design and deliver the most consistent brand experience. Follow these suggestions:

- **Spend extra time and effort to define your brand and what it stands for so that you and all in your organization know exactly the promise you're making and keeping.** Defining your brand involves creating your mission and vision statements, defining your brand promise, developing your brand definition and core brand message, and deciding on the brand character or personality that you'll put forth with every brand communication. Chapter 6 covers these tasks.

- **Develop a brand experience that never fails or fluctuates.** If you can't have the most dazzling brand identity and presentation materials, aim instead to have the most amazing and amazingly consistent brand encounters. Chapter 14 helps you ensure brand contacts that never let consumers down and never let them wonder what you stand for.

Pop Quiz: Are You Ready to Rev Up Your Branding Engine?

Is branding the right next step for your organization? If you answer "yes" to a good many of the following questions, you have good reason to turn the page and get started!

✔ Are you launching a company or product that will benefit from a clear identity and high awareness?

✔ Have you been in business for a while but feel you lack consumer awareness and understanding about who you are and what you stand for?

✔ Do you sell your offerings online or over distances but feel that prospects don't know your name or the distinct benefits you offer?

✔ Do you feel that people in your own organization are unclear about how to explain your offerings, your distinctions, your target market, and how you excel over competitors?

✔ When you look at how your organization communicates through advertising, marketing materials, personal presentations, and at each customer contact point, do you see inconsistencies in the look, message, and company personality being presented?

✔ Is the leader of your organization prepared to devote time, staff, energy, and dollars to develop, launch, and grow a brand?

And the final question is "Can you think of even one reason why people should choose your offering over competing solutions?" If your answer is a resounding "yes," ask yourself this follow-up question: "Do those in your target market clearly understand the distinct benefits you provide?" If not, turn the page and start building your brand!

Chapter 2

When and How to Brand

In This Chapter

▶ Branding products, businesses, services, and even yourself

▶ Following the branding process, step-by-step

▶ Seizing the best moment to brand or rebrand

*T*he short answer to the question of when and how to brand is this: Brand when you're ready to make a promise to customers, and brand by making a promise that you're absolutely, positively certain you can keep.

A *brand,* in essence, is a promise about who you are and what benefits you deliver that gets reinforced every single time people come in contact with any facet of you or your business.

Branding isn't a veneer that you slap on (usually in the form of a new logo) to mask or transform a product offering. Treating branding like some skin-deep solution to your business's problems is like putting lipstick on a pig: People see through the makeup, no matter how thick the application. Branding has to go all the way to the core of who you are and what you stand for.

Count on this chapter to lead you into the branding process, starting with a good overview of branding definitions and terminology. Then we move into a look at all the things you can brand and a lineup of the moments when branding is most essential and beneficial to your business and marketing success.

Branding Demystified

The $64,000 question among those breaking ground in the world of branding is, "So what is branding, anyway?" In a sentence, *branding* is the process of building a positive collection of perceptions in your customers' minds.

When people encounter your business's name, they automatically conjure up impressions and memories that determine what they believe about you. Their notions may be the result of communications you've had with customers, or they may be the result of good or bad publicity or word-of-mouth. Your customers may have a deep well of perceptions about you, or your slate may be nearly clear of any impressions whatsoever.

Regardless of whether the beliefs a customer holds about you are many or few, good or bad, or accurate or inaccurate, they comprise the image of your brand in your customer's mind — and they influence how your customer thinks and buys.

Your brand image lives in your customers' minds whether you intentionally put it there or not. Branding is the route to making sure that the brand image you have is the brand image you want.

Translating branding lingo

Branding terminology is a language unto itself. To get a feel for the complexities, just type "branding terms" into your favorite Internet search engine. We did that recently and got a whopping 12 million results! Assuming that you'd rather focus on key phrases instead of the full foreign language of branding, check out this need-to-know list of terms:

- **Brand:** A promise about who you are and what benefits you deliver that gets reinforced every time people come in contact with any facet of you or your business
- **Brand identity:** The marks that visually present your brand, usually in the form of a logo, symbol, or a unique typestyle
- **Brand image:** The set of beliefs about what your brand is and what it stands for that exists in the customer's mind as a result of associations with you and your name
- **Branding:** The process of building a positive collection of perceptions in your customer's mind
- **Brand position:** How your brand fits in with and relates to various other brands within your competitive market
- **Brand management:** Controlling the presentation of your brand identity and brand message across your entire organization and through all media and communication outlets
- **Brand equity:** The value of your brand as an asset, based on its qualities, reputation, and recognition as well as the commitment and demand it generates. A valuable brand results in customer relationships that secure future earnings by developing brand passion and loyalty.

Don't get overwhelmed when you hear people talk about brand message, brand promise, brand mission, brand strategy, brand extension, brand revitalization, rebranding, and a mind-boggling array of other brand terms. Armed with an understanding of the terms in this section, you can navigate branding conversations just fine. Throughout this book, we introduce other terms as you need to know them for specific branding situations.

Branding's essential ingredient

Originally we titled this section "Branding's Essential Ingredients." Lucky for you, we changed the plural to a singular. Brands are built around four fundamentals: product differentiation, relevance, esteem, and knowledge. But the magic ingredient that converts those fundamentals into a branding success story is *consistency*. If you bring consistency to your branding program, you end up with a brand that stands head and shoulders (no branding pun intended) above the others.

If you know what you stand for and project messages to your target market that constantly reinforce how your offering is different and relevant, you build knowledge and, eventually, esteem. As a result of your consistency, you win out over businesses that shift with the wind, regardless of how beautifully they've polished their identities or their marketing materials. In branding, consistency is more important than level of execution.

We've seen too many companies develop award-winning logos and impressive brand launch materials only to have their brand images go sideways when the customer has an actual brand experience. Remember the lipstick-on-a-pig analogy from this chapter's introduction: False promises don't work. Your brand must honestly express who you are and who you aspire to be every time the customer encounters you, your staff, your offices, your Web site, your customer service, your product, your marketing communications, your news coverage, and every other impression that you or others make on behalf of your brand.

Turn to Chapter 6 for assistance as you define your brand and put your desired brand identity into words you can live up to. Then turn to Chapter 14 for help pledging allegiance to your brand through a brand management program that ensures consistent presentation of your brand through every single customer encounter.

To Brand or Not to Brand

That is the question. Well, that's the question that hangs in the air until people hear this truth: If you can think of even one reason why customers should choose your offering over all the others, then you have at least one reason to brand it.

Whether you're marketing a product, service business, large company or corporation, or even yourself, the same branding process applies and the same branding benefits accrue.

Products

Products are tangible, physical items that you can hold in your hands or see with your own eyes before you make the purchase. Products fall into two categories:

- ✔ **Commodities** are products that customers can't differentiate from one another because they all seem to serve the same need, solve the same problem, and deliver the same value.

    If people can't see a clear reason to buy one product over another — if they think that all available products deliver the same value and quality — they buy whatever's available at the lowest price, which is hardly a formula for business success.

- ✔ **Branded products** are the opposite of commodities. Commodity products become branded products, usually known as *consumer brands,* when a manufacturer wins awareness in the marketplace that its product has compelling characteristics that make it different and better than others in the product category. Branding is a powerful tool that differentiates your offering in ways that create consumer preference and allow you to command premium pricing.

Airline tickets, desktop computers, and strawberry jam are all commodities. Until you read the name on the boarding pass, hard drive, or jelly jar, all competitors serve basically the same need in the same way. Yet customers make a conscious decision to choose one company's offerings over the others because of what they believe and trust to be true about their product of choice. Maybe they're won over by the frequent flyer club options, service or warranty program, promise of organic ingredients, or any of a zillion other distinguishing attributes.

The minute a marketer gets customers to believe "our product is different and better, and here's why," the marketer turns a commodity into a brand — and a better chance for sales success.

Want proof? Consider salt. Good old salt was the epitome of a commodity until 1914, when Morton promised that its product would run freely even in damp weather. With the slogan "When it rains, it pours," Morton launched a brand and a branding success story that spices up university marketing course lectures to this day.

For more proof that you can brand and differentiate nearly any product, look at the following examples of consumer brands that have distinguished themselves as leading choices in their product categories.

Commodity	*Consumer Brand*
Soft drinks	Coca-Cola
Water	Evian
Sneakers	Nike
Computers	Apple
Razor blades	Gillette
Cake mixes	Betty Crocker
Suitcases	Louis Vuitton
Automobiles	Mercedes-Benz

Always brand your product if you want it to be noticed, differentiated, and viewed as more than a commodity.

Product marketing success hangs on a brand

Consider this true commodity-to-brand success story from a Miami, Florida-based manufacturer that worked with coauthor Bill's company, Brand Navigation, and William Berenson Brand Architects (which is owned by this book's invaluable technical editor) to help it brand hangers. You read that right: Branded hangers. The Great American Hanger Company turned the functional, ubiquitous item that holds clothes in a closet into a differentiated lifestyle product of choice. Business publications took note of the company's success, and CEO Devon Rifkin understated the effort when he said, "No one has ever created a hanger brand." But he didn't let that stop him.

By promising "hanger solutions of extraordinary craftsmanship, unparalleled customer service, and timeless innovations" — including logo-emblazoned hangers, hangers covered in customized fabrics, and even hangers sized to the one-of-a-kind shoulder widths of guys like Shaquille O'Neal — The Great American Hanger Company carved a niche in a field previously crowded by dime-a-dozen hangers that most people pick up for free at the dry-cleaners. The result: 838 percent growth over three years; 2004 revenues in excess of $5 million; profiles in dozens of business and fashion publications; orders from hotels, cruise lines, restaurants, airlines, celebrities, and fashion designers; and the delivery of 10,000 hangers — the largest order ever received — to drape the wardrobe of pop diva Jennifer Lopez.

When you turn your product into a consumer brand you build perceived value, consumer trust, buyer preference, and the potential for higher profit margins. See the sidebar "Product marketing success hangs on a brand" for a great commodity-to-brand case study.

Service businesses

Services are products that people buy sight-unseen. Unlike tangible, three-dimensional products that shoppers can see and feel and try out before buying, people buy services purely based on their trust that the person or business they're buying from will deliver as promised.

When service is your offering, customers buy your brand. They buy into and trust your promise of superb service.

If you sell a service or run a service business, you absolutely, positively need to develop and manage a strong, positive brand image for the following reasons:

- ✔ **People buy your service based entirely on their belief in your brand promise.** People need to have faith in you, your ability, and your reputation before they decide to commit their business.

- ✔ **Before signing on the dotted line to purchase a service, customers need to believe that their expectations will be met.** If they know nothing about you or lack confidence in the quality of your service, they take their business elsewhere.

Examples of globally recognized service brands include Google, eBay, H&R Block, Charles Schwab, Merrill Lynch, and FedEx. For examples of local-level service brands, think of your region's leading law firm, best hair salon, most innovative homebuilder, or most trusted medical clinic. Each earned its reputation by building a clear identity and consistently conveying a believable promise that consumers trust in while they wait for the purchased service to be performed and their high expectations to be met.

Business brands

Many larger companies and corporations brand their businesses in addition to or instead of branding their products.

Procter & Gamble, for example, has built an overall corporate brand in addition to one of the largest portfolios of consumer brands in the world. Another example — on a smaller level and closer-to-home — is a land developer that builds brands for each new homeowner community in addition to a brand for the land development company that holds the individual brands.

Amazon.com: Branding service with a smile

Amazon.com has trained e-shoppers to believe that when they hit "proceed to checkout," they can count on consistently friendly and reliable delivery, service, and customer support. Amazon has built one of the world's leading service brands, identified by a visual symbol — the Amazon logo, which we show here — that was updated in 2000 to more fully reflect the company's A-to-Z service commitment.

Founder and CEO Jeff Bezos explained the new logo in a company news release: "To reflect Amazon's brand and its relationship with its more than 16 million customers better; the familiar logo was changed to communicate the company's mission of being the most customer-centric company in the world, most notably by depicting the ultimate expression of customer satisfaction: a smile."

Some of the millions of Amazon.com devotees add yet more symbolism to the logo: They say it reflects the genial expression of the company's most visible personality, the always-smiling company founder.

Table 2-1 summarizes how product and company brands differ from and complement each other.

Table 2-1	Comparison of Business Brands and Product Brands
Business Brand	**Product or Consumer Brand**
Builds trust with business stakeholders, including investors, associates, and employees	Builds emotional attachment with the customer
Helps prospective stakeholders decide: Is this company organized to deliver upon its promises? How strong and trustworthy is this company's leadership? Is this company innovative?	Helps prospective customers decide: How is this product relevant to my life? What does this product mean to me?
Projected through marketing tools and especially through personal contacts	Projected through product packaging, labeling, and advertising
Results in lasting investor, employee, customer, and stakeholder relationships	Results in product choice, purchase, and loyalty

If you can only build one brand — and that's the advice we give to any business that's short on marketing expertise or dollars — make it a business brand because business brands

✔ Lead to corporate or company awareness, credibility, and good reputations

✔ Pave a smooth road for new product introductions

✔ Inspire employees

✔ Attract the interest of job applicants, investors, and business reporters

✔ Contribute to *customer preference,* which means that people not only want to buy from your business but also often are willing to pay more for the association with a leading company held in high esteem

Individuals (namely, yourself)

Individual brands come in two types: personal brands and personality brands.

Personal brands

Personal brands reflect personal reputations. They differentiate individuals by creating awareness of who they are, what they stand for, what they do best, and how they contribute to the world around them.

Whether you know it or not, you have a personal brand. If people know your name or recognize your face, they hold your brand image in their minds. As proof, say the name of someone you know and pay attention to the thoughts that pop into your mind. The set of memories that arise comprise your brand image of that person. The person you're thinking of may have some lofty title, but if the first thing that comes to mind is "She's always late," then being late is an important part of her brand. On the more positive side, if you think "Everything she touches turns to gold," then success is a major part of the person's brand.

By developing a personal brand, you can

✔ Establish yourself as an expert in your field

✔ Enhance your visibility and reputation within your community or industry

✔ Differentiate yourself from competitors based upon your unique style and talents

✔ Gain influence in social or business arenas

Personality brands

Personality brands are personal brands gone big-time. They're individual brands that are so large and strong that they not only deliver wide-reaching personal celebrity but also create significant value when associated with products or services.

Oprah is a personality brand. So are Martha Stewart, Tiger Woods, Michael Jordan, George Foreman, Paul Newman, Jennifer Lopez, and Donald Trump, to name a few.

People who develop personality brands often use their visibility to present or endorse products, quickly increasing product visibility, sales, and brand equity as a result of association with the celebrity's name. The connections between personality brands and product brands break down as follows:

✔ **Some personality brands grow out of product brands.** For example, the late Dave Thomas became a personality brand as a result of the Wendy's brand marketing campaign. He then leveraged his personality brand to create attention for his Foundation for Adoption.

✔ **Some product brands grow out of personality brands.** For example, Newman's Own grew out of the personality brand of Paul Newman, the George Foreman Grill gained product notoriety as a result of the personality brand of George Foreman, and almost every celebrity sports brand grew out of the strong personality brand of an athletic superstar.

✔ **Some product brands spawn personality brands, which go on to spawn product brands.** For example, Walt Disney Studios and Disneyland led to the globally recognized Walt Disney personality brand, which is being brought back to shine over new lines of Disney products, subbrands, and services.

Obviously, only the most visible personalities can turn their names into megasized personality brands, but that doesn't mean that personality brands are exclusively for the big guys. Many community leaders become local personalities whose endorsements of projects or fundraising campaigns, for example, turn otherwise obscure efforts into overnight successes.

If you aspire to become a leader in your community or industry, keep that goal in mind as you build your personal brand. Develop a personal reputation that you can leverage into a greater good by becoming a small-scale personality brand in your own backyard or business arena.

A Bird's-eye View of the Branding Process

When it comes to branding, you should know what you're getting into before you really buckle down and get started. This section gives you a helicopter view of the branding process you're getting ready to launch; we feature the major steps involved and tell you where to turn in the upcoming chapters for step-by-step branding advice.

If you're a visual person, Figure 2-1 lays out the branding process in a clear, easy-to-follow manner.

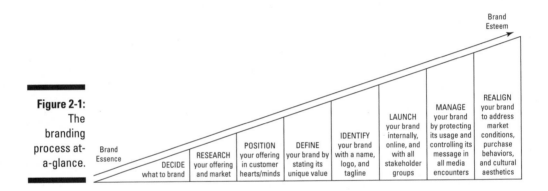

Figure 2-1: The branding process at-a-glance.

Brand Esteem

Brand Essence

DECIDE what to brand

RESEARCH your offering and market

POSITION your offering in customer hearts/minds

DEFINE your brand by stating its unique value

IDENTIFY your brand with a name, logo, and tagline

LAUNCH your brand internally, online, and with all stakeholder groups

MANAGE your brand by protecting its usage and controlling its message in all media encounters

REALIGN your brand to address market conditions, purchase behaviors, and cultural aesthetics

Step 1: Decide what you're going to brand

Are you branding a product, a service, a company, or an individual? If the distinctions are a bit blurry, flip back to the section "To Brand or Not to Brand" earlier in this chapter.

In addition to deciding what you're going to brand, you need to decide if the brand you're developing will be your one-and-only brand or if it will live alongside or under the umbrella of other brands in your organization.

Brand architecture 101

The relationship between your business and your brand is called *brand architecture*. In the same way that building architecture makes all the rooms of a structure work together, brand architecture neatly packages the segments of your company into a single, understandable entity. Most brands qualify as one of three types of brand architecture.

✔ **Parent-dominant brands:** Businesses that follow this form of brand architecture introduce each new product brand under the strong business brand identity of the parent organization. General Electric (GE) is a great example of a parent-dominant brand. Whether you buy a GE refrigerator, range, microwave, or washing machine, you're buying the General Electric brand. Under that brand, you can choose from the GE Monogram or the GE Profile line, but you always know you're buying GE because the parent brand dominates all its offerings.

Adopt a parent-dominant branding strategy if any of the following situations apply to your business:

- Your company has a modest marketing department and budget. If your resources are limited, build one strong parent brand to represent your core business and then introduce each new offering under the umbrella of your business identity. By doing so, you eliminate the need to create and manage the identity of multiple self-standing brands, which requires an intense investment of time, people, discipline, and dollars.

- All your products support a single business brand image and promise. For example, if your business brand issues a promise to deliver top-tier quality to the most discerning customers, you can't introduce a product that serves the bargain-basement market.

- You want to heighten the value of your business brand as part of a long-term plan to prepare your business for growth or sale. Parent-dominant products enhance the equity of the parent brand.

✔ **Parent-endorsed brands:** These brands enter the marketplace as their own brands but have the strong and visible endorsement of their parent organizations. For example, iPod is a parent-endorsed brand, as is Macintosh. Both enter the market carrying the strong, visible Apple logo, but the only name you see is the name of the brand you're buying at the moment: iPod or Mac. The brand emphasis is on the product, but the company brand adds instant credibility.

Consider a parent-endorsed branding strategy if any of the following situations apply to your business:

- You have the staff and financial resources to build a number of brands — one for your business and one for each product.

- You want to build strong visibility and equity for each individual brand, perhaps with a mid- or long-term goal of spinning off and selling the endorsed brand.

- You want to appeal to new target audiences whose interests may be easier to reach with a new brand than with the identity of your parent brand.

- You compete in an arena, such as the car industry, where all other businesses brand each line. In such cases, in order to achieve comparable visibility and esteem for your product lines, you may need to replicate the strategy of your competitors and introduce each line as a parent-endorsed brand.

✔ **Parent-silent brands:** These brands are owned by their parent companies but stand entirely on their own in the marketplace. For example, Crest, Folgers, Head & Shoulders, Oil of Olay, Pampers, and Pringles are consumer brands owned by Procter & Gamble, yet the parent company is virtually invisible as each brand is presented to consumers.

Building parent-silent brands is the most costly branding strategy of all. You need to build a strong, stand-alone brand for each and every product, *plus* you need to build a corporate or business brand that can carry its weight in the financial and corporate worlds and serve as a magic carpet for each new brand to ride in on until it establishes itself as a seemingly independent entity in the marketplace.

Unless you're a megamarketer with deep pockets, your brand will probably fall under the parent-dominant or parent-endorsed category unless — borrowing from the family tree language — it's an "only child" because you wisely follow the Rule of One explained in the next section.

Following the Rule of One

Unless you have a deep reservoir of staff, expertise, and marketing dollars, heed the branding Rule of One: Build one brand for your business rather than one business full of many brands. Introduce each new product or service as an offering under your business brand.

If you choose to brand separate products or services, build a separate business unit for each new brand. That way, each offering stands on its own, drawing on its own resources and building independent value that can contribute to your business brand equity or that you can spin off or sell in the future.

Step 2: Do your research

When you're clear about what you're branding, the next step is to analyze your offering and the market in which it will compete. Think of this as your discovery phase, which is comprised of two major steps:

1. **Find out everything there is to know about your market.**

   Begin by researching your prospective customers — who they are, where they are, and what motivates their buying decisions. Then analyze your competition to discover what solutions already exist in the marketplace and exactly how the offering you're branding is different and better.

2. Find out everything there is to know about your product or service.

You need to know what makes your offering unique, what attributes make it excel over competing alternatives, and how it solves your customers' wants or needs.

Flip to Chapter 4 as you embark on this fact-finding mission. Along with advice on how to proceed, that chapter has forms and questionnaires to use as you gather information about your brand offering and the market in which it will compete.

Step 3: Position your product or service

Positioning is how you find and win a place for your offering in the marketplace and in consumers' minds.

Consumers are so overwhelmed with product choices and marketing messages that they take in messages that seem distinctly meaningful. They make mind space only for products or services that provide unique solutions to problems or needs that aren't already being addressed by competing products.

To determine your market position, follow these four steps:

1. **Determine which distinct and meaningful consumer needs or desires only your product or service addresses in the marketplace.**

2. **Communicate your point of difference.**

3. **Win a unique position for your offering in the market and in the consumer's mind.**

4. **Perform so well that no competitor can compete against or unseat your position.**

Positioning precedes brand development. It defines how you'll differentiate your offering and slot it into an available space in the market and in your customers' minds.

Chapter 5 takes you on a step-by-step walk through the positioning process, including how to determine your market position, how to communicate your position, how to win your position in your consumers' minds, and how to protect your position so that your brand can claim and own a defined niche in which to live and grow.

Step 4: Write your brand definition

Your *brand definition* is a true statement about what your brand stands for. It describes what you offer, why you offer it, how your offering is different and better, what unique benefits your customers can count on, and what promise or set of promises you make to all who work with and buy from your business.

You have to know your brand definition before you begin to create materials that will become the public presentation of your brand in the marketplace. Otherwise the face of your brand doesn't match up with the base of your brand, and your brand communications lack credibility.

Figure 2-2 shows the relationship between

✔ **The base of your brand:** The culture, mission, vision, values, leadership, management, and organization that together create what your brand stands for

✔ **The face of your brand:** The part of your brand that rises into public view and translates the vast reality of your brand into a name, symbol, and message that employees, consumers, and colleagues can quickly and easily see, understand and believe

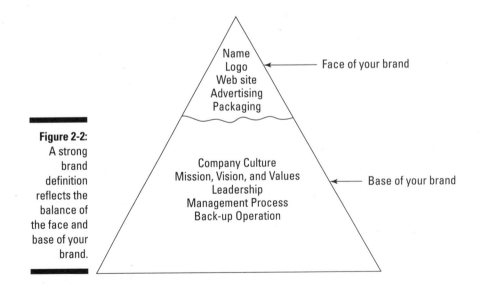

Figure 2-2:
A strong brand definition reflects the balance of the face and base of your brand.

The face of your brand has to sit firmly upon the strong base formed by your company mission, vision, and commitment to the promise you represent through your brand marketing.

As you get ready to define your brand, turn to Chapter 6 for help with every step involved.

Step 5: Develop your name, logo, and tagline

This is the point where branding gets exciting. The minute you give your brand a name and face — or logo — you can watch managers, employees, and others inside the company start to buy into the branding process. Here's a brief introduction to these important brand elements:

- ✔ **Name:** Your *name* is the key that unlocks your brand image in your consumer's mind. Turn to Chapter 7 for help creating your brand name, including advice for how to recognize qualities of a great name, pick or create your name, test the appropriateness and availability of the name you want, and turn the name you choose into a vehicle that conveys your brand promise and builds value for the brand it represents.

- ✔ **Logo:** Your *logo* is the brandmark or symbol that serves as the face of your brand on your signage, packaging, stationery, advertising, sales literature, and every other physical communication vehicle that carries your name into the marketplace. Coauthor Bill is the guru on this subject, and he's filled Chapter 8 with information on how to develop a great logo, avoid logo design taboos, apply your logo with consistency throughout your marketing program, and manage your logo so that no one tampers with or misrepresents its design.

- ✔ **Tagline:** Your *tagline* is the memorable phrase that provides consumers with a quick indication of your product, brand, and market position. Some marketers make their taglines an essential part of their identities, whereas other marketers don't create taglines at all. Taglines are particularly useful, though, for companies whose names or logos don't clearly convey the company position or personality and for businesses that rely heavily on e-mail or other communications in which logo presentation isn't possible. See Chapter 8 for help deciding whether or not your marketing would benefit from a tagline and, if so, how to create one for your brand.

Step 6: Launch your brand

Your brand launch happens in two phases, which take place in the following order:

1. **Internal launch**

   Before you even think of introducing your brand to prospects, explain it to all who have or feel that they have a stake in your business, including:

   - **Shareholders, managers, and employees:** These are the people most invested in your business and most apt to serve as ambassadors for your brand. Be ready to answer questions like "Why are we spending money on this?" and "How will this strengthen our business?" by linking your branding program to your business mission and goals. And by all means, take extra care with those who sell your product, providing them with a complete set of tools to help them present your brand position and story to prospects and customers (turn to Chapter 9 for advice).

   - **Key business partners and major customers:** These are people who have bought into your business as loyal advisors, supporters, and clients. Before they see your new brand on packaging or in ads, give them a preview. Chapter 9 helps you plan your approach.

2. **External launch**

   Your brand goes public when you unveil your name, logo, and slogan, and when you begin to tell your market the story of how your brand reflects what you stand for. Coauthor Barbara's the marketing guru on our author team, and she's designed Part III to guide you as you write the marketing plan for your launch and create the advertising, publicity-generation tools, sales materials, and online program that carry the announcement of your new brand into your marketplace.

Step 7: Manage, leverage, and protect your brand

This is the "care and feeding" phase of the branding process; it's the step that leads to a strong, healthy, resilient brand. Just like good parenting, good branding management can be summed up in a single word — consistency.

- ✔ Display a consistent look.
- ✔ Project a consistent tone.
- ✔ Deliver a consistent level of quality, demonstrated through consistent communications and consistent products and services.
- ✔ Be consistently true to your brand.

Consistency builds good brands. If you mess around with your brand, you destroy its strength.

Begin managing your brand from the moment you announce your name because

- ✔ The minute your name or news of your offering goes into the market-place, you begin making first impressions of your brand, whether they're the ones you intend to make or not.
- ✔ By understanding your brand definition and market position, you can project messages that build accurate perceptions from the get-go.
- ✔ By etching your brand onto a blank slate in the marketplace, you don't have to undertake the difficult task of erasing erroneous impressions and rewriting your brand image.

The chapters in Part IV help you stick to your guns. They're packed with information for keeping a tight rein on your brand, creating brand allegiance, leveraging value, and, when the time's right, revitalizing your brand to fit changing market or business conditions.

The chapters in Part V focus on how to protect your brand by establishing and standing up for your legal rights. They also help you create usage rules that protect your brand from well-meaning but misguided attempts by staff members, freelancers, printers, sign makers, and others who are all too willing to help you "refine" or "tweak" your brand image, which usually leads directly to an erosion of the consistency you're fighting to maintain.

Step 8: Realign your brand to keep it current

When you hear people talking about the need to redo their (or your) brand, don't listen in on the conversation, and don't use them as your branding gurus. For as long as your brand exists, it's your brand. It's the promise you made yesterday and the promise you'll make tomorrow. It's the essence of what your business stands for and the esteem it has built among all its stakeholders.

You can't just change essence; you can't just change your brand. What you can (and should) be willing to change is how your brand is presented. From time to time, you need to update your brand presentation (the face of your brand) to keep it relevant to the market in which it lives. Face it, market trends change. Purchase behaviors change (think of how the Internet turned how people buy upside down). Design looks or cultural aesthetics change. When they do, you need to realign your brand by updating its look and message but *not* by changing the promise you make.

Only on rare occasions do companies need to rebrand, which involves abandoning the essence of what they stand for and starting from scratch to build a brand new brand. This rare move is discussed in Chapter 17.

Here are a few examples of brand realignment:

- Coke changed its tagline from "The Real Thing" to just "Real" to sound more culturally relevant. It's the same message, but it has a realigned presentation.
- AT&T slightly evolved the look of the symbol and typeface it uses as its logo in order to appear lighter and more nimble following a merger with SBC.
- British Petroleum changed the definition of BP to "Beyond Petroleum" to address the market's growing environmental concerns.

None of these companies threw away their brands and started from scratch. They did what you should do when and if your brand presentation starts to get a little out of step with its market: Keep all the esteem you built through the first seven steps of the brand development process, and then protect your image with a regular assessment of whether it needs a slight realignment to match the market's evolving interests.

When to Brand

The following sections spotlight the major times that businesses launch or polish brands, along with advice for how to proceed and what to expect in each case.

Opening a new business

When you open a business, be ready to project your brand image from the first second that you throw open the company doors, hook up the phone lines, or launch your Web site.

While you're writing your business plan (if that term just threw you into a panic, run — don't walk — to get a copy of *Business Plans Kit For Dummies*, 2nd Edition, by Steven Peterson, Peter E. Jaret, and Barbara Findlay Schenck [Wiley]), write the plan for branding your business. Be sure to take into account the following advice as you do so:

✔ Follow the first seven steps in the branding process outlined in the preceding section of this chapter and detailed throughout this book.

✔ Take special care to figure out and understand exactly how you intend to position your business within the competitive landscape so that you provide a unique and valuable offering in an already crowded marketplace.

✔ Create all the primary branding tools before you ever open for business, including your name, brandmark or logo, stationery, Web site, sales material, and presentation tools to help you introduce your business and present your brand to funding partners, prospective employees, business partners, and new customers.

Introducing a new product

When you introduce a new product, you have to decide whether the product you're introducing will enter the market under your business brand or as its own brand, with or without a visible link to your business brand. (For more on this decision, refer to the section "Brand architecture 101" earlier in this chapter.)

If you decide to introduce your new product as a new brand, you need to follow every single one of the seven steps in the branding process, giving special consideration to the Step 2 discovery phase. You must do all the research and analysis necessary to determine your product position, point of difference, and marketing approach.

If you have an existing brand, seriously consider how you may fit your new product under your existing brand. Doing so allows you to leverage your new product introduction off of the visibility and value that your current brand already enjoys in the marketplace.

If you decide to introduce your new product as an offering under your established business brand, you need to take a few steps to ensure that your new product not only benefits *from* but also provides benefit *to* your business brand. Ask yourself these questions:

✔ Does the new product support and extend your established brand image?

✔ Have you done a careful competitive analysis to be sure that your new offering is distinctively different and better than existing products and that it will contribute to rather than weaken your brand image in your marketplace?

✔ Have you developed a product name and logo that fits within the framework of your business brand?

✔ Have you created product advertising and sales materials that conform to your business brand image and graphic identity?

The Rule of One is worth repeating here: Unless your business has strong marketing expertise and a well-funded marketing budget, limit the number of brands you build to one, and introduce all new products under that strong, single brand. The price of getting too ambitious is building no brand well and gaining little if any brand presence in your marketplace.

Fundraising for a nonprofit

Successful fundraising campaigns operate under the auspices of well-known, well-regarded, well-branded organizations. Before your organization launches a fundraising campaign, establish credibility and trust by first building a brand image for your organization that prospective donors know and believe in.

To build a brand image for your organization, follow these steps:

1. **Follow the brand building steps outlined earlier in this chapter to create awareness of your organization's overall mission, vision, and values and to build trust in your track record for leveraging donated dollars into good works.**

2. **Build a strong and emotional story for the new cause you're seeking to fund.**

3. **Introduce your campaign to the public, tying it to your overall mission and vision and leveraging the value and power of your organizational brand on behalf of your new fundraising program.**

Taking your business public

Don't even consider launching an *initial public offering,* or IPO, until you have a well-established and well-regarded brand. Investors direct dollars into businesses that they trust to be well-led, innovative, successful, and capable of rising to even higher levels of growth and profitability.

For proof that the sequence of branding before going public works, consider Google and Microsoft. By the time company shares were finally made available, investors were fighting over them because the brands were so strong and well-established.

Going global

Some businesses want to sell in international markets. Others want to establish themselves as global companies with operating presences in a range of countries. Either way, if your brand is going to travel, it had better be up to the task. Before your company crosses international borders, take these steps:

✔ **Create or realign your brand to fit the realities of the cultures it will enter.** Be sure that your name translates favorably, that the colors and shapes in your logo create positive impressions in the new environment, and that your brand messages are consistent with the culture of your new market. (Chapter 17 can help you make these adjustments to your brand.)

✔ **Plan, budget for, and launch a strong brand introduction in each new country or market area.** Gaining market share in a foreign market is a big task that begins with gaining name familiarity and belief in your business. Gaining brand awareness is an essential first step toward success. Make it your aim to quickly achieve the reputation of a trusted business with whom those in your new market want to work. (Chapter 9 offers plenty of advice for accomplishing this step.)

Raising venture capital

Venture capitalists are investors who look to invest in companies with strong leadership, strong business concepts, and strong positions in growing market arenas.

Don't even think of approaching venture capitalists until you have

✔ Clearly defined technology and products

✔ A business model capable of delivering predictable streams of revenue

✔ A management team with proven capability that's relevant to the size and kind of businesses you're trying to fund

✔ The ability to personally represent your brand by making an impeccable first impression

A brand is stronger than a giving request

Since 1881, the American Red Cross has won awareness and trust as the nation's premier emergency response organization, branding itself with the slogan "Together, we can save a life." When a humanitarian crisis hits, the Red Cross is the first name that comes to the minds of those who want to help. Its strong brand precedes its giving request.

When the Gulf Coast was ravaged by Hurricane Katrina in 2005, the Red Cross moved quickly to launch relief efforts. Within hours of the disaster, public service announcements aired nationally on television, with Aaron Neville's voice announcing that "Hope is stronger than a hurricane" accompanied by the dominant logo of the Red Cross. Within weeks, the giving public's emotional connection and strong belief in the Red Cross resulted in contribution pledges that exceeded $1.25 billion.

Use your business plan — the prerequisite to every venture capital request — to present your business and explain your brand. But also be prepared to make your personal presentation the embodiment of your brand personality. Ask yourself which would you rather invest in: an uncertain, messy-looking genius with a great idea or a focused, well-presented person of average intelligence with a great idea?

Merging with another business

Businesses merge, but there's really no such thing as a brand merger. Combining Brand A with Brand B doesn't result in Brand A+B. It either results in a retooled version of Brand A, a retooled version of Brand B, or an all-new Brand C.

Entering a merger is entering a politically sensitive area. As part of the merger negotiations, you need answer the following questions:

- ✔ Is the merger actually a takeover? If so, one culture and one brand will be subsumed by the other.

- ✔ Is the reason for the merger to acquire brand strength or to acquire physical attributes? If it's to acquire brand strength, then the stronger of the two brands is the one that must prevail.

- ✔ Can you afford the loss of established brand equity if you decide to create an altogether new brand as a result of the merger?

Depending on your answers to these questions, move into branding action by following one of these approaches:

- ✔ If the merger will result in the survival of one brand, turn to Chapter 17 for advice on revitalizing that brand and reintroducing it in its new and improved form.

- ✔ If the merger will result in an altogether new brand, start the branding process from scratch following the seven steps outlined in the section "A Bird's-eye View of the Branding Process" earlier in this chapter.

With either approach, dedicate extra time, effort, and dollars to gain complete understanding and buy-in from the staffs of both organizations before you take the retooled brand or the new brand public.

Chapter 3

Heating Up Your Branding Iron

- -

- -

*B*rands are indelible. When they're seared into customers' minds, they're long-lasting and durable. That's why this chapter is so important. It helps you plan your branding strategy before you leap into branding action. This chapter walks you through the steps of figuring out what you want your branding program to accomplish, what kind of brand identity you're seeking, and what it will take in terms of budget, manpower, and planning to reach the branding success you seek.

If you don't yet have a brand — that is, if you're starting a new business or getting ready to launch a new product — this chapter can help you plan your brand from scratch so you get your brand identity, image, and strategy spot-on from the get-go.

If you already have a brand — that is, if people already know your name and have impressions about what you stand for — use the information in this chapter as you assess whether the brand image you have is the one you want and, if not, how you can move your brand from where it is to where you want it to be.

Gearing Up to Brand, Rebrand, or Refine Your Brand

If branding is the hot topic in your organization, you're probably facing one of two situations: Either you're starting a business and want to create a new brand to go with it, or you have a brand but want a different (or somewhat different) one to better represent your offering in the marketplace.

Whether you're launching a new brand or you're in the process of refining an existing brand, you have to start by figuring out what people think when they hear your name or think about the industry or business arena you're entering. When you're clear about how people currently perceive your identity, then you can figure out what brand assets you have to build upon and what brand identity, in your dreams, you want to achieve.

Getting real about your current brand identity

The best starting point for brand development is a true and candid look at what people currently think of your brand and industry in the marketplace.

If you're starting a business and don't yet have a brand to analyze, instead assess the image of the business arena you're entering. For instance, if you're starting a children's museum, think about the mental images people have about museums in general and children's museums in particular. When you know the preconceived notions you're dealing with, you're in a good position to develop a strategy that leads to a brand image that reflects the unique attributes and differentiating aspects of the organization you're starting.

The point of your brand assessment is to determine answers to the following questions:

- What do people like or dislike about you, your business, or your business arena?
- What do they trust or distrust?
- What do they think you are and do?
- Why do they choose your offering?
- How do they think you compare with your competitors?
- How do they think you affect their lives for better or worse? How do they find your offering relevant and a good fit with their lives and needs?

Don't rely solely on your own judgments or those of your top management team to assess your current image. Instead, gather input from a wider range of people. Ask those who work on the front line of your business. Go to the people who answer incoming calls, take product orders, field complaints, and fix service problems. Then go talk to some customers or prospective customers, too.

Use the following questions in your interviews. They're designed to help you collect information on your current brand identity without making you or those you're interviewing feel self-conscious about their answers:

✔ In a sentence, how would you describe our business?

✔ How would you describe our products or services?

✔ What one reason, above all others, causes you and others to buy from our business?

✔ When you consider buying from our business, what three other companies or brands do you also consider?

✔ What one reason, above all others, do you think causes people to buy from one of our competitors?

✔ Do you think there is high or low awareness of our business or brand in the marketplace?

✔ Do you think there are clear and distinct differences between our offerings and those of our competitors? If so, what are a few of the distinct differences that make our offerings unique or more desirable?

✔ If you were to compare our business to a car, what car would it be, and why? What car would you associate with each of our three top competitors?

✔ If you were to compare our business to an actor or actress, who would it be, and why? Who would you associate with each of our three top competitors?

If your business is small and you have casual conversations with clients and prospects on an ongoing basis, you can ask the questions in informal face-to-face meetings. If your customer base is large or geographically diverse, you may need to pose the questions through written or phone surveys. Turn to Chapter 4 for advice on how to conduct customer research and when to call in professional assistance.

As you launch your research, first provide your own answers to these questions and collect answers from your key management team. Then put those answers aside while you pose the questions to employees, business associates, customers, and prospects. The differences between how you and others see your business and brand may be surprising and will lead to an honest assessment of the brand you currently have in your own mind and, more importantly, in the minds of others.

Taking stock of your brand assets and using them to your advantage

Before making adjustments to your brand image, you need to know what contributes to the value of the brand you currently own.

For a well-known example, consider the brand assets of Coke: the red packaging, the Coca-Cola script, the bottle shape, the name, the formula, the marketing position of "the Real Thing." Take any one of those assets away, and the brand is diminished. Evolve any one of those assets to fit emerging cultural attitudes or consumer tastes, and the brand is enhanced. Witness how "the Real Thing" became "Real" and how Coca-Cola has become Coke in marketing campaigns. The brand assets remain intact, and the brand value increases through enhanced relevance to changing marketplaces.

The worksheet in Figure 3-1 can help you assess your brand assets. As you enter your assessment of each asset, base your answer on your own opinion and on the opinions you collect from those in your company and customer base. Turn to professional researchers for help if your company is large or if you're realigning a brand that will have significant range and value in the future.

The resulting brand asset analysis allows you to decide which elements of your brand have significant value. These are the assets that you should keep or evolve in future brand realignments. The analysis also uncovers which assets have little recognition or regard and can go by the wayside with little or no loss of brand strength or value.

In your dreams! Defining your desired brand identity

Whereas the preceding sections help you analyze your brand assets and assess your brand image as it exists today, this section helps you define the brand image you want for the future.

As you envision your ideal brand image, realize that the brand you build needs to be a true reflection of your business's mission, vision, and values as well as the promises you make and keep in your marketplace. It also needs to be believable, which is why your strategy to achieve your desired brand identity needs to take into account currently held perceptions about your brand.

Branding isn't a game of leapfrog. You can't ask people to jump past what they currently believe and immediately land on a new perception about what you stand for. You have to nudge their beliefs in a new direction by building upon the images they currently hold as you help them adopt new levels of awareness, emotional attachment, beliefs, trust, and preference for your offering.

Use the chart in Figure 3-2 to list the attributes you think are important to your brand image along with how each attribute is currently perceived and how you want it to be perceived in the future. The far-right column asks you to rate the importance of each attribute to your desired image. Your responses will help you determine the priority you will place on enhancing perceptions of each attribute in your branding strategy.

BRAND STRENGTHS, WEAKNESSES, AND PRIORITIES WORKSHEET					
CAPABILITY	✔ Your brand's strength in this capability				IMPORTANCE of this capability to your success
	Poor	Fair	Good	Excellent	
Awareness How well-known or noticed is your brand in its market?					Low Medium High
Emotional Connection How deeply and emotionally do people relate to your brand?					Low Medium High
Distinction How well do people understand the attributes or promises that set your brand apart from competitors?					Low Medium High
Credibility and Trust How well do people believe and trust in you and your promises? How good is your reputation?					Low Medium High
Purchase Motivation How well does your brand inspire preference and pave the way for a purchase decision?					Low Medium High

Figure 3-1: Use this worksheet as you analyze your brand assets and how each contributes to the strength of your brand image.

Using key brand attributes to steer branding strategy

A few years back, we worked with the developers of a gated golf community featuring a prestigious golf course and homes that raised the bar of design quality and residential investments. Exclusivity was a key brand attribute to the community's developers and customers alike.

The problem was that the community was hard to find. It was away from main roads, so people considering home or homesite purchases needed detailed directions. The most obvious solution to this problem — posting highway signage or outdoor boards offering driving directions — was ruled out because it risked eroding the brand's attributes of exclusivity and prestige.

As a solution, the developers created a brochure that unfolded to a map leading prospects right to the property, with inset photos pointing out landscape and lifestyle attributes along the way. The cover read, "The ideal community is hard to find, unless you know where to look." Brochures were distributed to real estate agents and stocked in regional visitor bureaus. Additionally, a kiosk reflecting the construction quality of one of the community's homes was installed in the arrivals area of the regional airport. While waiting for their luggage, air travelers saw the travel route above the steering wheel of a Range Rover; a take-one box full of the map-brochures was placed underneath the image.

Problem solved. Prestige protected.

Figure 3-2: Use this worksheet as you assess your current brand image and work to enhance your image in key areas.

BRAND IMAGE ATTRIBUTES: ASSESSMENT AND RANKING WORKSHEET			
Brand Image Attribute	Current Perception	Desired Perception in 1–2 years	Strategic Emphasis
(List descriptors that capture the essence of your brand such as Performance, Design, Prestige, Reliability, Safety, Comfort, Luxury, Expertise, Innovation, and so on.)	✔ How your brand is currently perceived in your market and against your competitors	✔ How you aspire to be perceived in your market and against your competitors	✔ Importance of this attribute to the success of your brand
	Poor Fair Good Excellent	Poor Fair Good Excellent	Low Medium High
	☐ ☐ ☐ ☐	☐ ☐ ☐ ☐	☐ ☐ ☐
	☐ ☐ ☐ ☐	☐ ☐ ☐ ☐	☐ ☐ ☐
	☐ ☐ ☐ ☐	☐ ☐ ☐ ☐	☐ ☐ ☐
	☐ ☐ ☐ ☐	☐ ☐ ☐ ☐	☐ ☐ ☐
	☐ ☐ ☐ ☐	☐ ☐ ☐ ☐	☐ ☐ ☐

What's Your Goal? Prioritizing Your Brand's To-Do List

Not everyone setting out to build or fine-tune a brand has the same mission. Some, especially those representing big, hugely funded companies or top-tier celebrities, aim above all else to establish and maintain top-of-mind awareness to ensure that the spotlight in their category shines brightly and fully in their brand's direction. Others establish brands in order to forge or deepen emotional connections with customers, to differentiate their products from competing offers, or to develop the kind of preference and motivation that prompts purchase decisions and makes cash registers ring. And still other brand builders want their brands to do all of the above.

Your brand to-do list can be long or short, but you can't create it after the fact; in order to build a brand or fine-tune the brand you have, you need to know where you want to arrive. As you set your sights, determine which of the following brand functions best describe what you aim to achieve through branding:

- ✔ Build awareness
- ✔ Create an emotional connection
- ✔ Convey distinguishing attributes
- ✔ Gain credibility and trust
- ✔ Achieve buyer preference

If you need help organizing your thinking, use the worksheet in Figure 3-3. It lists the five key brand functions and provides space to rate your brand's current strength in each area and prioritize the functions you want to enhance through your future branding strategy.

Build awareness

If you're launching a new brand or working to strengthen a brand in a competitive category, increasing awareness may be among the highest priorities of your branding program. Brands large and small put awareness-building at the top of the branding to-do list for these reasons:

- ✔ **Awareness leads to marketplace dominance.** The most powerful brands owned by the biggest companies and celebrities hold their competitive positions based largely on how widely they're known and noticed. That's why marketers with the biggest brand names constantly reinforce their images through advertising, promotions, and publicity. They know that in order to maintain their market dominance, they must continuously strengthen the awareness or notice of their brands in their far-flung marketplaces.

✔ **Awareness makes selling easier.** Marketers who aren't working with names like Nike or Oprah work to build awareness not to become the best known brands in their marketing worlds but to build sales, pure and simple. Without brand awareness, you spend the lion's share of every ad, presentation, or sales call introducing your business and explaining why it's better than all other alternatives. Meanwhile, a competing company with established brand awareness can spend that time advancing information that moves the customer to a purchase decision.

After you build awareness for your brand, that awareness acts like a proxy for your business. When you can't be somewhere in person, your brand goes for you, getting you noticed and conveying your core message and business promise on your behalf.

Create an emotional connection

If your customers select your offering based largely on how they feel about owning your product or associating with your business, then creating an emotional connection needs to be an important part of your branding strategy.

Not all brands rely on emotional connections. Some brands succeed based on their high levels of credibility or on their abilities to distinguish themselves based on unique benefits that customers can't get from competing companies. These brands are chosen based on factual comparisons. They appeal to what people think; they involve decisions of the mind. Brands that rely on emotional connections appeal to what people feel; they involve decisions of the heart.

Consider the last time you bought dish soap. You looked at the lineup of bottles, glanced at the prices, saw that a soap brand you'd heard of was competitively priced, and made your selection. Your decision was rational; based on your awareness of the brand, you grabbed what seemed to deliver the best value for the dollars you were expending. You weren't looking for a happy marriage between you and the dish soap — you just wanted to know that you were choosing a good product for a decent price. Emotions didn't come into play. On the other hand, think of what you went through the last time you bought a car; gave to a charity; helped your son or daughter select a university to attend; or decided on a new home, laptop computer, or even expensive sunglasses. Suddenly, your emotions came into play. In addition to function, you weighed whether or not your choice would *feel* good — whether it would instill confidence, security, pride, or even a coolness factor. Ultimately, your emotions steered you toward your choice more than your mind did.

In setting your branding strategy, move emotional connection to the top of your list if any of the following apply:

- ✔ Your product is selected for the sense of satisfaction or security it delivers, the self-image it enhances, or the experience it provides — as much or more than for its factual attributes.

- ✔ Your product involves a major financial investment that contributes to the customer's ego or lifestyle. Not all high-priced items involve emotional connection (root canal, anyone?) but many do, including those that affect how buyers feel about themselves and how they appear to others.

- ✔ Customer loyalty is essential to your success. Face it, people stick with brands they love, and love, above all others, is the hallmark emotion.

Differentiate your product

When customers understand why your offering is different and better than all competing products, they have a clear reason to buy from you, and you have a secure market position.

If you're not 100 percent sure of how you stand apart from the competitive pack — or if you're sure but your customers seem confused or don't appear to find the distinction meaningful or motivating — then product differentiation needs to move up in the ranks of what you want to accomplish through your branding strategy.

Product differentiation is particularly important if you're facing any of these marketing challenges:

- ✔ Customers fail to see your offering as unique and distinctly beneficial.

- ✔ Your market environment is crowded with similar offerings.

- ✔ To win sales in your competitive environment, you frequently revert to a reliance on low pricing or discounting strategies rather than high value.

In some cases, simply fine-tuning your brand promise and marketing message is enough to win differentiation in the customer's mind. (Chapter 6 is full of information on these topics.) More often, though, to achieve meaningful distinction, you need to undertake at least some level of product modification in order to add meaningful attributes and benefits that your customer can't receive from competitors. Additionally, you many need to change the way you present your brand by changing your product packaging to magnify important distinctions that will pull customers in your direction at the moment of purchase. (If brand revitalization is in the cards, Chapter 17 can lead you through the process.)

Create credibility and trust

In any branding strategy, you absolutely must plan to establish or enhance credibility and trust. Brands, essentially, are reputations that result from promises made and consistently kept. If your brand fails to win on these two counts — if it fails to appear credible or trustworthy — it fails altogether.

When people buy services or when they buy online, they're buying based completely on trust that their expectations will be met. Therefore, every new service or online business needs to make credibility and trust a branding priority. Likewise, businesses that face credibility crises because they've failed to deliver on the promises they've made need to rebuild brand trust in a hurry.

To rate your brand's credibility and trust levels, ask yourself these questions:

✔ Do people believe we're credible and trustworthy?

✔ Do we appear credible?

✔ Do we act trustworthy?

✔ What promise do we make to customers?

✔ What guarantee or assurance do we extend?

✔ What additional promises can we make to build even higher levels of trust?

Your assessment of your current level of trust and your need to enhance the promise you make will determine the emphasis you put on heightening credibility and trust in your branding strategy.

Motivate purchasing

Brands are like great advance teams in that they establish interest, appeal, confidence, preference, and purchase motivation in a customer's mind before your product ever enters the arena.

For an idea of how brands work to presell products, consider this analogy: Looking back to the social scene of your high school days, which would you have preferred: a date with a person whose name you knew and respected, to whom you were attracted, and with whom you felt trust and a sense of pride in the potential association; or a blind date who didn't even come with an assurance from a good friend? In teen jargon, "Duh!" The answer's a no-brainer.

Faced with a selection, you and nearly everyone else opt for the safe choice. And the safe choice is the one you've heard of (awareness), the one that makes you feel good (emotional connection), the one with uniquely positive attributes (distinction), and the one you can rely on (credibility and trust).

Together, all the brand functions combine to create product preference and to motivate purchases, although all don't play equally in your branding strategy. If you're building a new brand, your initial branding emphasis will probably focus on developing brand awareness and differentiating your product. If you're refining or realigning an existing brand, you probably already have established strength in at least some of the functions. Therefore your future branding strategy will direct your efforts toward gaining strength in your current areas of weakness. The worksheet in Figure 3-3 helps you prioritize your efforts and design your strategy to motivate purchasing.

Figure 3-3:
Use this worksheet to assess the current strengths of your brand and to prioritize the strengths you want to achieve through your future branding strategy.

BRAND ASSET ANALYSIS WORKSHEET					
Assess the strength of your brand assets by assigning a rating of 1–5 (with 1 indicating poor value and 5 indicating outstanding value) in each of the following areas. Then determine whether your brand strength would be reduced if the brand asset were altered.					
Brand asset	Is it well-known?	Is it well regarded?	Is it well managed?	Would your brand strength be reduced if this asset were changed or eliminated?	
				Yes	No
Your brand name				☐	☐
Identifying elements					
Logo				☐	☐
Logotype/script				☐	☐
Slogan/tagline				☐	☐
Color scheme				☐	☐
Packaging				☐	☐
Your core message				☐	☐
Your dominance in a key market niche				☐	☐
Your relationship with key customer groups				☐	☐
Other				☐	☐
Other				☐	☐

Crunching the Numbers: Budgeting for Your Brand Building Program

Ask a handful of homebuilders how much it costs to build a home and you'll get a handful of different answers. The cost depends on the home being built. The same is true when the question is, "How much does it cost to build a brand?"

The variables involved in the cost of brand building include:

- **The amount of your own time and expertise you can commit:** Especially if your brand is local or your business is small, you can probably research your current brand image, define your desired brand identity, and determine the value of the brand assets you've already developed without bringing in professional help.

- **The extent to which your brand will venture:** If your brand will travel far from your home office and therefore will represent you when you're nowhere to be found, it had better be pretty impressive, which usually means that you'd better plan to make a more sizeable investment in branding than that required by a very small business with a small and geographically limited clientele.

- **The business level at which your brand will compete:** Playing in the major league is more expensive than playing in the minor league. If you intend to compete with established, well-known, superbly branded companies or organizations, you'd better invest in a brand that's up to the task, which means a do-it-yourself logo is out of the question, for example.

As you assemble your budget, flip back to Chapter 1 for an idea of the range of costs involved in each phase of the brand development process. Based on the variables listed, adjust the numbers to your unique situation as you assign costs for each of the following three phases of the branding process:

1. **Strategic development and positioning**

   This phase involves market research, brand identity research, brand aspiration research, and development of the positioning and branding strategies you'll follow to reach the branding success you seek. (If you plan to do a good portion of this work yourself, check out Chapters 4, 5, and 6.)

2. **Creation of brand identity elements**

   In this phase, professionals are worth their weight in gold. When it comes to creating, selecting, and protecting your name; designing your logo; devising your tagline; and developing the core marketing materials that will carry your brand into the marketplace, hire the best talent for the job.

If the job is development of a name and logo for a service business that faces only moderate competition in a localized market area, plan on a moderate investment. On the other hand, if the job is development of a name and logo that will travel not just past state lines but across international borders and through cyberspace to hundreds of thousands of business prospects, invest more heavily and amortize the cost for years to come.

3. Implementation of your brand strategy

When you've set your brand strategy and established your brand identity, implementing your branding program becomes part of your existing marketing program — and your existing marketing budget. Branding and marketing aren't separate in terms of message *or* money. Your brand strategy becomes the foundation for your marketing strategy, just as it becomes the basis of your business plan (see the next section).

If you don't have the heaviest hammer . . .

The old saying marketers use when dealing with small-budget clients is, "If you don't have the heaviest hammer, use the sharpest nail." How does that relate to branding?

If you don't have the biggest budget (or anything even close to a big budget), sharpen the focus of your branding program so that it works to achieve two brand functions above all others: target-market awareness and product differentiation. Make sure that every single communication that leaves your business helps those within your target market know who you are and why your offering is different and better.

The key to this strategy is focusing on your target market. If you don't have the biggest budget, don't try to talk to the biggest market. Tailor your brand and focus your communications on those who will make a difference to your success. Then as you send brand messages into your target marketplace, follow this advice:

✔ See that every single communication — online or offline, in person or through media — carries your brand identity without variation so that you etch a single, crystal-clear, professional brand image.

✔ Put your logo on absolutely everything that represents you and your brand in the marketplace.

✔ Add a tagline or slogan (see Chapter 8 for help) if your name doesn't adequately convey who you are, what you do, and why you're great.

✔ If you rely heavily on e-mail, add a signature line that presents your business name and tagline on your e-mail messages.

Building a brand image doesn't have to cost a fortune, but building a brand that doesn't cost a fortune *does* require target marketing and utmost consistency.

Making Brand Development Part of Your Business Plan

Your brand *is* your business; it's the presentation of what you are and what you stand for. Your brand is the way you present the promise your business makes to everyone it touches, whether as an employee, an investor, a customer, an associate, or a supporter in the form of a referring source, contributor, or friend.

Your business plan (you do have one, right?) is the blueprint for how you'll achieve business success. It includes the following components:

- ✔ **Your company overview,** which includes your mission, vision, values, key products, and business goals

- ✔ **Your business environment,** which includes your industry overview, market segmentation, customer profile, and competitive analysis

- ✔ **Your company strategy,** which includes your business model, goals, marketing plan, and growth strategy

- ✔ **Your company description,** which includes the products you offer, your research and operational capabilities, and your marketing strategy

In every one of these business plan components, your brand plays a starring role. It embodies your mission, vision, and values. It impacts your product development plans. It guides your market segmentation, customer targeting, and competitive strategy decisions. It determines what you do and say and how you look and feel. It keeps you true to your business promise.

When you build your business, essentially, you're building your brand, and vice versa. The two are interdependent and mutually beneficial.

Knowing the relationship between your mission, vision, and brand identity

This part confuses even the pros. The terms *mission, vision,* and *brand identity* all come with blurry edges that overlap and confound. For the record:

- ✔ **Your mission** is the broad purpose of your company and the affect it will have on others.

- ✔ **Your vision** is your long-term aspiration for your business. It's what you want to achieve through your business success.

- ✔ **Your brand identity** is a tangible expression that reflects and represents both your mission and your vision.

Those of us in the field of marketing spend hours trying to simplify the hierarchy of mission, vision, and brand identity, and here's a quick way to put the three in context: Your mission is the heart of your business, your vision is the eyes, and your brand identity is the face. (Chapter 6 helps you put all three into words.)

Committing to the branding process

Think of entering the branding process as entering a marriage — you have to agree to commit for the long haul.

Your brand is a reflection of your company's mission and vision. You'd think that if you know your company's mission and vision, identifying your brand and starting the branding process should be a piece of cake. But it rarely is. Many businesses reach for their mission and vision statements and realize that they never created them in the first place. Oops. Others have statements that, upon review, no longer accurately reflect where they want the business to go and what they want it to be. If either of these scenarios sound sounds familiar, don't be embarrassed. Instead, turn quickly to Chapter 6 for guidance in righting the wrongs.

Determining the kind of business you want your brand to reflect is a big and important decision that may take time and definitely takes patience. Set aside some time and head off on a planning retreat with all the people who make your business what it is. Together, you can define what you want out of your brand, how you'll measure success, and how you'll build a brand that can grow with your business and your customer base far into the future. When you embark on the planning process, turn to Chapter 6 for step-by-step advice to follow when creating your brand definition and brand promise.

Who's on First? Recruiting Your Branding Team

Your brand is the promise of what your organization is, what it stands for, and what benefits it delivers, and it's reinforced every single time people come in contact with any facet of your business. That means that everyone in your company is a representative of your brand. As you set out to create or revamp your brand, form a branding team that includes representatives from all aspects of your organization. Then, at key milestones along the way, bring your entire staff onto the team through updates and presentations.

Getting buy-in from the top down

Buy-in, participation, and leadership from the owners and top-level executives of your company are absolutely essential to your branding success.

Your brand is a reflection of the direction in which the top-level leadership is driving the company. If those in a position to make strategic business decisions don't understand and champion the brand you're building, they may as well lead the company away from its brand promise and toward a credibility train wreck.

Consider a photographic studio that builds a brand to reflect the expertise and exclusivity required to handle high-end corporate assignments that result in award-winning photos appearing in annual reports, internationally distributed brochures, and ads in the most prestigious publications. If the studio owner, in an effort to increase business, starts advertising to attract clients for wedding photos and high school graduation pictures, the prestigious attributes of the studio's brand promise to corporations go right out the window.

Your brand needs to be reinforced through every business decision and through every brand contact point. For that reason, it needs to have the interest and engagement of those who call the shots and keep the company true to its brand premise and promise.

Engaging all employees in the process

The only way to get company-wide commitment to your brand is to get company-wide awareness of your brand, backed by company-wide rules about how your brand is to be presented and protected.

Educate everyone from the CEO to part-time or freelance designers about your brand strategy, promise, identity, and presentation guidelines. Turn them into brand champions (use Chapter 13 as your playbook), and ensure that they know the rules for presenting your brand by following the advice for managing your logo in Chapter 8 and staying true to your brand promise in Chapter 14.

Take the time to put everyone on the same branding page. What they don't know *can* hurt you.

Part II
Building a Brand, Step-by-Step

The 5th Wave   By Rich Tennant

In this part . . .

Consider this part to be your brand construction guide. It starts by leading you through the equivalent of your environmental analysis, helping you research everything there is to know about your market conditions, customer preferences, and competitive conditions.

Next, it goes into site planning, helping you find and stake an available position for your brand in the market and in your customers' minds. Then architectural design begins and branding momentum revs up, first with the decision about exactly the kind of brand you're building, then with the selection of a great brand name, and finally with the design of the logo that will identify your brand at a glance and long into the future.

The only way to build a strong brand is to start with a solid foundation. This part helps you lay the cornerstone.

Chapter 4

Finding a Niche You Can Fill: Researching Your Market

*N*o matter what you're branding or whether you're building a new brand or revitalizing an existing brand, your effort has to start with market research, and here's why: Unless your budget is limitless (and we've yet to see one that is), you can't possibly try to talk to all the people who may have some interest in what you have to offer. You have to target both your message and your market.

Targeting your market involves figuring out which people are most likely to want what you're selling. You have to find out who they are, where they are, how they're best reached by media, what kinds of messages or offers will motivate them to buy, and, when they're ready to buy, what kind of buying and customer experience will make them satisfied and loyal to your brand.

If you have ESP or you're a genius with a crystal ball, you can guess at the answers. If you're like everyone else, you need to do some research, and that's what this chapter's all about. It helps you create a profile of your ideal customer and then determine your customers' purchase motivations, their preferred purchase channels and experiences, and the reasons they choose one brand over another in your category.

In the process of this research, you find your *market niche* — the select group of customers who share unique interests and needs that your offering alone can address. When you find your market niche, *presto!* You've discovered an open position for your brand in the crowded marketplace around you.

Defining Who Buys What You're Selling — and Why

You have to know your customers in order to know how to speak to them and how to create a brand experience that they find relevant, attractive, and motivating. If your market is comprised of teenagers and your marketing talks to seniors, you're communicating in a foreign language. That's an exaggeration, of course, but it makes the point of why this section is important.

Customer research is essential for of the following reasons, among others:

- **Customer research helps you define who your customers are and, better yet, who your most ideal customers are.** This information helps you design a brand strategy that attracts and wins more customers just like the very best ones you already have.

- **Customer research reveals the reasons your most ideal customers are attracted to your business.** With this knowledge, you can highlight in your branding strategy the attributes that your customers find most attractive, and you can design processes that enhance and complete the brand experience every time customers encounter your business.

- **Customer research reveals the reasons people *don't* buy your offering.** You can use this knowledge to fix deficiencies or differentiate between those who do and don't want what you're selling, which leads you straight to a market niche.

In the next sections, we focus on how to create a profile of who your customers are in factual terms and how to discover what your customers want and value, what motivates their purchase decisions, what buying patterns they follow, and what they prefer about the various brands in your category.

Your customer profile

Arriving at your customer profile involves a look at customer facts and figures, which usually fall into the categories of *geographics, demographics,* and *behavioral patterns.*

By knowing your customer geographics, you know *where* to reach your customers; by knowing their demographics, you know *who* to reach; and based on their behavior patterns, you know *how* to reach them.

If you're branding a new business, you don't have an established clientele to profile. Instead, describe the people you believe are most apt to buy from your new company based on what you know about customers in your industry and in the unique niche you're aiming to fill.

Mapping out geographics

To obtain geographic information, gather addresses off invoices, checks, or shipping labels, or ask customers for their zip codes during quick surveys. The findings tell you which neighborhoods, counties, states, or international regions are home to large concentrations of your customers. Analyze your findings by answering the following questions:

✔ **Do a majority of your customers live in a single geographic area?** The concept of *geodemographics,* or *cluster marketing,* stems from the premise that people who live in the same area tend to have similar traits, preferences, and buying patterns. If you notice that your customers cluster in concise market areas, study the economics and resident profiles of those market areas. You're likely to discover the values and purchase motivators of your customers.

✔ **Do customers from different market areas purchase from your business differently?** For example, suppose you discover that customers within close proximity to your business drop in for impulse and sale purchases, whereas those from farther away make appointments, stay longer, and buy higher-ticket items. With this information, you may conclude that convenience is a key brand attribute to those in the local market area, and expertise or exclusivity are key attributes to distant customers. Based on the market area you want to grow, you know which attribute to stress in your branding program.

Detailing demographics

Use personal observation or surveys to arrive at a factual analysis of your customer base. Focus on the following elements:

✔ **Gender:** What percentage of customers is male, and what percentage is female?

✔ **Age:** What percentage of customers falls into the following age groups: children, teens, 20–30, 31–40, 41–50, 51–65, and 65+?

✔ **Household composition:** Are most customers single, married, divorced, widowed, parents with children at home, couples without children at home, or grandparents?

✔ **Income information:** What income category do most customers fall into? Do most rent or own their homes? Are they retired, self-employed, professionals, or students?

✔ **Ethnic information:** Is most or a good percentage of your customer base of a specific nationality? What languages do they speak?

Uncovering behavioral patterns

Behavioral patterns usually stem from your customers' interests and beliefs.

- ✔ **Interests:** Do many of your customers share the same recreational interests? Do they tend to read the same kinds of magazines, watch the same kinds of TV programs, or listen to the same kinds of radio stations or music? Do they use the Internet?

- ✔ **Beliefs:** Is a good portion of your customer base members of the same kinds of groups, organizations, churches, political party, or other groups that they support and believe in?

What your customers want and value

When you know who you're trying to reach and where and how to reach them, you need to know *what* to say in order to address your customers' values, motivations, and purchasing patterns. The following questions can help you access the information you need:

- ✔ **What motivates your customers' purchase decisions?** Put differently, what needs or desires are your customers trying to fill when they purchase your product? Realize that the answer isn't always obvious. A couple may say that they like the design and quality of a particular new home when really they're motivated by the prestige of the neighborhood.

  To get to the root of your customers' purchase motivation, try to find out how your offering makes a customer feel. For instance, you may discover that the homebuyers like the design and quality of the home they're considering because it makes them feel prestigious or luxurious. By uncovering the feelings your product evokes, you know the basis of the buyer's motivation and the attributes to highlight in your branding strategy.

- ✔ **How do your customers approach your business?** Do they buy in-person, or by phone, mail, or online? Do customers decide to buy on their own or on the recommendation of or with the approval of someone else? Does your brand need to make a promise to the product consumer or to the purchase authority or referring agent? Or both? By knowing how customers reach your business and the factors that influence their purchase you'll be able to create a more effective branding strategy.

- ✔ **How do customers purchase your products?** By analyzing purchase patterns, you can uncover information about the brand attributes that matter most to customers.

  - Do most of your customers buy on impulse or after careful consideration? Careful consideration may indicate a need for trust and reliability assurances.

- Do they pay cash, charge, or buy on payment plans? Payment plans may indicate a greater sensitivity to price.

- Do they sign contracts or opt for multipurchase deals? Long-term commitments indicate high trust.

- If you offer an add-on warranty or service program, do most customers take the offering or decline it? Acceptance may indicate concern over ease of use or reliability.

- Are they interested primarily in price, or are their decisions made based on quality, prestige, convenience, or other values?

What sets your most ideal customers apart

Your most ideal customers are the people who buy the most from your business, cause the fewest problems, say the nicest things, and recommend you the most often. To determine if your most ideal customers have geographic, demographic, or behavioral traits in common (see the section "Your customer profile" for an explanation of those things), answer these questions:

✔ Do your most ideal customers tend to buy the same kinds of products or request the same kinds of options?

✔ Do they buy from your business simply to obtain your product or service, or do they think that your offering fulfills additional needs or interests — such as the ability to socialize, to feel the prestige of joining your exclusive or trendy clientele, to enrich themselves educationally through product samples or seminars, or to enjoy the level of your expertise or the safety of your trustworthiness?

✔ What attributes of your business do you think your most ideal customers value most highly: product quality, available features, convenience (your location or your purchasing options), reliability, staff expertise, customer support and service, price (high or low — some people are attracted to bargains and others to the highest level of premium offering), or other aspects of doing business with you?

✔ How do your most ideal customers buy? For example, do they buy on impulse, in bulk, on sale, and so on?

✔ Do your most ideal customers share any of the same demographic or lifestyle characteristics, such as gender, age, income, ethnicity, geographic location, beliefs, or values?

Who *might* be a customer? Inquiring minds want to know

In addition to studying your customers (check out the section "Defining Who Buys What You're Selling — and Why"), study your *inquiries.* Inquiries are prospective customers, and they're a great indicator of what kinds of messages and motivators attract interest to your business. To study your inquiries, do the following:

✔ **Track where your inquiries come from.** Use information from incoming phone calls, direct mail responses, in-person visits, and Web site activity reports to determine the geographic locales of people who are attracted to your offering. The findings may lead you to the development of new target market areas.

✔ **Pay attention to what kinds of marketing messages gain strong inquiry responsiveness, and then watch to see whether or not those inquiries result in sales.** You may discover that an attribute you tout in marketing draws a heavy response that doesn't convert to sales. Conclusion: On closer examination, your offering doesn't fulfill the inquiry's want or need. Either you need to enhance the strength of the attribute that drew the inquiry to you, or you need to shift your emphasis to a different, more-deliverable attribute in future marketing efforts.

✔ **Collect the names of those inquiring about your offering and then follow up with them to determine whether or not they purchased a product in your category.** Conduct a short survey by phone or mail to ask if they made a purchase, if they're still considering a purchase, or if they decided not to purchase. If they purchased a competing product, ask what distinguishing features or brand attributes led them from your offering to that of your competitors.

Why customers buy from you

Take all that you know about your customer demographics, geographics, behavioral patterns, and purchase values and motivations and answer this question: Why do customers choose to buy from you?

Commit your thoughts to paper using the format shown in Figure 4-1. Complete the form twice: once for your average customer and once for your most ideal customer. Use the information in the average customer form to determine how your brand must appeal to your current clientele. Use the information in the ideal customer form to determine which brand attributes to emphasize in order to shift your clientele to include more customers like those you currently consider the cream of the crop and also to enhance the brand experience that your most ideal customers count on from your business.

Figure 4-1:
Use this
form as you
create two
customer
descrip-
tions: one
that
describes
your current
customer
and one that
describes
your most
ideal
customer.

AT-A-GLANCE CUSTOMER DESCRIPTION
PROFILE: Our customers are predominantly __[gender]__ living in __[region]__ who __[a description of lifestyle facts such as: are married, own their homes, work as professionals, have young children living at home, and are members of business organizations and/or golf clubs]__ .
WANTS AND VALUES: Our customers value __[the attributes your customers value, for example Quality, Features, Convenience, Reliability, Expertise, Support, Service, Low Price, Prestige, or Exclusivity]__ .
MOTIVATIONS: The top reasons our customers buy from our business are: [we're conveniently located, they get to work directly with the owner/s, they want the best and perceive us to be more exclusive than our competitors, we get things done quickly and on budget, and so on] .

Digging Up the Info You Need

Of all the time and money spent on market research each year, the overwhelming majority is invested by a few huge companies. Hmmm . . . there's probably a correlation there: Big businesses get bigger by knowing and responding to customer wants and needs.

You can do the same, even without a huge research investment. If you're willing to devote time, you don't need a huge budget to unearth the information you need. You can start by looking for telltale signs within your own business and sales records. You can talk directly to customers (something that smaller business owners do on a daily basis anyway), and you can conduct do-it-yourself research.

Know thyself: Conducting a self-assessment of your offering

A successful brand strategy results in an accurate reflection of what you are and what you promise to those who come into contact with your business. That's why it's important to start your brand research by looking long and hard at your business to define your brand as it exists right now. Start by answering these questions:

✔ **What does your business do best?** What single thing above all others makes your business or product a great choice for customers? If you were to close tomorrow, what attributes that you offer would customers have the hardest time finding elsewhere?

✔ **What do customers buy most from your business?** Refer to your invoices, your order log, and your income statement. Where is the money coming from? Customers vote with their pocketbooks, so if most of your revenue comes from a single product or service line, that line probably represents the offering your customers value most highly.

✔ **What aspect of your business gets the most internal attention?** How do you or the leadership of your company allocate time and money to develop your business? Most companies prioritize efforts in one of the following areas: research and development, operations, marketing, distribution and delivery, management, organization, and customer service. What is the major emphasis in your company? Your answer probably points toward your business strength and a brand attribute.

✔ **What services do you offer or promise that your competitors don't?** A decade ago, who would have thought that delivering a pizza within 30 minutes would distinguish a brand? Domino's did. Who would have thought that promising to get a delivery to its destination overnight would set a company apart? FedEx did. Does your company make a promise — a promise that may feel like a minimal standard within your organization — that causes customers to choose and stick with your business? Look hard. Something as mundane as consistently putting jewelry in a robin's egg-blue box could be the factor that makes you the Tiffany of your category.

Tuning in to customer insights

To find out how your business is excelling and where it's lagging, you don't need to do formal research. Just talk to those who actually meet with your customers face-to-face — at the reception desk, at the customer service window, in the complaints or returns line, and on the sales floor. Or place yourself in a position to actually watch customers in action. What do they like? What attracts them? What confuses them? What causes them to look more closely? What causes them to turn away?

As you tap into customer insights, look for answers to these questions:

✔ **What requests do customers make that you currently don't fulfill?** Do customers wish you offered same-day delivery, easier parking, additional product features, streamlined service, or a real person on the other end of the line instead of your voicemail system? Ask everyone in your organization to add every request they hear to a *customer wish list*. You can't fulfill all requests — doing so could cause you to veer away from your brand identity — but you at least need to know what customers want so you can enhance your offerings when appropriate.

An example of customer input leading to brand enhancements comes right from our own Oregon backyard, where the High Desert Museum tuned in to customers and enhanced its reputation as a visitor destination. Museum volunteers and staff noticed that after about an hour and half at the museum, visitors started asking where they could get something to eat. A vending machine was the only answer, and you can bet that it did a brisk business. Still, after about two hours, guests drifted out the front door in order to find restaurants, leaving behind them the chance to join the museum membership or to shop longer in the museum store. But that was then, and this is now. Today, the museum has a full-service restaurant that serves visitors, allows for after-hours catered receptions, and enhances the museum's brand image as a place to spend not just a few hungry hours but a full day immersed in natural history and wildlife exhibits.

✔ **What complaints do customers register?** Establish a complaint log where employees can list customer complaints they receive or elements they believe to cause customer departures. You can only fix problems that you know about. According to research, for every complaint you hear, 26 customers have issues that they don't mention. So in addition to asking employees to record stated complaints, ask them to read unstated clues to dissatisfaction (see the next item in this list).

✔ **What hints of dissatisfaction do your customers give?** Ask everyone in your company to note compliments that customers share about your competitors. Ask them to record any positive mention of how things used to be ("Oh, for the good old days when a real person answered the phone"), and ask employees to let you know if they no longer hear the compliments that they used to hear frequently.

✔ **Which products are on back order? And which frequently get returned?** The answers to these two questions reveal what your customers want and don't want.

✔ **What displays, Web pages, or promotional offers get the most attention from your customers?** There's an old saying in marketing: "Sell what people are buying." In branding, the concept translates to something like this: Brand the attributes people want from your business. To uncover what they want, watch them move through your business. Watch the way they travel through your Web site, watch the promotional offers that win the greatest response, watch the carpet on your retail floor to see where it's most worn, and watch your shelves to see which ones are continuously depleted of inventory or which products are reordered continuously.

Conducting customer research

Sometimes you have to conduct more formal research in order to excavate the information you need to know from customers. Let this section guide you as you enter the realm of interviews, surveys, and focus groups.

Just watch! Observing customer behaviors

The section "Tuning in to customer insights" gets you started researching customer behavior simply by watching your customers in action. This section takes it a step farther and provides a few how-to tips and approaches for formalizing your customer observation research.

✔ **Watch how customers arrive at your business.** On at least a quarterly basis, consider the following:

- **If they arrive at your business online,** track the paths they take to your site. Do they follow links, and, if so, what do the links offer? If they come from search engine results, what terms are they researching? If they navigate through your site, where do they go? Your conclusions reveal how customers are attracted to your business.

- **If they arrive in person,** what kinds of cars do they drive? What kinds of clothes do they wear? Observe what shopping bags, if any, they carry. Do they arrive alone or with others? All are clues to customer interests and values. Based on your findings, you can enhance waiting areas, child play areas, refreshment offerings, or other amenities that cater to the ways your customers experience your brand and your business.

- **If they arrive via phone,** use caller ID features to pinpoint each caller's geographic location. Then work with your phone service provider to assess their phone experiences: How long do they stay on hold, how many hang up before getting through to someone in your business, and how many layers of automated responses do they go through before accessing the right information? Your findings tell you a lot about your inquiries (prospective customers), the satisfaction levels of your phone customers, and the interests they seek to address.

✔ **Watch where customers go when they're at your business.** This step is particularly important for businesses that serve customers on-site. Consider the following:

- **What do they do upon entry?** Do they ask about the nature of your business? If so, you know immediately that you need to enhance your brand awareness. Do they seem confused about what to do or where to go upon entry to your business? If so, you need to enhance your reception techniques or your directional signage. Do they encounter bottlenecks that cause initial negative reactions? Unless you're trying to convey that you're the busiest business in the world and that people would rather wait than go to a competitor, interpret your customers' reactions as the need for some service retuning.

- **What questions do they ask or hint at?** If they consistently ask about prices, or if they leave looking quizzically at the receipts in their hands, be ready to reassess your pricing or billing procedures.

If they have to ask repeatedly to touch the merchandise or to see samples of your work for other clients, understand that they have doubts about your offering and need the reassurances that only better displays and presentations can deliver. If they want to experience your product (a sure sign of engaged interest), be ready to offer anything from test-drives to testimonials that provide a sense of what it's like to be the proud owner of whatever you're selling.

- **Where do they stand or wait?** Go to the normal collection points in your business and see what your customers experience during wait times. Are they presented with brand messages? Are they encouraged to make add-on purchases? Are they asked to share their input about your business? If they do nothing but look around for what to do next, you're missing an opportunity to promote your brand or to collect information that allows you to make your brand stronger.

Just ask! Interviews and surveys

Before you take up your customer's time with an interview or survey, be clear about what you want the research to accomplish. Most research is intended to discover who your customers are and how to reach them, what your customers think of and want from products or services like the ones you offer, and how your customers may react to possible product or marketing innovations or revisions you're considering. As you collect information, follow this advice:

- ✔ **If you're collecting information to clarify your customer profile, you hardly need an in-depth interview or survey.** (For more on customer profiles, flip back to the section "Your customer profile" earlier in this chapter.) You can collect information through online or in-person customer registration forms, you can host contests that include the requested information on entry forms, or you can issue a customer information update request on a regular basis, perhaps accompanied by a small thank-you gift for those you count among your valuable customer base.

- ✔ **If you're working to assess levels of customer awareness, interest, or satisfaction, customer opinion surveys are a good tool for the task.** You can conduct short surveys in-person at the point of purchase, or you can collect more extensive information through questionnaires delivered via phone, mail, or e-mail.

For surveys that involve more than a few questions, most companies seek professional assistance as they develop their survey instruments. The tricky part is that although you want to collect information about your offerings in order to improve them, you don't want to fan any fires of discontent by spotlighting shortcomings or by unduly imposing on your customers' time. You also don't want to lead your customers to the answers you're seeking; if you do, the research is basically good for nothing. To balance your dueling desires for customer input and customer satisfaction, follow this advice:

- **Keep your survey short enough that it only takes a few minutes of your customers' time.** The exception is when you're dealing with highly loyal customers who are committed to your business and willing to invest heavily of their time.

- **Avoid general questions in favor of comparative questions that are more likely to elicit thoughtful and accurate responses.** For example, avoid a general question like, "On a scale of 1 to 10 with 10 being best, how do you rate our service?" Instead, ask, "On a scale of 1 to 10 with 10 being best, how satisfied were you with the service you received during your last visit to our business?"

- **Ask questions that help you understand how your customer relates to your product.** For example, you may ask, "On a scale of 1 to 10 with 10 being highest, how closely did our product live up to your expectations?"

- **Ask questions that reveal how you stack up against competitors in customers' minds.** For example, you may ask, "On a scale of 1 to 10 with 10 being highest, how convenient is our location compared to the location of other businesses where you can purchase similar products or services?"

✔ **To see how your customers react to a product or marketing idea, or to pinpoint subtleties in what they think or feel, consider chatting one-to-one in personal or phone interviews.** When conducting interviews, keep the following points in mind:

- **You waste everyone's time if you aren't truly open to any customer response to your idea.** If you (or those in a leadership position) already know what you're going to do and are simply seeking validation, save your time and money.

- **You may not be the best person to conduct the interview.** Generally, people are nice and polite and don't want to burst bubbles or hurt feelings. If a third-party professional researcher asks for your customers' opinions, the answers may be 180 degrees different (and more accurate) than what customers would admit to the owner of the idea.

Table 4-1 can help you determine when to seek professional help with your research program and when you can just go it alone.

Just listen! Using focus groups

Focus groups, by definition, are left to the professionals. A focus group is a gathering of customers or prospective customers who share input about a product or marketing idea with a professional moderator who guides the conversation, prompts input, and manages the discussion so it isn't dominated by one person or opinion. The only reason you should hold a focus group is if you want to weigh opinions, reactions, and risks before proceeding with an important product or marketing decision. Before holding a focus group, be clear about the information or idea you're presenting to the group and the kind of impressions you're seeking to collect before the session ends.

When to do it yourself and when to get research help

When you're dealing with market research, there are some things you can do yourself and others that you need outside help for in order to get the most accurate, useful results. Table 4-1 lays out various information-gathering approaches along with advice regarding when to involve professional assistance.

Table 4-1	Information-Gathering Approaches	
Desired Finding	*Method*	*When To Call in the Pros*
Customer profile	Information capture at first purchase, Web site registration, information requests on contest entry forms, information update requests, informal customer-intercept interviews	Seek assistance from Web site developers when creating online registration forms. You can handle the other methods yourself.
Customer awareness, interest, or satisfaction levels	Written or phone surveys	Seek professional assistance to develop survey questions that are clear and concise and don't lead or skew results and to analyze findings on complex issues.
Customer opinions or reactions to product or marketing ideas	In-person or phone interviews	Especially if the interview involves a sensitive issue, find a single, trained interviewer in your company or hire a professional so that all interviews are conducted in the same manner and by a person with whom the customer can be candid.
Customer input on product or marketing ideas	Focus groups	Involve a research professional to assemble the groups, to hold the sessions in rooms with two-way mirrors and recording capability, and to facilitate the discussion.

(continued)

Table 4-1 *(continued)*

Desired Finding	Method	When To Call in the Pros
Customer behaviors	Observation, document review	No professional assistance is necessary. Watching your customers or studying their order history is relatively easy and requires no customer interaction.

Where else to turn for facts and figures

Thanks to the Internet, the resources available to help you gather information about your market and customers are virtually without limit. Following are a few ways to focus your research efforts.

Go Web surfing

When you hit the Web, start with these recommendations and then let your imagination and your search engine take over:

- ✔ **Visit the Web sites of your competitors.** Check out how they present themselves, the brand attributes they highlight, and the new moves they're announcing to see what you're up against.

- ✔ **Go to government Web sites.** Start with www.census.gov for information on the population and resident characteristics in practically any U.S. community. Then move on to the Web sites of the business development departments that serve your target market areas, from your state's economic development department to the business resource center at your local chamber of commerce.

- ✔ **Search for organizations that serve the interests of your industry.** Enter your industry into a search engine and check out some of the top results in order to access facts and figures about the business arena in which you operate. For instance, when we enter "golf industry statistics" in our favorite search engine, one of the first results is the Golf Research Group, "the world's leading consultant and publisher of business information to the golfing industry." As another example, we enter "cellular phone industry statistics" into the search engine and one of the first results is for the Cellular Telecommunications & Internet Association, "the international association for the wireless telecommunication industry." Similar industry groups probably serve your business arena.

Hit the library reference shelves

In addition to reference materials specific to your industry, check out these two marketing sourcebooks:

✔ **ESRI Community Sourcebooks:** These volumes contain population, demographic, and income data as well as other consumer information for every U.S. zip code, Direct Marketing Area (DMA), and Metropolitan Statistical Area (MSA). The information is valuable as you work to forecast demand for your products, note population trends, and analyze the composition of your target market area.

✔ **The Lifestyle Market Analyst:** Published by Standard Rate and Data Service (SRDS) and Equifax, this guide provides demographic and lifestyle data organized by geographic market area, lifestyle interests, and consumer profiles.

Putting It All in Perspective

Knowing as much as you can about who you're trying to reach and what your target customer wants and needs helps you make essential decisions as you create your branding strategy. But beware: People can smell a fabricated fake. You have to *be* what you say you are. If your customers want "cool and trendy," you have to be cool and trendy before you amplify that message in the marketplace. You have to be able to walk your talk.

The most powerful brands are created by those with strong personalities, aspirations, and passions. A great example is Martha Stewart. On an episode of the show *The Apprentice,* she reprimanded one of the contestants for relying too heavily on research findings. She used her own organization as a counterpoint, explaining that rather than creating products in response to customer desires, her company created unquestionably great products and *then* created customer desire. The same statement applies to most every current and historic great brand leader, from Steve Jobs to Walt Disney to Oprah Winfrey. All have strong opinions and clear visions. Even when they were told that their ideas wouldn't fly, they proceeded, and then they created the desire that led to the best branding case studies in the world.

Use research not to create your brand message but to fine-tune it. Start with passion, and build from there. If your brand doesn't have your heart and soul in it, no amount of research can give it a successful life.

Seizing Marketplace Opportunities

Chapter 2 features an illustrated view of the branding process as it moves from brand essence to brand esteem. The final leg in the branding race is to realign your brand to address market conditions, purchase behaviors, and customer aesthetics, and that final phase is never done. Your brand lives in the here and now, and the only way to keep it alive and healthy is to constantly keep it attuned to the wants, needs, interests, and opportunities that exist in the world not just of today but of tomorrow.

Your brand is a player in pop culture, so the more you tune in to the changing world around you, the more your brand will remain current — and relevant.

To keep your brand on top of marketplace opportunities, you don't have to be a seer who forecasts the future. You just have to look beyond the known environments of your business and social arena for new ideas, needs, products, fads, trends, and market frenzies. To put yourself in position to seize opportunities, follow these suggestions:

- **Stay close to your customers.** Only by listening and observing can you know what they want but can't find or what new needs they're dealing with that marketers haven't yet addressed.

- **Get close to your noncustomers.** It sounds counterintuitive, but you need to keep an eye on what people who are the polar opposite of your customers are into. Urban youth certainly didn't fit the customer profile of high-end fashion boutiques, but it didn't take long for the grunge look to affect haute couture anyway. To keep your brand current, widen your marketplace view. Tune in to what may feel like the foreign language of teenagers even if your market is comprised of senior citizens. Read technology publications even if your business arena is in the professional services.

- **Be ready to update and align your brand to the changing market environment.** Check out Chapter 17 for help with this task.

- **At all times, watch for unmet needs and unserved market segments.** A branding success opportunity may await you if you can fill a hole in the market. See the sidebar on *DOS For Dummies* for a prime example.

DOS For Dummies launched a global phenomenon

Way back in 1987, when computerese was a foreign language and computer manuals were practically impossible to understand, a frustrated customer was overheard wishing for a simple how-to book that explained the DOS operating system. According to lore, he said, "Something like DOS For Dummies." In 1991, Dan Gookin's book with that very title hit bookshelves. Booksellers were leery that the title would insult their customers, but they agreed to stock the book after they saw how well it was selling.

Today, 150 million books later, the *For Dummies* phenomenon is a branding case study. If you want proof that brands emerge with full strength when they address real and unmet needs and when they're propelled by the founder's passion and powerful belief, look no further than the yellow and black book you're smartly holding in your hands.

Chapter 5

Filling Your Niche: Positioning Your Brand

In This Chapter

▶ Determining your brand's point of distinction

▶ Finding an available, meaningful market position to fill

▶ Getting real about your competition

▶ Putting your brand position to the test

*D*epending on who's counting, today's average consumer faces a barrage of up to 3,000 advertising and promotional messages every single day. People cope with the onslaught in two ways. First, they tune out messages that don't appeal to their wants and needs. Second, they brush off messages for offerings they already buy from trusted suppliers unless — and here's the whole point of finding and protecting a position for your brand — the offering being presented is uniquely and attractively different and better.

To get through the noise and clutter of today's marketplace, you have to win a competitive position by presenting your offering as unique and different in a way that truly matters to customers. Then, after your brand wins a place in your customers' minds, you need to hold on to your position by delivering a brand experience that's so perfectly suited to customer desires and expectations that your clientele sees no reason to let any competing brand into the space you fill.

Branding expert Walter Landor, the creative and strategic genius behind many of the most famous brands you know today, is widely quoted for his assertion that "Products are made in the factory, but brands are created in the mind." This chapter helps you find an available space to create your brand in the minds of your customers.

The Marketing Muscle of Positioning

From playing with childhood puzzles, you know that you can't force a square peg into a round hole. You also can't force a square peg into a space already filled by another square peg, right? In order to fit a new peg into a puzzle, you need to find an open space and fill it with a piece that matches up perfectly. When you do, the piece drops effortlessly into the open slot and sits securely in place.

The same principle applies to the human mind. You can't fit an idea into a customer's mind unless it matches up with a need or desire that the customer genuinely cares about and that isn't already addressed perfectly by another idea or offering.

Positioning is the process of finding an unfulfilled want or need in your customer's mind and filling it with a distinctively different and ideally suited offering.

Finding a Position of Your Own: The Birthplace of Your Brand

To build a brand, you have to build a positive collection of perceptions in your customers' minds. As with any construction project, before you can actually do the building, you have to select and prepare the site. That's the role positioning plays in the branding process.

Before you can define, identify, and launch your brand, you have to find the position where your brand will live in your customers' minds and hearts. (Flip back to Chapter 2 for an illustration of the branding process and to see how positioning paves the way for your brand definition and identity.)

As you seek your position, follow one of the following four most common positioning approaches that we explain in this section.

Fulfill an unfilled need

Think of this as the find-an-itch-and-scratch-it approach. You study your customer wants and needs, see a desire that isn't addressed by any existing product or service, and move quickly to beat any competitor to the solution.

The resulting brand, created in response to an existing desire, slides right into an available slot in the customer's mind — as long as you seize the open position before anyone else stakes claim to it.

WeightWatchers is a great example of fulfilling a need. Founder Jean Nidetch turned a living room conversation about how to lose weight into a brand that's now 40 years old and known around the world for its weekly support group meetings that help customers lose weight and keep it off.

Specialize to create a new market niche

Marketers that follow this positioning route aim to provide the absolute best solution to a very exclusive or narrow segment of the market. This approach is the polar opposite of trying to be all things to all people. Specialty brands exist in large, crowded fields; rather than trying to compete with the pack, a business finds a way to serve a well-defined portion of the market in a uniquely attractive way. As a result, it creates a *market niche,* a select group of customers who have similar wants and needs that have been overlooked by competing businesses.

EasyJet created a market niche when the company set out to cater to the cost-conscious, plan-it-yourself traveler with self-proclaimed "cheap flights." EasyJet called itself "Europe's leading low-cost airline," marketing to low-budget, no-frills customers with the tagline "The Web's favorite airline."

Transform an established solution

This evolutionary approach to positioning involves taking a solution that currently exists in the marketplace and transforming it into a new solution that's so different that it spawns a whole new product category. Examples include the transformation of computers into laptops, cars into electronic or hybrid machines, and the coffee shop into an upscale European-style café experience, to name a few.

Creating a new solution to an already-addressed desire or need takes enormous insight into the popular culture and plenty of marketing power to get the word out. To succeed with this approach to positioning, you need to have or hire people with the capability to spot fads and predict trends. You also need plenty of money — both to evolve currently available products into a new innovation and to promote the resulting new product with such velocity and strength that you can lay claim to the first position in the new product category before competitors have time to leap into the arena.

The iPod is a perfect example of this type of positioning. Apple responded to the market's desires for miniaturization, maximum capacity, and mind-boggling design in 2001. Apple CEO Steve Jobs unveiled the iPod as a Mac-compatible product that puts "1,000 songs in your pocket." By 2005, the iPod was the best-selling digital audio player in the world and an essential accessory in the minds of people who had never before even considered carrying their music around with them.

Discover an all-new solution

Creating an all-new product or service to fill a want or need that no else has even noticed or thought to address is the revolutionary approach to branding. All-new solutions come from the minds of people who see the same problems everyone else sees, but they ignore conventional thinking and come up with entirely new solutions. Most brand-new brand ideas are built upon existing ideas; a few examples are car radios, TV dinners, and exercise bikes.

Gaining a market position, awareness, and adoption for a brand-new idea takes patience and a massive marketing investment. After all, you're not just introducing a product, you're introducing a whole new paradigm for which the market may or may not be ready.

The Segway Human Transporter is a great example of this revolutionary approach to branding. It was introduced by inventor Dean Kamen in 2001 to "transform a person into an empowered pedestrian" and to create a whole new way to move people on "fun, smart transportation."

Figuring Out What You Do Better Than Anyone Else

The key to your market position is your *point of difference,* also called your *point of distinction* or your *unique selling proposition* (USP).

Your unique attributes are what set you apart from your competitors and attract clients to your offering. Without clearly defined and communicated distinctions, people basically view a product as a commodity chosen simply for its availability or lowest price and easily passed over for any similar offering that seems to fill the same bill with less effort or expense. (See Chapter 2 for plenty of information on commodities.)

To avoid the one-is-as-good-as-another trap, take these steps:

- ✔ **Find something true about yourself, your business, or your product that can define and differentiate you while also addressing a genuine market interest or need.**

- ✔ **Make customers aware of the unique benefits or value that they receive only when they work with your business or buy your product.** For example, take note the next time you're invited to participate in a taste test, when you watch an ad showing how much better one paper towel sops up moisture over another, or when you see before-and-after photos proving a product's effectiveness. These demonstrations are ways that marketers work to make you aware of the unique advantages that only their products deliver.

- ✔ **Reinforce your positive point of difference every single time the customer encounters your name, your product, or your staff or in any other way comes into contact with your brand experience.**

Just being different isn't enough for a successful positioning strategy. An automobile manufacturer that introduces the only car to burn gasoline at a rate of one gallon every two miles has a point of distinction but no point of attraction. To position your brand, you need both attraction and distinction.

- ✔ The **attraction** comes from providing values and attributes that customers genuinely want or need.

- ✔ The **distinction** comes from providing values and attributes that customers can only receive when they work with your business or buy your product.

In order to win a meaningful, distinctive position in the market, you need to shine a spotlight on your most outstanding attributes. So what are they?

To conduct a self-assessment of your offering, use the worksheet in Figure 5-1. (If you need help digging up the information you need, flip back to Chapter 4.) Enter your company's greatest strengths in the left-hand column. Then use the following columns to enter assessments of how well you, your management team, your staff, and your customers feel that your offering distinguishes your business and set you apart in your competitive marketplace. When you see a resounding "best" across the board, you know you've landed on an attribute of distinction.

ASSESSING THE STRENGTH OF YOUR BRAND ATTRIBUTES: WORKSHEET				
✔ How each attribute rates against the attributes of competitive offerings				
Attribute	Your opinion of this attribute	Opinions of top managers	Opinions of front-line staff	Opinions of customers
	Best Good Average	Best Good Average	Best Good Average	Best Good Average
Enter the most outstanding aspect of your best-selling product or service	☐ ☐ ☐	☐ ☐ ☐	☐ ☐ ☐	☐ ☐ ☐
Enter the product aspect you've spent the most time or money developing	☐ ☐ ☐	☐ ☐ ☐	☐ ☐ ☐	☐ ☐ ☐
Enter the value most customers seek from your offering (such as quality, features, convenience, reliability, expertise, support, service, low price, prestige, or exclusive price)	☐ ☐ ☐	☐ ☐ ☐	☐ ☐ ☐	☐ ☐ ☐
If you closed tomorrow, what one attribute would your customers miss most or find hardest to replace?				

Figure 5-1: Honestly assess the strength of your brand attributes.

Deciding Which Customers You Serve the Best

Positioning involves focusing — not just on what you do best but also on the market segment you serve best. Instead of trying to please all people in all ways, great brands please some people — a defined segment of market — in an extraordinary way because of the unique and meaningful attributes and experiences the brands offer.

Which segment of the market do you serve best? To find out, compile your answers in the Customer Profile worksheet illustrated in Figure 5-2. If you're not sure of your answers, flip back to Chapter 4 for advice on how to conduct research about where your customers are, who they are, what they value, and how they prefer to buy products like the ones you're offering.

CUSTOMER PROFILE WORKSHEET

Geography
Where are your customers? Do they live or work in specific neighborhoods, regions, states, or countries?_____

Demography
Gender   __% Male   __% Female

Age   __% Children   __ % Teens   __% 20–30   __% 31–40
              __% 41–50   __% 51–66   __%65+

Education   __% Current Students   __% High School Diploma
              __% University Degree   __% Post-Graduate

Household Information
Are customers predominantly single, married, divorced, or widowed? _____
Are they parents with children still at home, couples without children at home, grandparents, and so on?_____
Do they rent or own their homes, and what kinds of homes do they live in?
_____

Income
What income category do most customers fall under? _____
What are their professions: Are they retired, self-employed, professionals, or students? _____

Ethnic Information
Is your customer base of a specific nationality? What languages do they speak? _____

Behavioral Patterns
Interests
What are the recreational interests of your customers? _____
What magazines do they read, programs do they watch, and music do they listen to? Do they use the Internet? _____

Beliefs
Do your customers participate in particular groups, organizations, churches, political parties, or other associations? _____

Buying Patterns
Do your customers decide to purchase on their own or upon the advice of others, and whom? _____
Do they buy on impulse or after careful consideration? _____
Do they pay cash, charge, or buy on payment plans? _____
Would you say they're more price-conscious or status-conscious? _____
Do they put greater value on quality or service than on price? _____

Figure 5-2: Use this worksheet as you create a customer profile to focus your branding strategy on the type of person and the market niche you serve best.

Finding Your Place in the Competitive Landscape

To position your brand, you need to look at how your offering fits within your competitive landscape, including

- ✔ How your customers think your offering ranks
- ✔ How you think your offering ranks

In a perfect branding world, your customers' beliefs and perceptions about your offering match precisely with what you believe to be your brand's distinguishing characteristics and attributes. However, for all but the best-built and best-managed brands, the matchup is less than perfect. In fact, you're probably holding this book because you sense a gap between what you think makes you different and better and how you think your offering is perceived in your marketplace.

If people misunderstand your brand, you can't just wave a magic wand to change their minds. You have to move strategically from the position your brand currently occupies in customers' minds to where you want it to be. You also have to be sure that the position you want your brand to hold in the marketplace isn't already taken by some other brand.

Putting your brand on the positioning map

Use a positioning matrix like the one illustrated in Figure 5-3 as you work to determine where your brand fits in your competitive landscape.

Figure 5-3 shows how Di Lusso Bakery Café, a client of Bill's company, Brand Navigation, mapped its position in its competitive environment of coffee shops and casual eateries. Using a framework that plotted competitors based on type of customer experience (ranging from global brand to local cafe) and café atmosphere (ranging from old world to contemporary), Di Lusso determined that its desired brand position was more old-world and more local than its two major competitors.

Create a similar map for your brand using attributes that matter most in your competitive arena. For instance, a specialty food products brand may position competitive offerings along axis lines based on food preferences (traditional to gourmet) and pricing (affordable to premium). A ski resort may position competitive offerings along axis lines based on type of ski experience (one-day recreation to destination resort) and price (affordable to premium).

Brand Positioning Matrix

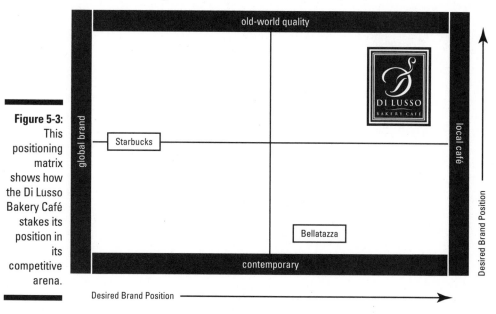

Figure 5-3:
This positioning matrix shows how the Di Lusso Bakery Café stakes its position in its competitive arena.

If you're creating a branding strategy for an existing brand, as you place your brand on your positioning matrix, be reasonable about the position it currently holds in the minds of your customers. Moving your brand from its current position to a new position isn't like moving furniture. You can't just pick your brand up and slot it into a new space. Your customers — not you — move your brand to a new position based on the impressions they receive consistently over time. To change your market position, you need to build upon what customers currently believe by conveying messages, making impressions, and delivering experiences that logically move your brand toward your desired competitive position. The chapters in Part III help you plan your repositioning strategy and get the word out.

Determining your point of difference

Your *point of difference* determines your position in your competitive environment. It defines the precise segment of the market that you serve best and how your offering is distinctively unique from that of businesses or products that provide similar but different solutions and experiences.

Package your position as an experience

In any competitive arena, a number of brands compete for the same space on the positioning matrix by claiming to be the friendliest, to have the highest quality, to offer the lowest prices, or to excel in any other attribute you can think of. Yet one brand prevails and wins recognition from the marketplace, mystifying all the competitors who truly think and can even prove that their attributes in the area of distinction are better.

So what tips the customer's perception toward one competitor and away from the others? As in most other things in life, firsthand experience trumps all other forms of communication. In spite of the fact that a number of competitors offer similar services, prices, or quality, in each arena, one brand delivers an experience that expresses the attribute in such a way that customers believe it to be the best. And that belief gets reinforced every time the customer encounters the brand in any way or at any time.

As you define your unique point of difference and stake your position, create an experience that allows your customer to feel the difference firsthand. For example, if you say that your position is economy, create a warehouse environment and experience. If your position is exclusivity, create an exclusive experience that includes individualized service and second-to-none responsiveness.

The brands that win the positioning war are those that get their strategy right, convey their distinguishing attributes with utter consistency, and deliver an experience that differentiates them from all the others. Help your customers constantly experience your difference, and your unique position is reaffirmed every time the customer brushes up against it.

Many businesses, especially many small businesses that desperately want to increase sales, try to make their products attractive to anyone and everyone. They're afraid to pinpoint their distinctions or target precise market segments for fear that they'll miss sales opportunities. In fact, the reverse is true. If you can't tell customers what you do best, they have no reason to choose your offering. If you try to tell them you're best at everything, your claim isn't very credible.

Before you begin the process of putting your brand into words (see Chapter 6), you need to define your point of difference in your competitive environment. Use the following template:

> [*Name of your business, product, or service*] is the [*your distinction and the generic term for your type of offering*] to provide [*your unique features or benefits*] to [*your customer profile*] who choose our offering in order to feel [*your customers' emotional outcome*].

In this statement, your distinction may be along the lines of "best," "first," "only," "most-recommended," or "highest-ranking." The generic term for your type of offering may be "café," "mouthwash," "how-to manual," "homebuilder," "sports drink," or "Web designer." Examples of customer profiles include "local residents with global mindsets," "upwardly mobile young professionals seeking enhanced status,"and "parents wanting to provide their children with opportunity and enrichment." Finally, your customers' emotional outcome may be "secure," "successful," "self-confident," or "indulged."

No copycats! Avoiding the fate of a me-too brand

This section is brief because the headline just about says it all. A *me-too brand* is one that offers exactly what another brand offers with no distinctive attributes other than the fact that it's presented by a different marketer.

If you try to slot your brand into a market or mind position already taken by a competitor, you face a long and tough uphill battle. Trying to unseat a competitor requires that you convince customers to move away from their current choice first. Only then can you convince them to move toward your offering. That's double the marketing work with half the assurance of marketing success. After all, telling customers that what they believe is wrong is a slow way to make friends and influence perceptions.

An equally bad idea is trying to leverage off someone else's brand. By likening your brand to someone else's, all you do is cast a spotlight on a competitor and point out your own second-string position.

The best alternative is to find your own position by filling an unfilled need, specializing to serve a market segment or niche, or creating an all-new solution. (Flip back to the section "Finding a Position of Your Own: The Birthplace of Your Brand" earlier in this chapter for a rundown of these approaches.)

Testing and Protecting Your Position

As soon as you're clear about your customer profile, your place in your competitive environment, and the point of difference that sets you apart and provides customers a reason to buy from you and you alone, you're ready to write your *positioning statement*. A positioning statement describes your offering, your market, and the point of difference or unique distinction that sets your offering apart from competing alternatives.

Your positioning statement defines the niche that only your offering fills in the marketplace and the distinction that you'll highlight in all marketing efforts. Your positioning statement isn't a public announcement; rather, it's an internal marketing compass. After you establish your positioning statement, use it within your company to guide all your branding and marketing communication efforts.

Before writing your positioning statement, answer these questions:

✔ Is your point of difference unique and hard for a competitor to duplicate?

✔ Do your distinctions or differences truly matter to your customers?

✔ Does your offering synch well with economic and cultural trends?

✔ Will customers believe your claims about your offering? Why *should* they believe you? Can you support or prove your claim?

If you can answer "yes" to these questions, it's time to sharpen your pencil or open your word processing program to start writing your positioning statement. Your positioning statement should contain the following points, in order:

1. Name of your company or product

2. Your business description

3. A summary of your point of difference

4. Your customer profile

Here's an example positioning statement: *Valley Homes home construction is the first company to build energy-efficient, custom-designed, affordable homes for Central Valley residents seeking to build quality, one-of-a-kind residences on the homesites of their choice.*

After writing your positioning statement, evaluate its accuracy by asking

✔ Is it believable?

✔ Is it consistent with what people who know your business believe to be true about you, the way you operate, and the benefits you deliver?

✔ Can you consistently deliver the distinct attributes as they're stated?

✔ Can you package and deliver your point of difference with such consistency that, every single time customers encounter your brand, your distinction is reinforced and the experience reminds customers of why they chose and remain loyal to your brand?

Steer clear of positioning landmines by making sure that your positioning statement avoids these problem areas:

✔ Be sure that no other brand already owns the position you're trying to claim.

✔ Be sure that your point of difference is one you can protect. For instance, don't base your position on having the lowest price because a competitor can always best you on that front.

✔ Be sure that you don't build your position around an attribute you can't control, such as being the "only provider of XYZ service." Unless you can set up a barrier to entry by competitors through a license or some other protection, you leave yourself vulnerable to having the very attribute you built your brand upon eroded by a quick move by a new player in your game.

When your positioning statement passes these tests, you've found a place to build your brand. Congratulations! Now you can start putting your brand promise and brand definition into words (see Chapter 6).

Chapter 6

Putting Your Brand into Words

In This Chapter

▶ Knowing your business mission and vision

▶ Defining your brand

───────────────────────────────

*B*uilding a brand and building a home have two things in common: Both need a site to occupy — a house lot in the case of a home and a market position in the case of a brand — and both require a plan that you can follow in order to achieve the desired outcome.

The process of finding a place to build your brand both in your marketplace and in your customers' minds is called *positioning;* it's the first important step in branding and the topic of Chapter 5. Planning the brand you intend to create is what this chapter is all about.

In this chapter, we help you lay the foundation for a brand that accurately reflects the essence of what you stand for and how you operate. We begin with a look at your mission and vision statements (and help you write statements if you don't already have them). Next, we help you define the promise you make to all who deal with you and your organization. After that, we guide the crafting of your brand identity statement and your core brand message. Finally, we help you write the brand character statement that influences all expressions of your brand — your name, logo, tagline, advertising, Web site, the products and services you offer, the staff you assemble, the customer experience you deliver, and the reputation you develop as a result.

Dusting Off Your Business Vision, Mission, and Values

Your brand is a reflection of what you stand for, so it has to align perfectly with the values and purpose of your business or organization.

If you're unclear about what your business is, why it exists, who it serves, and what it promises, this section is especially for you. It's also a must-read if you have a good sense of your vision and mission but haven't yet committed anything to writing. This is the time to put ink on paper.

To arrive at a brand that perfectly reflects the essence of your company, you need to write three essential statements:

- ✔ **Your vision statement,** which defines your long-term aspirations. It explains why you're doing what you're doing and the ultimate good you want to achieve through your success. Think of your vision as the picture of where you ultimately want your work to lead you.

- ✔ **Your mission statement,** which defines the purpose of your company and the effect you intend to have on the world around you. It states what you do for others and the approach you follow in order to achieve the aspirations you've set for yourself, your organization, or your business. Think of your mission as the route you'll follow to achieve your vision.

- ✔ **Your business promise,** which summarizes the positive difference you deliver to all who deal with your organization. Internally, your business promise guides the development of all elements of your brand. Externally, your business promise is sometimes translated into and presented as a motto or tagline.

For an example of how a vision and mission translate into a tagline, consider the Cystic Fibrosis Foundation, an organization working to cure a genetic disease that affects approximately 30,000 children and adults in the United States. The Foundation's brand statements are as follows:

- ✔ **Vision:** To identify the resources and people needed to cure cystic fibrosis.

- ✔ **Mission:** To assure the development of the means to cure and control cystic fibrosis and to improve the quality of life for those with the disease.

- ✔ **Brand tagline:** Adding tomorrows every day.

Use the information in the following sections to write statements that guide your organization and the development of your brand.

Refocusing your vision

Your brand is the tangible expression of your vision. It's the banner that waves what you're passionate about and what you aspire to achieve. Just as the images on a country's flag symbolize the core of what is important to that culture and nation, your brand symbolizes the core of what's important to you and your organization.

Whether you've written it down or not, you probably have a vision of the good that you, your business, or your organization hopes to achieve in your world. Likewise, you probably have a set of principles and values that guide how you operate and what you are and aren't willing to do to achieve success.

As a prerequisite to writing your brand identity statement (see "Mission Possible: Defining Your Brand" later in this chapter), put your values and vision into words. Your values and vision are fundamental to what your business is and stands for, and therefore they're essential to the brand image that's reflected to the public.

The values you value

Start by clarifying your *values* — your beliefs about your responsibility to your employees, clients, business associates, and community. The worksheet in Figure 6-1 can guide your thinking.

VALUES WORKSHEET

Use the provided values as a point from which to launch your thinking as you list all the values that steer your decision-making and the direction of your organization. After you compile a list of all values you believe play a significant role in your business decisions and plans, put a check mark alongside the few that you feel take precedence over all others.

☐ Satisfied customers	☐ Maximum profits	☐ Long-term success
☐ Enjoyable business atmosphere	☐ Healthy, satisfied, fulfilled employees	☐ Dominant market position
☐ Leading technologies an innovations	☐ Industry and market recognition	☐ Environmental protection
☐ Product quality	☐ Ethical standards	☐ Contribution to community
☐ _____	☐ _____	☐ _____
☐ _____	☐ _____	☐ _____
☐ _____	☐ _____	☐ _____
☐ _____	☐ _____	☐ _____

Figure 6-1: Determine the values that influence business decisions in your organization.

Your statement of values can take the form of a simple list that declares the principles that steer your company. For example, the Whole Foods Web site dedicates a page to a list of the company's core values, including the following:

- ✔ Selling the highest quality natural and organic products possible
- ✔ Satisfying and delighting our customers
- ✔ Supporting team member happiness and excellence

✔ Creating wealth through profits and growth

✔ Caring about our communities and our environment

Envisioning your highest hopes and aspirations

Your *vision statement* puts into a single sentence the reason your business exists. Regardless of whether you move offices, make operational changes, update your logo, revise your marketing message, or undertake any number of other strategic or tactical changes, the vision of what you're aiming to achieve, the good you intend to do in your world, should remain stable.

Many organizations post their vision statements on their corporate Web sites. Following are a few examples:

✔ Habitat For Humanity Australia: A world where everyone has a decent place to live.

✔ Boys & Girls Clubs of Canada: Leading the way to a brighter future for Canada's children and youth.

✔ Volvo Car Corporation: To be the world's most desired and successful premium car brand.

✔ Virginia Tech: To do things that matter and that have a profound impact on our changing world — whether it is in the classroom, the laboratory, or a village in a developing country.

As you develop your own vision statement, take some time to answer these questions:

✔ Why do you and those in your organization get up and go to work every day? You could earn a living at any number of places, so what is it about your organization that keeps you loyal and motivated?

✔ Ultimately, what good are you aiming to affect in your world? What lasting difference do you want to make?

✔ What ultimate benefits do your products and services deliver?

Use your answers to compile a short vision statement that summarizes what you feel is the highest purpose of your business.

Building your brand on the strong back of your business mission

Your vision is your ultimate dream; your mission is how you'll achieve your aspirations.

As you can see from the two examples in this section, there's no one format to follow in writing your business mission. All that really matters is that your mission statement covers the following points:

- The products or services you provide
- Who you serve
- How you are unique
- What benefits or greater good you promise

As an example, consider the vision of the Boys & Girls Clubs of Canada: *Leading the way to a brighter future for Canada's children and youth.* A brighter future for children and youth is the organization's ultimate aspiration. The road map to get there is contained in the organization's supporting mission statement: *The mission of all Boys and Girls Clubs of Canada is to provide a safe, supportive place where children and youth can experience new opportunities, overcome barriers, build positive relationships, and develop confidence and skills for life.*

As you write your own statement, don't get hung up on the format or on the idea that your statement has to look just like anyone else's. For instance, look at how different the mission of the Boys & Girls Club is from the mission of the Peace Corps, which reads:

> *Three simple goals comprise the Peace Corps mission:*
>
> *1. Helping the people of interested countries in meeting their needs for trained men and women.*
>
> *2. Helping promote a better understanding of Americans on the part of the people served.*
>
> *3. Helping promote a better understanding of other peoples on the part of all Americans.*

As you begin to strengthen your mission statement or write one for the first time, the worksheet shown in Figure 6-2 can help. It presents questions to help focus your thinking before providing a framework into which you can enter the components of your statement.

As you polish your statement into its final form, use language and a format that reflects the nature and tone of your business. Some statements are formal, and some are relaxed; some are short, and some are long. No matter how your mission statement looks or sounds, be sure to

- **Avoid jargon.** Instead, use language that anyone inside or outside your company can easily understand.

- **Avoid generalizations in favor of specific descriptions.** Rather than say "We serve elderly Americans," say "We serve elderly, recently widowed Americans who are living independently in their own homes."

STATING YOUR MISSION WORKSHEET
In a sentence, how do you describe what your company does?
In a phrase, what product or service do you offer?
In a phrase, what group of people do you serve?
What benefits or positive outcome do you promise to those you serve?
When thinking about your offerings compared to competitive offerings, what words would those who know your business well use to explain how you are different or better?
Mission Statement Framework [*Name of your business*] provides [*description of the product or service your business offers*] for [*describe the group of people you serve*] who seek [*define the positive benefit you deliver*] and who prefer our solution over available alternatives because we [*describe your point of difference as described in Chapter 5*]

Figure 6-2: Use these questions and framework as you assemble your mission statement.

✔ **Show passion.** Write your mission statement in a way that inspires others to want to come on board and be part of the good work you're doing.

Polishing your business promise

Your *business promise* is the pledge upon which you build your brand and stake your reputation. It's what you assure those who come into contact with your business — whether as employees, suppliers, investors, associates, or customers — that they can count on you to deliver. It's the expectation that you live up to every time people experience your brand, whether through advertising, promotions, buying experiences, service encounters, or any other contact.

Your promise is the essence of your brand. Don't make the common mistake of thinking that your logo is your brand identity. Your logo is a visual representation of your brand and an important element of your brand identity, but it's just one component. When people think of your brand, they may visualize your logo, but your promise is what motivates them in your direction.

While-you-wait service is a promise. The best on-time arrival record is a promise. "You'll never wait in line" is a promise. "You're a name, not a number" is a promise. Each one puts a company's reputation on the line by assuring that the brand will live up to the high expectations it sets for itself, or else. The promise becomes an internal rallying call for excellence and a magnet for new business.

Your promise is essential to your branding strategy. If you're not already sure of the promise you make to all who deal with your business, consider these questions:

- ✔ Why do customers choose your business? What do they seek from you that they can't get elsewhere?

- ✔ How do you think your most satisfied customers describe your products or services? What words do they use when they pay compliments or when they fill out satisfaction surveys?

- ✔ How do you think your most satisfied customers describe the feeling they get when they work with your business? Would they use words like "efficient," "fun," "friendly," "competent," "creative," "convenient," "reliable," "exciting," "amazing," or others?

- ✔ What attributes of your company do you think customers like best and would find the hardest to replace if your business weren't available to them?

- ✔ If customers had to choose one word or phrase that describes what they consistently expect and receive from your company, what would it be?

Answer these questions on your own, ask managers and staff members to answer them, and then go to a few key customers and ask for their input. Explain what you're up to. Tell them that, as part of your branding strategy, you're clarifying the way your business promise is interpreted in the market, and you'd appreciate their responses to the preceding questions.

When you're done with your analysis, take these steps:

1. **List all the reasons customers choose your business and the attributes they count on only your company to deliver.**

2. **Circle all the attributes you're confident that you can deliver consistently and upon which you're willing to stake your reputation.**

3. **Put a check mark next to those attributes that are compelling to customers and to your internal team — the ones you can rally behind and take pride in offering.**

4. **Take the checked items and make a short list of business attributes that are most assured, most compelling, most believable, and most consistent with the character of your company.**

Your final list of business attributes provides the basis upon which to form your business promise. Following are a few examples to get you started:

- ✔ Sony Ericsson: "Sony Ericsson will always deliver the best mobile business experience. That is our promise to you."

- ✔ BMW: "Sheer driving pleasure."

- ✔ Wal-Mart: "Always low prices. Always."

- ✔ John Deere: "You can count on equipment that's as productive as possible. Up and ready to work when you are. And designed to minimize your daily operating costs. Nothing runs like a Deere."

- ✔ Umpqua Bank (a Northwest boutique bank): "Serious about service."

No one likes someone who breaks promises. As you put your promise into words, make sure it's one you can deliver upon consistently every single time people come into contact with your brand, whether as customers, employees, suppliers, associates, or prospects. Staying true to your word and consistently upholding your promise is essential to building business trust and loyalty.

Beginning with your point of difference (see Chapter 5), use the following template to write the business promise you'll incorporate into your branding strategy.

> [*Name of your business, product, or service*] is the [*your distinction and the generic term for your type of offering*] to provide [*your unique features or benefits*] to [*your customer profile*] who choose our offering in order to feel [*your customers' emotional outcome*].

> We consistently deliver the unique attributes and benefits our customers count on, and we promise our customers [*the promise customers can absolutely count on from your company*].

Defining your brand character

Your *brand character* is like the personality of your brand. Some brands are serious or even somber, and some are whimsical, fun, or playful. Some brands are youthful, and some are like silver-haired sages.

As a first step in defining your brand character, ask yourself this question: How would your brand be described if it were a person who walked into the room? Sophisticated? Fashionable? Flamboyant? Reserved? Important? Playful? Or one of countless other descriptions? Keep your answer in mind as you go through the rest of this section.

As you define your brand character, realize that the character you convey must be an accurate reflection of your business vision, mission, values, and promise.

If your brand character, which is reflected through the look and tone of your brand expressions, is inconsistent with what your company actually is and stands for, you'll face two problems.

✔ Your brand expressions will roam all over the map, serious at one time and playful at another depending on the mood and whim of whoever is producing them, and you'll wind up with a schizophrenic brand identity as a result.

✔ The brand identity you project into the marketplace will be inconsistent with the brand experience people encounter when they actually contact your business, leading to a lack of credibility and a poor reputation.

Follow these steps to write a brand character statement that guides the development of all expressions of your brand:

1. **Review your vision statement to refocus on the highest aspirations of your business.**

2. **Review the top values you support.**

3. **Review the promise you make in your marketplace.**

4. **Based on your vision, values, and promise, write a one-sentence brand character statement.**

   Use the following format: Our brand is [*insert a description of the character of your brand*], a trait we reflect through brand expressions that are [*insert a description of the mood and tone that all your marketing will project*].

If you have difficulty defining your character, ask yourself these questions:

✔ If you were to compare your business to a car, what car would it be, and why?

✔ If you were to compare your business to an actor or actress, who would it be, and why?

Your answers help you determine words and personality traits that define the character of your business and brand and steer the creation of all brand expressions within and outside your company.

From your name and logo to the way your staff dresses, the look of your surroundings, your marketing materials, and the experience you provide, all contacts with your brand should reinforce a single mood, tone, and personality.

Mission Possible: Defining Your Brand

Your *brand identity statement,* also called your *brand definition,* shrinks all your thoughts about your business mission, values, and promise into a concise statement that defines what you do, how you differ from all other similar solutions, and what you pledge to deliver to those who deal with your business.

Your completed brand identity statement serves as the steering wheel for your branding strategy. It influences every turn you make in presenting your brand — from giving it a name and logo to producing ads and marketing materials to creating the experience that customers will encounter when they come into contact with your brand from any direction.

What to incorporate

As you write your brand identity statement, be sure that it reflects the following information:

- ✔ The three things you want people to know about your business:
  - What you offer
  - Who you serve
  - How you're best at what you do
- ✔ Your point of difference (how you serve your target market differently and better than all other options)
- ✔ Your business promise that will be upheld through all brand experiences
- ✔ Your brand character or personality that will be communicated through the mood and tone projected in all brand expressions

The anatomy of a brand identity statement

Your brand identity is the face of your brand. It includes your name, logo, tagline or slogan, advertising, marketing materials, signage, and every other way that you express your brand in your business and in your marketplace.

Your brand identity statement defines your brand identity. It describes the people your brand must relate to, the attributes it must highlight, and the promise and character it must convey. To write a brand identity statement that guides your branding strategy, use this format:

> [*Your name*] promises [*your target market*] that they can count on us for [*your unique attribute or benefit*] delivered with [*information about the character, tone, and mood you convey*].

Grading your statement

Before accepting your brand identity statement as the one that will guide your branding strategy, see if you can answer "yes" to these three questions:

- ✔ Does the statement illuminate your difference? Does it make it clear how you differ from other solutions in your business arena?

- ✔ Is the statement customer-centric? Does it clarify what you provide and promise to others rather than what you aspire for yourself?

- ✔ Can you project the statement with a unified voice across all markets and media? And can you fulfill its promise through every contact with your business and as part of the overall customer experience with your brand?

Putting your brand identity statement to the test

After you commit your brand identity statement to paper, it's time to test it internally within your business and with key customer groups.

In personal meetings and focus group sessions, confirm that the brand identity statement you've crafted resonates with those who work with and buy from your business. (For information on conducting research, turn to Chapter 4.) In this final test, probe the following questions:

✔ Is the promise you make the same as the promise customers count on from your business?

- Do people believe that your business consistently delivers on its promise?

- Do they believe that the promise is upheld through all contact points, including your physical place of business, phone greeting, online presence, customer service, return policies, staff members, communications, and every other way in which you interact with those in your market?

- If they were to explain to someone else the promise your business makes, how would they express it?

✔ Are the unique attributes or benefits highlighted in your brand identity statement consistent with those that others most associate with your business?

✔ Is the character that you've summarized in your brand identity statement consistent with the character that others believe you exude?

✔ If you uncover slight differences between the promise, benefits, and character defined in your brand identity statement and the attributes others believe to be true about your business, what adjustments to your business would align the two mindsets?

If your brand will serve a concise, easy-to-reach, and relatively small market, you can test your brand identity statement on your own, using the research advice presented in Chapter 4. For brands that serve larger markets or face major competition from established and recognized brands, invest in professional assistance to test your statement before putting it to work as you name your brand, design its logo and tagline, and create the marketing materials and brand experience that will present it day in and day out in your market.

Chapter 7

Naming Your Brand

• •

In This Chapter

▶ Realizing the power of a great brand name

▶ Brainstorming and choosing your brand name

▶ Claiming your name on the Web

▶ Registering and protecting your name

• •

*I*f you haven't yet named your brand, you just opened to what may be the most important chapter in this book.

Naming your brand is by far the most challenging, momentous, and necessary phase in the process of branding. Before you can proceed to develop a brand identity, you need a name that's appropriate, available, appealing, and enduring. Truly, naming a brand is as important — and as difficult — as naming a baby.

Other elements of your brand — including your logo, tagline, and color scheme — may evolve over time, but your name will remain constant. From the day you announce your name, it's the key that unlocks your brand image in the minds of your consumers.

This chapter sheds light on the value of your brand name, how to recognize the characteristics of a good name, and how to come up with and protect a name that works well from the start and long into your successful future.

What's In a Name?

The right name distinguishes you from all other businesses, and ideally, it establishes your personality, brand character, market position, and the nature of your offering. The very best name accomplishes the following objectives:

✔ It reflects the brand character you want your business to project.

✔ It's descriptive of your offering.

✔ It creates an association to the meaning of your brand.

✔ It's easy and pleasant to say.

✔ It's unique and memorable.

Not all great names score a ten in all areas, but nearly every good name scores on most fronts, and only a rare few successful names strike out completely on any one of the preceding characteristics. In this section, we help guide your selection — or creation — of a name that meets the criteria for your brand.

What the right name does

The right name establishes your brand from the day you announce it and grows with your business and your vision as you evolve into a larger, more established organization that possibly reaches into new market areas, new geographic regions, and even new product areas.

In the same way you wouldn't want to give a baby a name that doesn't transition to adulthood, you don't want to give your brand a name that hinders your development in the future. For that reason, most forward-thinking marketers avoid names like First Avenue Dry Cleaning, for instance, unless they're absolutely certain that they'll always be on First Avenue and that they'll always focus on dry cleaning as their primary offering.

In choosing your name, the following three criteria weigh heavier than all others:

✔ Your name should convey or support your brand image.

✔ Your name should convey or be consistent with your brand promise.

✔ Your name should have the capability to appreciate as an asset that can be harvested through premium pricing, through licensing, or even through the sale of shares in your business or the outright sale of your brand name to a future owner.

Conveys or implies your brand image

If you're at all unclear about your desired brand image, flip back to Chapter 6, which leads you through the process of crafting the brand identity statement that steers all decisions regarding the expression of your brand and the image you create in the marketplace.

Bending the brand name rules, at a price

Some businesses inherit, live with, or even choose names that go against some or all the textbook criteria for a great brand name — and they end up with great brands anyway. How do they do it? They invest marketing time and money to build a story around their names, and in the process they build affection, loyalty, and equity for names that, without significant marketing support, would have probably made it into Chapter 21 of this book as examples of branding mistakes to avoid.

An outstanding and well-known example is the brand name Smucker's. In 1897, Jerome Monroe Smucker started pressing the fruit from Johnny Appleseed's tree plantings at his Ohio mill and selling the resulting fruit products from the back of a horse-drawn wagon. Before long, Smucker's name became associated with his personal guarantee of product quality, a promise that evolved over the years into the hallmark of a brand that's now distributed worldwide and ranks as North America's market leader in the categories of jams, jellies, preserves, and a range of other specialty items.

Of and by itself, the Smucker's name would hardly pass most brand name tests or research studies. But over time and with excellent marketing, the name has become a renowned brand success story. To quote from company literature: "We still proudly display our name on every jar because . . . with a name like Smucker's, it has to be good."

Note: Before bending the rules to give your brand a name that doesn't quickly and clearly convey your brand in a pleasant and easy-to-recall manner, realize that you'll need to invest heavily in marketing efforts to create the associations that don't stem naturally from your name choice.

Your brand identity statement follows this framework:

> [*Your business*] promises [*your target market*] that they can count on us for [*unique attribute or benefit*] delivered with [*information about the character, tone, and mood you convey*].

Write down your brand identity statement and commit to it before beginning the naming process. By defining your brand first, you can select a name that's consistent with the three elements of your brand identity statement: your target market, your promise, and the tone and mood used to consistently convey the character of your business.

A name that doesn't directly or obviously reflect your brand identity statement — that doesn't obviously convey or imply the nature of your target market, your brand promise, or your brand character — can turn out to be a spectacularly strong brand name if (and this is a big if) you're willing and able to invest the marketing budget to win market awareness, acceptance, and enthusiasm for what it means. As proof, consider names such as Apple, Google, Amazon, and Yahoo!, along with a good many of today's other best-known brands. The names themselves don't convey promises or differentiate offerings, yet they label today's megabrands thanks to terrific awareness-building and brand management programs that have injected the names with meaning in consumers' minds.

At the other end of the spectrum, consider great brand names like Internet Explorer, Dunkin' Donuts, and Mail Boxes, Etc., which instantaneously convey their brand purposes even to those who may have never heard the names before.

Either approach works, but the smaller your marketing budget, the wiser you are to settle on a brand name that automatically conveys your brand essence. Doing so allows you to avoid the costly need for extensive market education to create meaning for your name.

Advances your brand promise

Your brand name should convey, imply, or support your brand promise. There's no hard-and-fast rule about the degree to which your name must reveal your promise. However, if your name only hints at what you do and offer, then you'd better be prepared to invest marketing time, effort, and money to tell the story not communicated by your name.

Some brands clearly put the brand promise right into the brand name. Well-known examples include:

- ✔ Jiffy Lube service centers
- ✔ DieHard automotive batteries
- ✔ Terminix pest control
- ✔ Krusteaz easy-to-make pie crust mix
- ✔ Lean Cuisine entrees
- ✔ Powerade sports drink
- ✔ Coppertone suncare products
- ✔ Miracle-Gro plant food
- ✔ Seattle's Best coffee
- ✔ Ziploc storage bags
- ✔ Clear Eyes eye drops

Some brands imply the promise that customers can count on through names that are completely consistent with the benefits they deliver. Examples include:

- ✔ Gymboree: The celebration of childhood

- ✔ Victoria's Secret: Romantic, stylish, and feminine lingerie

- ✔ Foot Locker: Athletic footwear and apparel

- ✔ Sunkist: Quality, fresh-tasting, better-for-you citrus products

- ✔ The Home Depot: One-stop shopping for home improvement and construction

- ✔ Legalzoom: A law firm specializing in low-cost divorce services that calls itself the nation's leading online legal service

Still other names neither convey nor imply the brand promise. Instead, they support the brand's commitment by being consistent in character and presentation to the brand's offering. Here are a couple examples:

- ✔ Yahoo!: The name doesn't say or imply "search engine" or "Web hosting," and it doesn't convey a brand promise. Instead, the name paves the way for an online experience that's fast, fun, and successful.

- ✔ Pier One: The name doesn't say or imply "distinct, casual home furnishings and décor at a good value," which is what the company promises. Instead, it conjures up the idea of an environment where customers can, in the company's words, "discover the 'spice' they need to personalize their homes."

Regardless of whether your promise is directly presented, implied, or simply supported through your brand name, make sure it's pegged to a commitment that's small enough to keep but big enough to grow with your business. You can probably think of a brand that promised to be the "hometown" business only to chase opportunity in a nearby market area where, eventually, the headquarters moved and the hometown promise evaporated.

Becomes an asset

Good brand names accumulate value that pays off in a number of ways.

- ✔ As a well-managed brand gains awareness, its promise becomes trusted, and that trust carries a value for which consumers are willing to pay a premium, leading to stronger sales and higher profits.

- ✔ As a well-managed brand gains market recognition, it becomes valued by other marketers who want to cross-promote with or even license the brand name to benefit from its strong and positive image, leading to marketing and business opportunities.

✔ As a well-managed brand grows into a market success story, others want to own part of it, leading to a public offering or outright purchase of the brand, at which time the original brand builder can harvest the brand's value through a complete or partial sale.

For advice on leveraging your brand's value, see Chapter 16. But first, put yourself in position to build your brand into an asset by following these naming tips:

✔ **Give your brand a name that can grow and live for years.**

- **Avoid names that limit your product range.** Unless you're absolutely certain that you'll never want to sell anything other than lamps, for instance, be careful about calling yourself The Lamp Store.

- **Give your brand some geographic elbow room.** The advantages of not tying your name to a single geographic region are twofold. By avoiding a name like Milwaukee Printing Services, you allow your business to open into new market areas without the burden of an out-of-town name or the need for a new name altogether, and you keep yourself out of the lineup of all the other business names that start with Milwaukee in the local phone directory.

✔ **Especially if you think you may want to sell your business in the future, give your brand a name that isn't your own (referred to as *Me, Inc.* in the branding business).** At the time of sale, a good portion of your brand equity resides in *goodwill,* which is the positive value of your name and reputation. If your brand name is *your* name, the new owners will probably want rename it, and they'll want to pay less as a result.

✔ **Give your brand a name that's unique, memorable, and easy to recall.**

When naming happens

Most brands get their names at one of the following three times:

✔ **When a new business or product is being introduced for the first time**

This is when most brands are named and is likely the situation you're facing as you read this book.

✔ **When an existing business or product wants to face its future with a new name that isn't burdened with a negative connotation**

For example, Kentucky Fried Chicken renamed itself KFC, freeing it to market offerings beyond the range of fried foods and chicken. Another example is Phillip Morris, which became Altria to distance itself from its tobacco heritage.

✔ **When an existing business or product wants to embrace growth opportunities precluded by the limiting nature of its existing name**

For example, Federal Express became FedEx, giving itself a shorter name that better exemplifies the company's speed promise while at the same time deemphasizing the word "federal" to better reflect the brand's worldwide market. Likewise, the plastic card in your billfold didn't always carry the brand name VISA. It used to be called BankAmericard, a name that was abandoned in the mid-1970s in favor of a name that was shorter, instantly recognizable, pronounceable in any language, and had no country or language affiliations.

Types of names

The brand name selection process usually results in a name that fits into one of the following categories:

✔ **The owner's name or names:** An owner's name can serve as the basis for a business name, such as Joe Smith's Piano Tuning Service. On a far larger scale, an owner's name (or two owners' names, in this case) can serve as the basis for a merged business name, such as ExxonMobil.

Especially for small business sole proprietors, building a new brand on the name of an owner is an easy approach. The name is likely to be available, easy to register, and capable of advancing the promise that the owner stands by the company's products or services.

The downside to using an owner's name is that, without significant marketing, personal names rarely develop the kind of widespread awareness and sky-high credibility that translate to premium pricing and future sale value.

✔ **Abbreviation names:** People think of quick, easy-to-recall names like IBM or AOL and believe that a similarly short abbreviation or acronym will work for them. In both these examples, though, extensive marketing efforts had to be made before the names meant something to consumers. Unless you're willing to invest accordingly, avoid this route. Either you'll end up with a string of initials that mean little to consumers or you'll end up with a generic name like ABC Equipment Rental, which exudes no personality or promise and has only one benefit — putting you first in alphabetical lists in the phone book. That's hardly a brand building strategy!

✔ **Geographically anchored names:** These are dime-a-dozen names that work to capitalize on a known local landmark or geographic indicator. Think Central Coast Bank, Pleasantville Grocery, and Cascade Mountain Insurance. Most names of this kind blur into a group of like-named entities. Only a few stand out as esteemed brands, and those that do are almost always the ones that invested the most time and money to market their names into distinguishing brands.

✔ **Descriptive names:** These are names that describe a business's offering or brand promise. Head Start Child Development Programs, U-Haul, Budget Rent A Car, and Clinique are examples of names that convey the nature of the brand's offerings and business promise.

✔ **Borrowed interest names:** These are names that use existing words that don't directly reflect the brand's offerings or promise but that can be linked to a brand's essence and promise through marketing efforts rather than through direct translation. Good examples include Apple, Nike, Yahoo!, and Starbucks.

✔ **Fabricated-word names:** These are names that combine acronyms, words, or syllables to form previously unknown words and brand names. Google, Verizon, Microsoft, and Mozilla are all are easy to repeat, easy to recall names that have been imbued with meaning due to their business's efforts. Because they're newly invented words, fabricated names are usually available for trademark protection, and the domain names that contain them are likely to be available, too.

Naming advice to follow

As you brainstorm name ideas, be aware that great names — and names you should avoid — have a number of qualities in common. Table 7-1 shares some qualities of remarkable names as well as naming mistakes to avoid.

Table 7-1	Naming Advice
Qualities of Remarkable Brand Names	*What to Avoid*
Easy to spell and pronounce	Unique spellings or pronunciations that consumers won't remember
Short enough to fit easily on marketing materials and to say on the phone	Abbreviations that have no meaning without significant marketing investment
Unique and easy to remember	A generic name that's hard to distinguish and almost impossible to protect
Reflective of your business offering or promise — either directly, indirectly, or through association	A copycat name that borrows from well-known bigger brands, causing marketplace confusion and risking lawsuits

Qualities of Remarkable Brand Names	What to Avoid
Consistent with your brand character	A name that limits the brand's opportunity to expand its offerings or geographic sphere
Capable of growing with your business over time	Owner names, especially if you plan to sell your business in the foreseeable future
Capable of expanding to apply to new products or geographic areas	A name that's long and likely to be called by abbreviations that may not be consistent with the brand's character
Available to trademark	
Available as a domain name	

Picking (or Inventing) Your Brand Name

When it comes time to actually name your brand, get ready to spend some time and even some money, especially if your brand's going to span a large market area, compete against major brand names, or support a major vision that will take decades to achieve and therefore will live long into the future.

Whether you choose to name your brand on your own or to seek professional assistance from a professional marketing firm or branding group, involve your own team in the process by following these steps.

1. **List the attributes you personally want to reflect in your brand name.**

   Consider the following:

   - What terms out of your brand identity statement do you most want your name to convey, reflect, or support?
   - What aspects of your brand promise would you like your name to advance?
   - What words define the character you want your name to convey?

2. **Bring together key business partners, managers, and staff members, and ask them to answer the three questions listed in Step 1. Then ask them what kinds of names come to their minds.**

Before you even begin the brainstorming process, or before you involve professional assistance, this initial internal reaction focuses you on the brand essence, attributes, and character that seem true to those who are most involved with your business and its differentiating attributes.

3. **Decide who will actually decide on your name.**

   Will the final choice rest with a single person or with the team? Will it require a unanimous vote, or will the majority rule? Will one person have veto power?

4. **Involve all who will have a say — especially the key decision maker — in the naming process.**

You're setting yourself up for trouble if the person who will ultimately approve the name fails to participate in the process and lacks understanding of the reasons behind the name being presented.

Rounding up good ideas

Whether you're naming your brand on your own or involving a professional branding consultant or marketing firm, begin by giving thought to the kinds of names you think do and don't suit the character and vision of your brand.

Begin by assembling the team that will name your brand or that will work with the professional consultants. Consider holding a retreat to get the creative ideas flowing. Not every idea will be a good idea; that's the nature of brainstorming. But the process produces lists of the kinds of names you think fit well with your business. From there, you can proceed to narrow down the choices, or you can turn your initial ideas over to a professional branding consultant or marketing firm.

Brainstorming

At the beginning of a brainstorming session, participants usually are shy about getting creative or throwing out what may seem like wild and crazy ideas. Allow them to ease into the process by starting the session with a discussion of what kinds of feelings the participants would like people to have when they hear your brand name, whatever it turns out to be.

Have an easels or white board available and write down every emotion you hear. Then group them into categories, such as reputation, expertise, features and benefits, or any other labels that seem to fit over clusters of words that emerged from the discussion.

Then leave the categories in sight as you begin to brainstorm names that may induce the desired responses.

As you brainstorm name ideas, encourage creativity by following these tips:

✔ **Give every idea its time and space.** The quickest way to kill creativity is to shut down ideas with comments like, "That's been done before," "That won't work," or "That's not what we're looking for."

✔ **When an idea seems to come out of left field, encourage alternatives.** Prompt more ideas with comments like, "What other words describe that same concept?" and "How can we say that and fit within our brand character?"

✔ **Probe ideas.** Ask participants to describe the underlying meaning of the names they're presenting. Sometimes in their descriptions they'll uncover other names that are even more appropriate.

✔ **Encourage alternative perspectives.** Ask participants to stand in the shoes of others and to think of how they'd describe your brand from the point of view of a child, a celebrity, an older consumer, or others who may not be represented by the brainstorming group.

Record the results of your brainstorming session and review them as soon after the session as possible. Circle the ideas that match your brand identity statement. They make up the short list that you work from as you narrow choices and begin to assemble name ideas (see the section "The hard part: Narrowing your list to the best options" later in this chapter).

Finding inspiration

To find a unique name, reach outside your usual work environment. Give the following ideas a try:

✔ **Get out of your regular surroundings and go to the kinds of places where your target customers spend time.** If they eat in fast-food restaurants, go order a soda or a meal, take a table, and observe. If they're avid shoppers, go to the mall or to your downtown shopping area. If they commute mass transit, buy a ticket and take a ride or two.

As you observe target customers, pay attention to the books they're reading, the shopping bags they're carrying, and the labels they're wearing. Jot down names. They may unlock ideas for a name for your brand that fits well with the interests and mindset of your customer base.

✔ **Go to the magazine rack in your local bookstore or public library and pull copies of magazines that you think your customers read.** Flip through and note ideas, names, or words that you think fit your brand character and your brand identity statement.

✔ **Go to stores or pick up magazines that are well outside the interest area of your customers.** If your customers are interested in high fashion, go to a fish and bait shop, for instance. Look around at brand names. The exposure may trigger interesting new concepts.

✔ **Look through English and international language dictionaries, and flip through a thesaurus.** In the English dictionary, look up words that describe your brand and study the word origins, seeing if they trace back to Greek, Latin, or other roots that may provide the basis for good brand names. In international dictionaries, look for translations of your brand promise or attributes that may make great names. In the thesaurus, look for synonyms for words that describe your brand.

Throughout your search, take note of the kinds of names that catch your eye or ear. Are they names that convey or imply promises, names based on borrowed interest, or names that are fabricated from syllables and sounds to create one-of-a-kind new words? Your findings can guide your name decision.

The hard part: Narrowing your list to the best options

Here's where the naming process gets tricky. Narrowing your list of potential names down to a few best choices is tough and emotional. You know that you're making a lasting decision, and until the name is announced and met with great fanfare, you can't really be certain that it's the ideal name.

When creating your short list of names, follow this advice:

✔ Include only a few top contenders unless you're planning to undertake a trademark search, in which case you need a longer list because many will be knocked out during the legal process.

✔ Keep your top name contenders tightly within your brand naming circle until you're ready to reveal your name selection. Then (and only then) you may want to show also-ran names as part of the rationale you present to build support for your top choice.

Not even the greatest name contenders can hold up to the scrutiny that follows a leak during water-cooler conversations. For that reason, don't let the names out of your committee until you select one and it's ready for presentation, backed by all the rationale for why it's a great choice and how it will excel in your marketing arena.

Putting your top contenders through a preliminary test

When you arrive at a short list of names you believe fit your brand well, put each one through the following series of questions and investigations.

✔ **Does it accurately depict or support your desired brand image?**

- Does it convey, imply, or accurately reflect your differentiating attributes and brand promise?

- Does it reflect your brand position? For instance, if your position is being the most professional, creative, responsive, efficient, or prestigious in your marketplace, does the name sound adequately professional, creative, responsive, efficient, or prestigious?

- Is it a credible reflection of your business today? For example, if you're a local firm, including the word "global" in your name may be quite a stretch.

- Can it grow with you as you achieve your highest aspiration and the vision of your business?

✔ **Is it easy to say?**

- Write each leading name on a piece of paper and ask a few confidants to read it out loud. Do they pronounce it correctly? Does it sound pleasing to the ear? (To avoid feeding the internal gossip mill, ask people outside your business.)

- Pretend that you're answering the phone and use the name in a greeting. ("Good morning, XYZ Company. May I help you?") Does it roll off the tongue, or is it awkward to say?

- Pretend that you're introducing yourself as the president or vice president or chief inventor of the company. How does the name sound in professional conversations?

✔ **Is it easy to spell?**

- Say each leading name candidate out loud to others and ask them to write it down. Do they spell it correctly?

If the name's misspelled from time to time you may well select it anyway, deciding that you can market your way around the problem. But be sure to make note of and save the various misspellings. As you establish your online identity, you can try to grab domain names for each of the erroneous spellings and automatically redirect them to your official Web site. (You can find more on online branding in Chapter 12.)

✔ **Is it unique?**

- Pick up your phone book and the phone book for the biggest city in your market area. Go to the section in the white pages where your brand name would appear to see how many similarly named businesses already exist. Then conduct a similar exercise using business directories, including everything from chamber of commerce or economic development directories to industry registers.

- Enter the name in a few Internet search engines and scan the results to see if the name currently applies to other businesses.

✔ **Does it translate well?** Should you decide to go into e-commerce or to serve international markets, does the name you're considering have a positive connotation in other cultures? If you think you'll be targeting specific international audiences in the future, ask people familiar with the languages and cultures of those groups to react to the name. If you don't know anyone to ask, consider asking a language professor at a local university for input.

✔ **Do you like the name?** You'll be living with this name for a long time, so you need to be comfortable with it. If the name really rubs you the wrong way or embarrasses you in any way, move on to another selection. But if it feels awkward to say or write, realize that you may simply be resisting change. The fact that it sounds different is good and even necessary to stand out in the crowded market environment.

✔ **Can you protect it?** The final section of this chapter describes how to check availability, stake your claim, obtain your domain name, and protect your brand with a trademark if it will be crossing state and national borders. If the name's not available or protectable in your market area — whether that's your hometown, state, region, country, or the world — the sooner you know, the sooner you can strike it off your list and move on to the next best choice.

Building consensus around your top-choice name

To win support for your name selection, don't surprise your decision makers with a last-minute presentation. Keep them in the loop throughout the process so that, as a top choice emerges, they're familiar with the name, the rationale for its selection, and the ways that it works on behalf of your business.

As you reach outside your decision-making circle to present the name to your entire company, turn to Chapter 9 to find out how to launch your brand internally.

Grabbing a Domain Name, If You Can

Your domain name is the string of characters that people type into their Web browsers to reach your site. Ideally, you want your domain name to read `www.[yourbrandname].com`, but in today's crowded online world, the chance of getting your dream address is far from guaranteed.

For an initial test of availability, open your browser and enter the domain name of your dreams in the address line. If you're taken straight to a Web page, your desired domain name is already taken — sorry. If, instead, you get a message that no such page exists, you've hit the equivalent of online pay dirt. In that event, register the name, quickly. Even if it doesn't actually become your brand name, the cost of registering and protecting it just in case is miniscule compared to the value of reserving the name in case you decide it's your winning brand name choice. (Expect to pay anywhere from a few dollars to $75 to register a domain name for a three-year period. For a complete list of domain name registrars, go to `www.internic.net/regist.html`.)

To conduct a more thorough availability search, turn to a domain name registry site. Network Solutions (`www.networksolutions.com`) is one of many that offer free name searches. Enter the name you want and wait a few seconds to see if it's available. If it's not, the site invites you to "see options to get unavailable domain names." Click that option to see advice for making offers on already-registered names.

If your desired brand name isn't available as a domain name, you can either simply strike the name from your list or, if the name is owned by a *cyber squatter* (someone who reserves all kinds of names until someone is willing to buy the rights to them), you can contact the owner to see about purchasing the address. Be aware, however, that this can be a time-consuming and costly process.

If your desired brand name is already taken, avoid taking these alternate routes:

- Don't try to secure the name you want simply by replacing the `.com` with `.net` or `.org`. Here's why: Rather than conducting an online search for a company's address, many Web users take a shortcut by typing the company plus `.com` into their browser address lines. Therefore, if you adopt a domain name that consists of your brand name plus `.net`, savvy Web users will reach a wrong address. Oops.

- Don't try to reserve some clever variation of your name by adding hyphens or using alternative spellings. For instance, don't try to license `www.branding-for-dummies.com` if `www.brandingfordummies.com` is already taken. People won't remember how to make the adjustments, and as a result, they'll never find you online.

Turn to Chapter 12 for much more information on how to establish your brand online.

Fitting Your Name into Your Brand Architecture

Before you settle on a brand name, consider how and where the brand will fit within your business, which is known as *brand architecture* (see Chapter 2).

Most brands fit into one of these architecture categories:

- **Independent brands:** These are stand-alone brands that represent every offering and activity of the organizations they represent. Most small businesses create independent brands for the simple reason that they're easier to build, manage, and market. At the same time, many very large organizations also present all their offerings under a single brand. The Red Cross is a good example.

- **Parent-dominant brands:** Parent-dominant brands are closely and very visibly tied to the name and credibility of the top-level brand. For example, a nonprofit organization that hosts a well-known annual fundraiser probably treats the yearly event as a parent-dominant brand of the organization.

- **Parent-endorsed brands:** These are uniquely differentiated offerings that are closely affiliated with their parent brands. Even though they're known by their own brand names, parent-endorsed brands are clearly linked to a better-known umbrella brand. An example is Sony PlayStation.

- **Brand extensions:** These brands piggyback on the recognition of an established parent brand but build awareness and interest in a new and different target market segment. A few examples are Arm & Hammer Deodorant, Starbucks Coffee Liqueur, and RainX Windshield Wiper Blades.

Successful smaller businesses build only one brand — for good reason. Building, managing, protecting, and consistently conveying a single brand takes time, money, and tremendous dedication. Creating multiple brands doubles or triples the branding work and often results in a lack of focus on the primary brand that drives the company's success.

Roundabout advice from Mark Twain

Consider this quote from Mark Twain:

Sufficient unto the day is one baby. As long as you are in your right mind, don't ever pray for twins. Twins amount to a permanent riot; and there ain't any real difference between triplets and an insurrection.

Twain could well have been talking about brands rather than babies because one brand is sufficient for most smaller businesses, and more than one brand is more than most small businesses can handle and manage well.

Unless your marketing expertise is high and your budget large, stick to a single brand. Make all additional products, events, or other brandable offerings that you present subbrands that live under the strong umbrella of your one-and-only brand.

Rather than create multiple brands, build a single, dominant brand that presides over a number of product lines, events, fundraising campaigns, or other brandable entities while reinforcing your primary brand at all times. Then as you name each new offering, be sure that the name you select complements the promise of the top-level brand. If it doesn't, throw it out of the running and move on to other names that fit with the identity and character of the brand under which all other products fit.

Catch It If You Can: Protecting Your Name

After you select your name and put it through the wringer to see if people can spell it, say it, remember it, find it online, and relate well to it in your home culture as well as in other cultures, it's time to begin the process of registering and protecting the name to ensure that it will belong to you and only you for as long as it lives in the marketplace.

Screening to see if the name you want is already taken

Just because you love a name doesn't mean you can adopt it and start using it. First, you have to jump through some legal hoops to make sure that the name isn't too similar to an existing business name or trademark in your market area. Conducting a name-availability search on your own and without legal help isn't enough to assure that the name you want is available, but it helps you uncover which names definitely are already in use. With that knowledge, you can create a Plan B before investing heavily in a name that may not work for your brand.

Follow these steps to do your own initial name-availability search:

1. **Conduct a preliminary online search for the name.**

   Start by entering your desired name plus .com in the address line of your Web browser to see if you're taken to the site of an existing business. Then enter the name into a number of different search engines to see if businesses with your top-choice name appear in the search results.

   If another business already uses the name you want, you may still be able to use it as your own so long as your market area or industry doesn't overlap with that of the other business. However, proceed with caution and the understanding that you're risking marketplace confusion by giving your brand the same name as another business's brand.

2. **Search your state's database of registered business names.**

   This database is kept by the office of your secretary of state, corporations division, corporate registry, or a similar department depending on the state or region in which you're headquartered.

   Banks require that you have an approved name before opening a business bank account, and they can usually tell you exactly which government office to call for name registration assistance. One call can tell you whether the name you want is already taken in your immediate market area. If the name's available, you can complete a registration form, pay a fee, and protect the name for your use in your immediate market area.

3. **Screen the name with the United States Patent and Trademark Office, which maintains a massive database of pending, registered, and expired federal trademarks.**

   Go to www.uspto.gov, click on Trademarks, then Search Trademarks, and enter the name you want. For global and international information, go to www.uspto.gov/main/profiles/international.htm.

4. **Conduct a preliminary domain name search.**

   A number of online resources allow you to conduct a free search of domain name registries. Enter "domain name search" into your favorite search engine, ask advice from the firm that hosts your Web site, or visit sites such as www.neetworksolutions.com or www.allwhois.com to conduct free on-the-spot searches.

Legal mumbo jumbo

Following are definitions for a few of the terms you're bound to hear during the name-protection process. This information comes from the Web site of the U.S. Patent and Trademark Office. For more information, visit www.uspto.gov or check out *Patents, Copyrights & Trademarks For Dummies* by Henri Charmasson (Wiley).

✔ **Copyright:** Protection provided by the government to the creators of original works, giving the owners of the copyright the exclusive right to reproduce the work and to protect the way it's reproduced, published, performed, distributed, displayed, and sold. U.S. copyrights are registered by the Copyright Office of the Library of Congress and are indicated by the symbol ©.

✔ **Trademark:** A word, phrase, symbol, design, or a combination of these used to identify and distinguish a business and its products or services.

✔ **Registered trademark:** A trademark that's registered with and protected by the U.S.

Patent and Trademark Office. Registered marks are indicated by use of the federal registration symbol of a circled R (®) or by the designation "Reg. TM." You may use the federal registration symbol only on or in connection with the goods and/or service listed in your federal trademark registration and only after the U.S. Patent and Trademark Office has officially registered your mark (not while your application is pending).

✔ **Service mark:** A trademark that identifies the source of a service rather than a product.

✔ **Mark:** A term that refers to trademarks or service marks. Anytime you claim rights to a mark, you may alert the public to your claim by inserting the designation "TM" (trademark) or "SM" service mark. You may use these terms regardless of whether you've filed a mark application with the U.S. Patent and Trademark Office.

Treading the trademark ropes

After you register your business name with government offices in your local market area, you're safe to use your name, but your name isn't safe from use by others outside your immediate market areas.

If you plan to do business across state or national borders, you should obtain a trademark to prevent others from infringing on your identity by using a similar name, logo, or other identifying feature of your brand.

You can obtain extensive information and advice on trademarks from these online resources:

✔ **U.S. trademarks:** www.uspto.gov

✔ **Patent offices throughout Europe:** patlib.european-patent-office.org/directory/overview.pl

✔ **Establishing a trademark in a number of countries:** `www.uspto.gov/main/profiles/international.htm`

Anyone who tells you that the arena of trademarks is an easy one to navigate is wearing rose-colored glasses. We've been through it enough times to strongly advise you to look over the sidebar "Scheduling a root canal for your brand name" and to seek legal assistance from an attorney who specializes in trademark protection.

Your business attorney probably can assist you or refer you to a good legal specialist for help with getting a trademark. Or you can use the Lawyer Locator tool on the American Bar Association's Web site (`www.abanet.org/lawyerlocator/searchaop.html`). This tool allows you to locate attorneys specializing in intellectual property in the state or country of your choice.

Scheduling a root canal for your brand name

Coming up with a name that appeals to consumers and gaining a nod of approval from your trademark attorney is a challenging, frustrating, and even painful process. Part of the dilemma is that consumers generally prefer names comprised of familiar words that create instant connection and understanding, whereas attorneys prefer unusual and coined names — the farther away from any word ever heard before, the better.

If a trademark is important to you (and if your brand will travel nationally or globally, it's not just a matter of importance but of necessity), follow this name development and trademarking process used by leading brand development specialists:

1. **Establish your strategic objective based on your desired brand position and character.**

2. **Develop anywhere from 500 to 1,000 potential names, using the various approaches cited in this chapter.**

3. **Select your top 50 name choices.**

4. **Send your list to an attorney who specializes in naming and trademarking.**

The attorney will conduct an initial trademark search in your business arena and in related areas of business to determine whether using the name may leave you vulnerable to litigation from other brand holders now or in the future. In most cases, by the time the drilling's over, only two or three of your 50 name entries end up on a "good chance of approval" list. The price for conducting the initial screening for each name usually runs around $25 to $30.

5. **The attorney puts names that make it past the initial screening through an exhaustive availability search.**

This phase generally runs around $3,000 to $4,000 per name and results in a detailed risk analysis. If your top-choice name is deemed clear to use without risk of an infringement suit from another trademark holder, authorize your attorney to run — not walk — to register it as your own. If its use comes with some infringement question marks, work with your attorney (and within the comforts of your own risk tolerance) to determine whether or not to proceed to adopt the name with or without a trademark.

Chapter 8

Designing Your Logo and Tagline

*L*ogo design is the point at which the branding process acquires fanfare. The minute people in your organization see your brand emerge in a logo that embodies your name they begin to get enthusiastic about what may have previously felt like a whole bunch of navel-gazing. To most people, logo creation is the fun part of branding. It's also the part that unduly gets the most energy and enthusiasm.

If you opened straight to this chapter with the hope that you could give your brand a face without wading through the process of researching, positioning, and defining your brand identity, realize that branding isn't like a game of Monopoly. You can't just jump to "Go." The only way you end up with a logo that accurately reflects the essence of your brand is by defining the essence of your brand *before* you begin the logo design process. If you haven't yet done so, do yourself and your brand a favor by going through the steps presented in Chapter 6. They help you clarify your understanding of your brand's mission, values, vision, culture, and character so that you can create a symbol — a logo — that serves as an accurate presentation of who you are and what you stand for in your marketplace.

If, however, you've taken the necessary steps and are truly ready to create a brand logo, dive right in. This chapter contains all you need to know.

Planning Your Logo: The Face of Your Brand

Your *logo* is the graphic design — in type or symbol form — that conveys your brand name and character in your marketplace.

The best logos are unique, simple, and strong representations of the companies they identify. To those seeing your signage, letterhead, packaging, ads, brochures, and any other communication that carries a visual representation of your brand, your logo is the face of your organization.

This section is full of advice on how to proceed with your logo design, but above all else, remember these three all-important points:

- **Keep your logo simple.** Simple logo designs work best for a number of reasons:

    - They actually stand out in the sea of visual complexity and chaos that exists in today's busy and saturated marketplace.

    - They enjoy longer lives than trendy, complicated logos that go out of style and require redesign to keep them in step with market tastes.

    - They contribute more significantly to a brand's awareness and recognition than logos that need to be updated every few years. Look at the long-standing logos of well-known and leading brands, such as Nike, Microsoft, and the Red Cross; they display an amazing amount of visual restraint.

- **Design a logo that can be presented consistently across all communication channels.** You want your logo to work well on your business checks, your vehicle signage, your Web site, your TV ads, and even your company uniforms or other apparel.

- **Don't do it yourself unless you're a design professional or you want your logo to look like it represents a hands-on business that, in fact, created its own logo.** Self-made logos are kind of like self-made TV ads; most of them are obvious for their lack of polish.

If you're not sure whether a do-it-yourself logo will present your company adequately, review your business vision (see Chapter 6 if your vision isn't totally clear in your mind). If your vision is to provide the lowest-cost, quickest, bare-bones solution in a low-competition market area, a self-created logo may work just fine. However, if your highest aspirations for your business involve a long life and a broadly recognized reputation for top quality in a competitive field, investing in a professionally designed logo is a moderate down payment on your success.

Matching your logo to your brand and business

Whether you do it yourself or hire a professional to develop your logo, you need to think in advance about what image you want your logo to convey.

Any graphic designer can tell you that clients who give no direction, saying that they'll simply know the right logo when they see it, burn through a lot of unnecessary time and money while they wait for the perfect look to miraculously emerge.

Instead, begin your logo-design task with some clear initial input about the type of image you want to develop. Use the worksheet in Figure 8-1 to assemble your thoughts and give your designer — whether that person is yourself, someone on your staff, or an experienced professional — good directions to work from.

LOGO DESIGN INSTRUCTIONS: WORKSHEET

To accurately reflect our brand, our logo should incorporate the following considerations:

Our logo needs to be consistent with the nature of our primary product or service, which is

_____

Our logo needs to be consistent with our brand promise, which is

_____

Our logo needs to accurately reflect our brand character, which we describe as

_____

Our logo needs to be consistent with the mood and tone we are committed to deliver through all our brand expressions. We describe our brand mood and tone as

_____

Our logo must reflect and be compatible with this brand identity statement:

We promise [*target market*] that they can count on us for

[*unique attribute or benefit*] delivered with [*information on your*

brand character, tone, and mood].

Figure 8-1: Use this worksheet to establish your logo creation guidelines before beginning the design process.

Choosing your logo approach

Most logos take one of the following forms:

- ✔ They feature the name of the business in a unique type presentation called a *wordmark*.

- ✔ They feature the initials of the business in a symbol called a *lettermark*.

- ✔ They feature a symbol that represents the business, called a *brandmark*.

- ✔ They combine these three logo approaches, for instance using a lettermark or a brandmark as the focal point of the logo, accompanied by the full name of the company — and sometimes the company slogan or tagline as well — in a unique configuration that becomes the company's brand symbol.

Take care when combining elements in your logo design. Too much results in an overdone, visually complicated, confusing logo. If you do combine elements, be sure that each component is visually clean and strong. For good examples, consider the multielement logos of fashion industry brands. For example, Chanel's unadorned wordmark is used in conjunction with the iconic overlapping double Cs to create a strong symbol and fashion icon.

Figure 8-2 presents examples of each of the logo approaches.

Spelling it out with a wordmark

A wordmark (sometimes called a *logotype* or *typographic symbol*) turns your brand name into your logo by presenting it in a unique typestyle, often with some artistic element that adds flair and memorability. Wordmarks are gaining in popularity among brand builders, as explained in the sidebar "What's in a logo? Increasingly, a name."

The best wordmarks are easy to read and distinctive. A few examples of widely and easily recognized wordmarks include the logos of FedEx, Google, Kellogg's, and Yahoo!.

Consider a wordmark especially if any of the following circumstances apply to your marketing situation.

- ✔ You want your logo to build recognition for your name.

- ✔ Your marketing budget is lean, and realistically, you aren't able to gain widespread recognition of a symbol, so you're better off gaining recognition of a distinct presentation of your name instead.

- ✔ You intend to develop subbrands under your primary brand, and you want a strong wordmark that can serve as an umbrella over each line.

Figure 8-2:
Logos feature wordmarks, lettermarks, brandmarks, and sometimes a combination of elements, as shown in these examples.

*Logos courtesy of: **Western Title & Escrow**, design by Brand Navigation, LLC; **Nexsys**, design by Brand Navigation, LLC; **SportsVision**, on file U.S.Gov, design by Brand Navigation, LLC; **Devonshire Associates Ltd.**, design by Brand Navigation, LLC; **Trimstone**, courtesy of Stoneworks of Art, design by William Berenson/Brand Architecture and Brand Navigation, LLC; **The Great American Hanger Company**, design by William Berenson/Brand Architects and Brand Navigation, LLC; **PowerLight**, design by Brand Navigation, LLC.*

Using your initials in a lettermark

Lettermarks turn a company's initial or initials into a brand symbol. In some logos, the lettermark appears all on its own, as in the IBM logo, which long ago dropped any reference to the name International Business Machines. Other stand-alone lettermarks include the logos of GE, CNN, and Louis Vuitton.

In other logos, the lettermark appears along with a wordmark that presents the full name of the brand, such as in the logo of McDonald's, which features the restaurant name along with an oversized "M." Another example is the logo of Kodak, which features a large K into which the name Kodak fits.

Lettermarks are good logo choices in the following circumstances:

- ✔ You want to make your name the primary emphasis of your logo, but you feel that your name is too long to be a good wordmark.

- ✔ You want to add a stylized monogram to a fairly straightforward presentation of your name in order to convey your brand personality.

- ✔ You have the budget necessary to gain awareness for your lettermark so that, in time, people see the mark and think of your business and its name.

Creating a brandmark or symbol

Brandmarks range from fairly literal to abstract designs. The best brandmarks become so associated with the brand names they symbolize that, in time, consumers automatically think of the brand name when they catch a glimpse of the logo. Think of the Nike Swoosh or the Mercedes symbol as examples of the power of great brandmarks.

You can create a brandmark by using free or almost-free resources available through clip-art or do-it-yourself logo sites or software, but the savings can be quickly eaten up by the investment you'll need to make to infuse a generic symbol with meaning for your brand.

Of all the logo approaches, developing a brandmark requires the highest level of professionalism, design expertise, and investment.

If you decide to go the brandmark route, you're best off hiring an experienced designer to create a customized, trademarkable symbol for your brand. And you should realize that, even with a one-of-a-kind, tailor-made mark, you need to make a strong marketing investment in order to establish meaning for your symbol in the eyes and minds of your consumers.

Consider a brandmark when these circumstances apply to your business:

✔ Your name is too long or cumbersome for a wordmark.

✔ A lettermark doesn't fit the character or image of your brand.

✔ A symbol will help you communicate the benefit, promise, distinction, or character of your brand.

✔ Your market spans the globe, and you seek a symbol that can represent your brand regardless of the language of the consumer.

✔ You have the budget required to build your logo into a recognizable, meaningful symbol that communicates with such strength that it can carry meaning even if it doesn't appear with your name.

Most brandmarks fit into one of these categories:

✔ **A representation of the business name.** For example, the Circle K brandmark is a "K" in a circle, and the Target logo is, unmistakably, a target. The Apple logo is an apple, the Red Cross logo is a red cross. The Shell logo is a shell, and the Greyhound logo is a greyhound. The list goes on and on.

✔ **A representation of the brand's primary offering.** For instance, a cruise line may adopt a brandmark of an ocean liner, and a catering service may use a knife and fork or a wine glass as its symbol.

✔ **A representation of the brand's promise.** For instance, an educational program may feature a symbol of a child holding a book, and a health spa may feature a symbol representing a toned body. Morton's salt adopted the symbol of a little girl sprinkling salt in the rain.

✔ **An abstract symbol that, over time and through marketing, is instilled with meaning for the brand it represents.** Examples of this kind of brandmark include the "good hands" of Allstate Insurance, the rings of the International Olympics, the Nike Swoosh, and the bespectacled triangle-faced man on the cover of the book you're holding. All are highly visible brandmarks that are meaningful to consumers because of diligent use and marketing by the brand holders.

Developing Your Logo Design

If you want to try to do it yourself, you can enter "do-it-yourself logo creation" into any search engine to obtain lists of logo-generating Web sites and logo development software. If you're artistically inclined and if you have the time to spend, proceed on your own, taking great care to follow the advice in the upcoming sections on logo design and logo taboos.

What's in a logo? Increasingly, a name

When you think of logos, you probably think of visual symbols or brandmarks because that's how logos entered the business world in the 1800s. Back then, the manufacturing break-throughs of the 19th century allowed for large-scale production of goods for the first time. With mass-production came product supplies that could be sold not just in home market areas but also in far-flung locations.

To successfully sell in distant markets, though, companies needed to gain consumer aware-ness and brand recognition in new areas where personal sales presence often wasn't possible.

Putting their names on their goods wasn't good enough because many 19th-century consumers were unable to read. So marketers used sym-bols to convey their brands. They adopted and presented meaningful brandmarks that could be easily understood even by those without liter-acy. The famous bell of the Bell Telephone

System (known to all as Ma Bell back in those pre-deregulation days) was one of the early symbols to gain widespread prominence.

Over the years, the need for a reliance on sym-bols ebbed. As literacy rates climbed, compa-nies began to present stylized versions of their names instead of or alongside symbols repre-senting their brands.

As the calendar turned to the year 2000 and the Internet became a major communication chan-nel, new companies increasingly adopted new words that would work as Internet domain names and as their brand names. Rather than asking the market to learn a newly fabricated name *and* a new symbol, the companies turned their names into their logos, presenting their brands with wordmarks instead of brandmarks. Google and Yahoo! are two globally recognized examples.

If you think your time is better spent running your business and acquiring customers rather than trying to create your own logo, hire a graphic designer, ad agency, or branding firm to do the creative and design work for you.

Whether you do it on your own or with professional assistance, start devel-oping your logo design by completing the worksheet shown in Figure 8-1 so that you or your logo design team members understand the brand your logo must reflect before the creative process begins.

Also, provide the following information to help guide creation of a logo that fits your brand and its market:

✔ **A description of your clientele:** For instance, are your customers pre-dominantly male or female, professional or blue-collar, urban or subur-ban, or of a particular age group or income level?

✔ **Three to six words that you think best describe your brand and offer-ing:** For example, "stylish," "high quality," "contemporary," "classic," "casual," "professional," and so on.

✔ **Samples of logos you like and don't like, along with some idea of why you feel the way you do about each one:** Designers can't read minds, so the more input you provide, the faster and better the process will go.

✔ **Your preliminary thoughts regarding design, color, and shape considerations:** If you know that your logo will need to work well in horizontal signs, for instance, or if you know that you hate the color brown, say so early on, not after you see the first round of design suggestions. Give creative professionals everything they need to do the job right from the start, when creativity is at its highest. Doing so avoids making them feel like their creative solutions are being killed through a thousand little cuts. Providing certain information upfront also saves you time and money because you arrive at a solution that fits your brand and meets your needs without rounds and rounds of costly revisions.

Design ingredients

As you go through the design process, be aware that the typestyle you select, the colors you adopt, and the shape the logo takes all have a bearing on the way it communicates and works for your brand.

What's your type?

Some typestyles look bold, some look progressive, some look refined or even elegant, and some look playful or creative. The typestyle you choose — and the way you arrange the type in your logo — has a tremendous impact on the impression your logo makes. Follow these tips:

✔ **Choose a typestyle that matches the character of your brand.** If your brand character is buttoned-down and professional, choose a typestyle that looks professional and even formal. If your brand character is casual, choose a typestyle that looks casual, too.

For a quick orientation to the world of typestyles, open your word processing program and pull down the menu for fonts to see samples of a wide variety of typestyles. Notice that some styles feature small lines adorning each character. These lines are called *serifs,* and the typestyles that feature them are called *serif* styles. Other typestyles are devoid of any letter enhancements, or *sans serif.* Courier and Times New Roman are examples of *serif* typestyles; Helvetica and Geneva are examples of *sans serif* typestyles. In general, *serif* typestyles convey a more traditional character whereas *sans serif* typestyles are more modern.

When choosing your typestyle, opt for a look that can withstand the test of time. For instance, the FedEx wordmark is derived from the Helvetica type and has been altered to make it more distinctive. Helvetica was designed by the typographer Max Miedinger in 1957. How's that for proof that classic styles have longevity!

✔ **Customize the presentation of your name in your logo.** Look at the wordmarks in Figure 8-2, and you'll see that some incorporate design elements into the type presentation. Others present the type in what, at first glance, seems to be a straightforward presentation. But don't be fooled. There's a world of difference between the look of a beautifully produced wordmark and the look of type straight off your word processor. Type produced directly from a word processor is evenly spaced so that all letters and words are the same distance apart. Type that's professionally arranged is adjusted so that letters are placed in uniquely pleasing configurations. The difference is almost imperceptible, yet it makes a dramatic difference in the appearance of a wordmark, and it's one of the reasons logo designers earn their fees.

A primer on colors

Your logo's color scheme can become an essential element of your brand identity. Coca-Cola *is* red; IBM *is* blue; John Deere *is* green. For that matter, think of your favorite college or pro team. Put the players in different colors, and fan confusion sets in.

As you choose colors for your brand identity, consider the following:

✔ **Establish a color scheme that differs from the scheme used by your major competitors.** People relate to color so strongly that you'll cause confusion by trying to adopt the same or similar colors that are already associated with another key player in your market arena.

✔ **Choose a color scheme that reflects your brand character.** If your market is comprised of young children, logo colors that resemble decorations on a birthday cake may be ideal. But the same colors would hardly work for the logo of a respected plastic surgeon or a leading corporate law firm.

Most consumers perceive neutral tones such as grey, taupe, navy, dark green, or burgundy as subdued, mature, and professional. Pastels convey calmness. Blues and greens are cool. Red, orange, and yellow are warm and energetic.

✔ **Choose colors that match your brand and the expectations customers have when selecting your offering.** For example, if your brand and your customers' expectations are professional, choose colors that are subdued and cool. If you offer and your customers seek lively entertainment, choose colors that are energetic.

✔ **Consider how your colors will be interpreted in other cultures or countries if your brand will be marketed outside your immediate market area.**

✔ **If your logo will appear on apparel or logo-emblazoned specialty items, consider how the colors will look on uniforms, golf shirts, ball caps, coffee mugs, or the dozens of other places it may end up.** If the colors can't be reproduced consistently, alter your color scheme accordingly. Alternatively, decide on an acceptable range of colors in which the logo can be presented without breaking your logo management rules (See the section "Managing your logo" later in this chapter for more information.)

✔ **The fewer colors you employ, the easier your logo will be to manage.** Logos with full-color illustrations or photos require full-color printing — an expensive and time-consuming process that you should adopt only after serious consideration. Plus, the Internet further restricts color options because the Web's color palette is limited.

✔ **No matter what color scheme you adopt, be sure your logo works beautifully in plain old black and white.** After all, that's how it will look on your business checks, in photocopies, in many small-format ads, and in numerous low-cost communications that will carry your brand identity far and wide.

Logo shapes and sizes

Most logos need to work well in a horizontal configuration that's about half as tall as it is wide. In other words, they need to look good on a standard business card, in the return address portion of a business envelope, and on the shirt pocket of uniforms or logo apparel.

Whatever configuration your logo takes, be sure it can reduce down to the size it will appear on a business card, which is where it will appear most frequently. If it becomes blurry or unrecognizable in a small size, redesign it to simplify the elements so that it reads well even in its most minute presentation.

Logo design evaluation

When reviewing logo designs, put them through a preliminary test to see if they incorporate the traits of most good symbols.

✔ **Do you think the logo makes a good impression for your business?** Does it make an impression that's equal to the professionalism and standards of your company?

✔ **Is it easy to see and remember?** Try this test when reviewing a logo design: Look at the logo, then set it aside and try to draw a quick rendition on a scrap of paper. If you come up with a sketch that's close to the design, then you can be pretty sure that the logo is memorable.

✔ **Does it work in a single ink color and at a small size?** If the rendition you're looking at is in color, run it through the photocopier and see if it looks good in black and white and at a size that fits on a business card. Check to be sure that none of the fine lines disappear in the reproduction and reduction. If they do, then the logo artwork is probably too weak to withstand a broad range of applications.

Logo design taboos

Economy is a virtue in almost every arena except logo design. The biggest mistake that new brand marketers make is saddling themselves with logos that scream "homemade." Follow this advice to avoid the most common logo-design pitfalls:

✔ **Don't have your cousin's nephew design it or do it yourself.** Remember, your logo is what visually represents your brand and the caliber of your offering. If you want to compete with great brands, hire an expert who specializes in logo design.

✔ **Don't let the design get too fussy.** Keep it simple. The best brands are clean and refined, conveying leadership and longevity.

✔ **Don't resort to clip art.** The archives of available symbols that you can drop into your logo are huge, but they're generic, say little about your brand and its character, and are sure to show up in someone else's logo at some point in the future.

✔ **Don't be a copycat.** Use other logos for inspiration, but invest the time and money necessary to create your own unique mark. For one thing, you end up with a unique logo. For another, you avoid the legal landmines that infringing on another company's brandmark are likely to set off.

Your logo makes the difference between a strong and a weak first impression for your business. It also makes the difference between a brand of choice and a product purchased simply for its price or availability. Want proof? Take the alligator off the shirt, and what is Izod selling? A shirt like any other shirt you can get anywhere. With the alligator, the shirt becomes an association with the success and stature of the Ivy League.

Preparing your logo artwork

If you feel up to the task of designing your own logo, follow this advice:

✔ If you create your logo by using the templates available in publishing programs, carefully customize colors, symbols, and typestyles so that you end up with a unique logo look for your business.

✔ Use the same design software that professionals use. Adobe Illustrator, CorelDRAW, and Macromedia Freehand are known as *vector-based graphic design software,* which means that your final logo design can be enlarged or reduced without design distortion or loss of quality.

If you go the preferred route and hire a design professional for your logo design and development, take these steps:

1. **Choose a professional whose expertise, size, and fees fit well with your needs.**

   Options range from freelance artists to small design studios to local, regional, national or global ad agencies to internationally renowned identity developers. You can spend anywhere from several hundred dollars up to the million-dollar range. If you want a logo that competes well in a local market, set aside a small budget and find a local resource. If you aspire to make the list of the world's top brands, turn to the talents of award-winning brand specialists, and invest accordingly.

2. **Review past work samples to be sure that the designer's style matches with your expectations.**

3. **Be clear about your budget and obtain cost estimates before authorizing design work to begin.**

4. **Stipulate that you will own all rights to your logo after you pay in full for its design and production.**

5. **Upon approval of your final logo design, obtain copies of the artwork in EPS format for printing purposes and in JPG and GIF formats for online use.**

Putting Your Logo to Work

After you create and approve your logo design, apply it consistently to every single communication that carries your name into the marketplace. Use the worksheet in Figure 8-3 to keep track of all the places your logo needs to go. Then aim to get your logo into place on all items on the list just as quickly as possible.

Avoid introducing your logo in a piecemeal fashion, applying it to some brand presentations immediately and others over time. If some communications carry your logo and others don't, or if some carry outdated versions of a revised logo while other carry the latest iteration, you're setting yourself up for a weak identity and marketplace confusion.

LOGO APPLICATION CHECKLIST	
✔ All items that apply to your business	✔ All items that apply to your business
Advertising ☐ Newspaper ads ☐ Magazine ads ☐ Phone directory ads ☐ Business and industry directory ads ☐ Community publication ads ☐ Online ads ☐ Billboards and outdoor sign ads ☐ Transit ads ☐ Direct mailers ☐ Newsletters ☐ Other:	**Signage** ☐ Exterior building signage ☐ Interior building signage ☐ Entry door and department signage ☐ Vehicle signage ☐ Posters and point-of-sale materials ☐ Product displays ☐ Trade show displays ☐ Other:
Sales Material and Literature ☐ Brochures ☐ Handouts (menus, take-one cards, and so on) ☐ How-to instructions and manuals ☐ Package enclosures ☐ Web site ☐ Other:	**Stationary and Correspondence Items** ☐ Letterhead ☐ Notepads ☐ Envelopes ☐ Mailing labels ☐ Business cards ☐ Fax cover sheets ☐ E-mail signature files ☐ Forms for estimates, invoices, purchase orders, and so on ☐ Other:
Audio-Visual Materials ☐ Videos, DVDs, CDs ☐ Speaker support materials ☐ Presentation handouts ☐ Other:	**Publicity Materials** ☐ Media kit folder ☐ News release sheets ☐ Company backgrounder and media kit enclosures ☐ Other:
Apparel ☐ Logo-ID gift or sale clothing items ☐ Uniforms ☐ Other:	**Specialty Items** ☐ Shopping bags and packaging ☐ Gift items and giveaways (pens, mousepads, coffee cups, and so on) ☐ Other:

Figure 8-3:
Use this worksheet as a checklist for all the places your logo goes.

Saving Face: Giving an Existing Logo a Makeover

Sometimes a logo gets tired. Perhaps it's been used inconsistently and, as a result, it's lost the ability to present your brand in a clear manner. Maybe it's failed to keep pace with changes to your brand's product offering, character, and target market. Or maybe it's just plain gone out of style over the years.

If you think that the time has come to repair your logo, begin by evaluating your needs. Consider whether you need an evolutionary or revolutionary re-design. In other words, think about whether you seek a quick nip and tuck or an extreme brand makeover.

To come to this conclusion, ask yourself the following questions:

- ✓ What image do you want to project, and how does your logo fall short?

- ✓ What about your business has changed since your logo was created? Is your target market different? Has your product offering changed? Do you still make the same business promise? Is your brand character still the same?

- ✓ Can you update your current logo to reflect your updated situation without making a radical identity change, or do you need an altogether new symbol even though the complete change may result in short-term market confusion?

- ✓ What elements of your logo are most important to your identity? The symbol? The colors? The wordmark? If you could keep only one portion of your logo, which would it be? (Chapter 17 presents before-and-after logo redesigns that show how others made their logo redesign decisions.)

- ✓ Do you have the budget required to change your logo throughout all brand communications?

Look back at Figure 8-3 for a list of all the places your brand logo goes. In addition to the cost of redesigning your logo, you need to be prepared to update every single place your logo appears, and the sooner the better. Trying to apply a new logo on a catch-as-catch-can basis is a formula for brand management disaster. Instead, aim to update your logo in all appearances in as short a period as possible.

As you get ready to revitalize your brand, turn to Chapter 17. It provides indicators to watch and situations to monitor as you determine whether or not to retool or retire your brand identity, how to critique your logo, how to revive your look, and how to manage the rebranding process so that it's as transparent and effective as it can possibly be.

Managing Your Logo

To maintain a strong graphic identity for your brand, your logo has to appear exactly the same every single time it's reproduced, with no exceptions.

The minute you present your logo with a different typestyle, or in a different color combination, or with a different embellishment of any kind, you lose consistency and, with that, the power to convey your brand identity with clarity.

To ensure that your logo is presented without variation, create a set of usage guidelines to be followed by everyone who produces marketing materials for your business. This section provides an outline to follow to manage your logo.

Creating logo tools, standards, and usage rules

As a first step toward controlling the presentation of your logo, create logo artwork that must be used consistently by all who create materials on behalf of your brand. Then stipulate that your logo must be reproduced from these approved files and not from second-generation versions that risk degradation of the clarity and quality of the design.

Beyond use of the approved artwork, also control how your logo can appear by establishing usage guidelines in each of the following areas.

Presentation of your logo as a single unit

Too often, those creating materials for your company will want to take liberties with your logo by increasing the size of one element and decreasing the size of another, or by moving elements into different positions to alter the shape of the logo in order to fit it into a space it otherwise doesn't fit. Ban such individualized treatments by providing artwork for your logo in several allowable shape variations — perhaps one for use in horizontal placements and one for use in vertical placements — along with the stipulation that any alternative configuration must be approved prior to usage.

Placement of your logo

Define how your logo can appear in printed materials.

- ✔ **Clarify how much open space must exist between your logo and surrounding design elements.** For instance, a company with a wordmark that begins with the letter "T" may require that the logo be surrounded by open space at least equal to the size the "T" appears on the page. This rule ensures that the logo isn't crowded by surrounding artwork.

- ✔ **Define whether or not you allow your logo to appear on its side or in a diagonal placement, or whether it must always run parallel to the bottom of the page, whether in a horizontal or vertical configuration.**

- ✔ **Define the smallest size in which your logo can appear.** Especially if your logo involves type or fine lines, it may become illegible at small sizes, which reflects poorly on your brand image.

Color treatments

In your logo usage guidelines, define the ink colors in which your logo may appear.

- ✔ In black and white applications, stipulate whether or not you allow the logo art to appear in white on a black background (called a *reverse treatment*) or whether the logo itself should appear in black, with no reverse option.

- ✔ When printing your logo in black ink, clarify whether you allow it to appear on colored paper or in colored backgrounds and, if so, whether background colors are limited to a range of recommended or allowable colors.

- ✔ When your logo appears in colors, spell out what colors are allowed. If your logo is to appear in green, for example, take the guidelines a step further by telling exactly which shade of green, giving the ink number from the Pantone Matching System (PMS) used by most printers. Also stipulate how to build the approved color through the four-color printing process (called CMYK for cyan-magenta-yellow-black) by defining what percentage of each of the four inks a printer should use to create the desired tone. Further, define how to arrive at the color through the RGB (red green blue) process for computer screen display.

Backgrounds and shadow effects

Many of the best-managed logos bar reproduction of color logos over backgrounds that compete with the logo design. When backgrounds are necessary, you may want to stipulate that the background must be dark enough to allow the logo to be reversed out of the background, causing the logo to appear in white rather than in the standard color treatment. Also, consider whether or not you allow your logo to be presented with a shadow effect.

Naming a brand cop

People don't fiddle with your logo to be mischievous; they think they're being helpful or creative on your behalf without realizing that their help is actually a hindrance to the strength of your brand identity. That's why usage rules are so all-important. It's also why you need to circulate your usage guidelines and name a person within your company who must approve any usage that deviates in any way from the approved usage of your logo.

Chapter 18 includes detailed information on writing and enforcing your brand usage guidelines.

Creating a Tagline

A *tagline* is a phrase that accompanies your brand name to quickly translate your positioning and brand identity statements into a line that means something to consumers. A tagline is meant to provide consumers with an indication of your brand and its market position in just a few memorable words.

Discovering what makes a great tagline

Great taglines have a number of common attributes. When writing your tagline, see that it meets these criteria:

- ✔ **It's memorable.** You hear it, memorize it quickly, and repeat it with ease.
- ✔ **It's short.** Great taglines often have as few as ten syllables so that they're quick to recite, easy to tuck in alongside logos, and short enough to include in voicemail greetings and small-space ads.
- ✔ **It conveys a brand's point of difference by telling what sets it apart from others.** A great example of this element is Avis Rent A Car and the tagline "We try harder."
- ✔ **It clarifies a brand's market position and key benefits, especially if the brand name doesn't quickly communicate the brand's offerings and distinctions.**
- ✔ **It differentiates a business from all others.** In fact, a great tagline is so unique that it doesn't work when linked to a competitor's brand name.
- ✔ **It reflects the brand's identity, character, promise, and personality.**
- ✔ **It's believable and original.**

A great tagline manages to excel on most or all of these fronts while also avoiding a couple of major tagline mistakes.

- ✔ It invokes positive feelings without running the risk of triggering sarcastic retorts.

- ✔ It appeals to consumers even more than to corporate committees. In other words, the tagline doesn't get bogged down with the input of a dozen executives who inadvertently turn the slogan into a corporate rallying call rather than a consumer magnet.

- ✔ It adds to the meaning of the brand name without repeating any of the same words or concepts.

Deciding whether you need a tagline (and you probably do)

Taglines are increasingly important as a means to carry your brand identity where your logo can't go, like your e-mail messages, classified ads, voicemail greetings, and other nonvisual communication channels. In those environments, your tagline becomes the single transmitter of your business's brand and position.

Some brand names tell a pretty complete brand story (for example, Coppertone, Jiffy Lube, U-Haul). Other brand names benefit from some quick explanation, which is where taglines come to the rescue. Plus, even seemingly self-sufficient brand names gain dimension through their slogans.

To determine whether you need a tagline, answer these questions:

- ✔ Does your business offer consumers distinct advantages that aren't conveyed in your name?

- ✔ Would your brand character be more clearly presented with a line that travels with your brand name?

- ✔ Is your company best at something that you want consumers to know about but that isn't conveyed by your name?

If you answered "yes" to any of these questions, a tagline may well be a strong addition to your brand name, logo, and marketing program.

Tag (line), you're it! Coming up with your slogan

For a look at some of the best slogans in use today, go online to the Advertising Slogan Hall of Fame at www.adslogans.co.uk/hof. From AT&T's "Reach out and touch someone" to the Yellow Pages' "Let your fingers do the walking," the site posts the top ten slogans of recent years along with an A-to-Z list of great taglines and a wealth of tagline development advice.

In crafting your own tagline, consider the following:

- Know your positioning statement. What meaningful and available niche in your market do you fill better than any other brand? (Turn to Chapter 5 if you're not sure.)

- Based on your unique position, come up with a list of quick, memorable one-liners that convey your special distinction.

- Put each of your tagline contenders to the test by seeing if they live up to the qualities listed in the section "What makes a great tagline?" For additional help analyzing your tagline ideas, go to the Sloganalysis page of the AdSlogans Web site (www.adslogans.co.uk/sloganalysis), where you can access a free diagnostic tool to help you weigh the strengths and weaknesses of taglines you're considering.

Part III

Launching Your New Brand

"IT'S A MACINTYRE PLANK"

In this part . . .

This part is like the Mission Control for your brand launch. These chapters help you direct all the steps involved in taking your brand to market — from strategic planning to internal organizational preparation to development and implementation of the public relations, advertising, and online marketing programs that propel your brand into public consciousness.

Before your brand takes flight, follow the advice in this part to maximize its market exposure and your resulting brand success.

Chapter 9

Countdown to Takeoff: Planning Your Brand Launch

*I*f your new brand were to consist simply of a new name, a new logo, and maybe a new tagline, it would be ready to launch as soon as the ink was dry on your new stationery, ads, and supporting marketing materials. But, guess what? Branding isn't that superficial.

Brands aren't skin-deep applications that you apply over your organization to give it a new, improved, and more compelling identity. Brands go all the way to the core of your business. They're reflected not just by your logo, ads, and sales communications but, even more importantly, by every contact with your business — whether before, during, or after the purchase.

That's why this chapter helps you launch your brand from the inside out, bringing every aspect of your business into alignment with your brand promise, personality, and character before you raise the curtain and intro-duce your brand in your marketplace.

This chapter leads you through the phases of your brand launch: preparing for your brand debut, writing your brand launch marketing plan, launching your brand internally, and moving your brand into the public eye.

Committing to Internal and External Brand Launches — In That Order

When it comes to brand launches, we've seen extreme successes and real flops, and the difference, almost without variation, comes down to whether or not the launch took place within the organization before it traveled to the outside world. If an internal launch doesn't occur first, a brand fails to win the kind of internal buy-in necessary to imbed the brand message into the entire brand experience.

Although your logo is a very important aspect of your brand, it's only one representation of your identity. Your brand is conveyed through everything the world sees and hears and encounters. How you answer your phones, how you treat your employees, how your employees treat your customers, how it feels to deal with your business, the look of your workspace or Web site, the music that plays in the background — these are the expressions that make your brand message and promise a reality. To create the experience that accurately reflects your brand, your internal team needs to embrace your brand before it sees the light of the world outside your doors.

Preparing for Your Brand Launch

Whether you're launching a new brand or revitalizing an existing brand, your brand identity needs to be announced as part of a complete brand story. If your new brand identity leaks out in bits and pieces, people within your organization are likely to think one of two things:

- So what?
- They spent all that time and money on *that?*

After you've decided on and approved your brand name, logo, and tagline (see Chapters 7 and 8), hold that information close to your vest while you put your brand through final tests and prepare it for unveiling.

Knowing your story, chapter and verse

Before you enlist the understanding, interest, and support of others, be sure you're 100-percent ready for your internal launch by assembling short statements that describe each of the following brand elements. Summarize the following:

✔ **Your market position:** Chapter 5 helps you work through the homework involved to arrive at a statement that tells what you offer, who you serve, and the unique benefits you offer in your competitive market arena.

✔ **Your brand promise:** If your brand promise isn't already clearly established, turn to Chapter 6 to define the reasons customers choose your business, the benefits people count on you to deliver, the experience they expect to receive, and the promise they can absolutely count on from your brand.

✔ **Your brand character:** Chapter 6 helps you arrive at a one-sentence brand character statement that defines the personality of your brand and the mood and tone that will be reflected through all brand expressions, including every contact and experience with your brand.

✔ **Your brand definition:** Also called your *brand identity statement,* this short definition wraps your target market, market position, point of difference, brand promise, and brand character into a single sentence that directs all your branding efforts. Your brand definition is an internal steering device, not an external marketing message. It's a single sentence that guides your brand's development, following this format: [*Your name*] promises [*your target market*] that they can count on us for [*your unique attribute or benefit*] delivered with [*information about the character, tone, and mood you convey*].

Putting your brand launch into context

You're probably reading this book because you're in the midst of creating a new brand or revising an existing brand, either through a brand identity face-lift or through a complete rebranding effort — which we liken to a branding mulligan, where you write your last brand off and start all over again.

Either way, you need to be clear about why you're doing what you're doing. What's more, those who work with you, either as employees or as shareholders or customers, need to be clear about what you're doing and why the effort is worthwhile to the value of your organization.

To prepare for your brand launch, ready your answers to the following questions.

Why are you undertaking this branding effort?

Most branding programs aim to achieve one or more of the following outcomes:

✔ **Build awareness:** Awareness leads to marketplace dominance and easier sales efforts, so awareness is usually a top objective in any brand launch.

✔ **Create an emotional connection:** Brands need to build emotional connections with their prospects, especially brands that deliver products that contribute to a sense of personal satisfaction or security. Additionally, brands aiming to enhance customer loyalty often target the emotional connection, realizing that customers remain true to brands they love.

✔ **Differentiate your offering:** For brands in crowded market categories — where many competitors offer similar products, services, and promises — differentiation is usually a key brand launch objective.

✔ **Create or enhance credibility and trust:** Every service or online business needs to make credibility and trust a key branding priority because service and online purchasers are, essentially, buying based on nothing but trust. Customers can't see, hold, or try out a service or online offering before saying "yes" or clicking Proceed to Checkout. Instead, they buy based purely on the belief that the company will deliver on its promise.

✔ **Motivate purchases:** Rapid sales growth is a key objective for those introducing new consumer brands, largely because the retail marketplace offers only a small window of opportunity for a new brand to prove marketplace acceptance before it's booted off the shelf for some other brand that delivers greater sales volume for the retailer.

For help determining your branding priorities, turn to Chapter 3. It includes a worksheet to help you determine the strategic importance of various brand functions to your branding success, while also helping you assess the pre-launch strengths of your current brand if you're undergoing a brand revitalization or rebranding program.

What do you expect your brand launch to achieve?

After you set your branding priorities (drawing from the list in the preceding section), you need to set objectives for what you want your brand launch to achieve. The more clearly you establish quantifiable outcomes for your brand launch, the more quickly you win buy-in from shareholders, funding partners, top-level executives, and the staff who will help you make your new brand a success.

✔ **If you're starting a new business or brand,** you're starting from zero, with no existing brand awareness, emotional connection, credibility, brand differentiation, or sales momentum. Therefore, setting objectives is a matter of determining how quickly you intend to reach certain levels of success in each priority area.

> ✔ **If you're realigning or rebranding an existing brand,** begin by assessing your pre-launch situation in each of the brand functions. Your existing success levels become the benchmark against which you measure the success of your brand launch.
>
> Chapter 3 can help as you determine your current success levels. For help conducting research or enlisting professional assistance, turn to the research sections in Chapter 4. When you know your benchmarks, you can set your brand launch objectives by defining the increases you intend to achieve above the pre-launch level in each priority area.

In either case, be realistic about how much change you can effect over the brand launch period and how much it will cost in terms of marketing investment to gain the level of awareness and sales motivation you set out to achieve. The market adopts change incrementally, which is a nice way to say *slowly,* so set your objectives with your eyes wide open about the momentum you're likely to achieve.

Aim to monitor your success not just at the completion of your brand launch but several times over the next year. Doing so allows you to measure how your brand is doing in terms of increases in sales, distribution, market share, and pricing, and also in terms of consumer awareness, preference, perceived value, perceived point of difference, satisfaction, and desire to purchase, repurchase, or refer to others.

Depending upon the size of your organization, you can conduct this research on your own following the survey and interview advice in Chapter 4, or you can turn to the professional assistance of a research firm. You can find research firms through major city phone directories or by asking for referrals from advertising agencies and branding firms.

What about timing?

If your brand launch will gain momentum with a tie-in with a major conference, trade show, or industry event, or if it will benefit from introduction at a certain date for some other reason, make that date clear when you launch the brand internally.

It's easy for people in your company to get complacent about something that seems like an aesthetic change, but if they realize that, on a certain date, the curtain needs to rise and the brand needs to be ready to go in order to achieve awareness and momentum, they'll step on board with a greater sense of mission.

What's your message?

Before unveiling your brand internally or externally, be completely certain about the single message you want the market to take away from your brand launch program. By clarifying your brand introduction message in advance, all brand communications — formal and informal, from the CEO to the front-line staff — align, contributing to a strong, clear impression. To create your message, follow the framework shown in Figure 9-1.

BRAND INTRODUCTION MESSAGE WORKSHEET

1. The purpose of our brand introduction is to convince [*insert a brief description of your target market*]

_____

that our brand offering [*insert your value proposition by describing how your offering helps customers make or save money, improve effectiveness and efficiency, enhance safety, security, or success, or enjoy other valuable benefits*]

_____

2. We back our value proposition by [*insert a description of how you prove and reinforce your value proposition throughout your organization*]

_____

Figure 9-1:
Craft a clear
brand
introduction
message.

3. To reinforce our brand promise and character, all our brand communications and every experience with our brand conveys the mood and tone of [*insert a description of the voice and personality that all communications with your brand will convey*]

_____

Producing prototypes to introduce your brand

As you prepare to introduce your brand, be ready to show how your brand will appear in the marketplace over the coming weeks and months. Do this by creating *prototypes,* also called *mock-ups,* of everything from signs to ads to Web pages to uniforms, apparel, specialty items, and product packages. By showing samples of how the brand will look in actual applications, you allow people on your internal team to engage and interact with the brand. By seeing how the identity works, they begin to put their attachments to previous brand identity representations, or their doubts about the newly adopted identity representations, out of their minds.

Don't skimp on the production of your prototypes. If the samples you show aren't impressive, the reaction to your brand won't be impressive either. Invest in prototypes that look as much like the real thing as possible. The designers, ad agency, or brand consultants who help you with your branding program can provide these prototypes.

Checking your internal readiness

In branding, what you say pales in comparison to what you do. The experience your customers have with your brand trumps your logo presentation, advertising, and marketing efforts in a heartbeat. In fact, given the choice between a beautifully presented brand identity that's backed by an uneven brand experience and a marginally presented brand identity that's backed by a brand experience that's impeccably reinforced at every touch point, we and most other brand consultants would vote for experience over identity any day.

To prepare your organization to consistently deliver on your brand promise, create an inventory of all the ways people encounter your business. Evaluate each contact point to see that it accurately reflects the mood, tone, and promise of your brand. To get your evaluation started, begin with this list:

- ✔ **Telephone:** Do you answer phones promptly, consistently, and with a message that reinforces your brand? Do voicemail recordings throughout your company convey a common tone and message?

- ✔ **In-person arrival:** Are directions to your business clear and in keeping with the character of your business? Is your business location a good reflection of your brand? Does your front door (or your Web site's home page, if your business exists primarily online) make a strong, accurate first impression? Upon arrival, does your entry area (or your home page) make a strong statement for your brand? Are people greeted promptly and in a manner that reflects your brand promise?

- ✔ **Within your business:** Is the look, sound, and even the smell of your business in keeping with your brand character? Do your employees reflect your brand identity by the way they look and act, the clothes they wear, and the way they interact with customers?

- ✔ **Correspondence:** Have you standardized mail and e-mail correspondence so that all communications, whether they come from a salesperson, an invoice clerk, or a service representative, create an echo chamber for the quality and caliber of your brand?

✔ **Service:** The service cycle involves eight steps — initial contact, establishment of rapport, product presentation, sale negotiation and transaction, payment, product delivery, follow-up to confirm customer satisfaction, and ongoing customer service and communication. Monitor how well your brand is reflected at each of these contact points. If at any one your customer has an uneven experience with your brand, your brand promise is eroded and the strength of your brand is weakened.

The minute you feel your organization is ready to deliver a consistent brand experience at every customer touch point, you're ready for brand launch.

Previewing your brand story with priority audiences

Prior to the public launch of your brand and again on at least an annual basis, take your brand story to your most important outside audiences: Your investors and your best customers.

Taking your brand story to investors and analysts

We don't mean to sound too much like Yogi Berra, but the best thing you can do to enhance market investment in your brand is to build and manage a great brand in the first place.

The financial world watches the Interbrand and *BusinessWeek* annual surveys on power brands (see Chapter 22) for a reason: Investors realize that a good way to monitor a firm's earning potential is to monitor the strength of its branding program.

In addition to watching how a brand stacks up in national studies, investors watch how well brands send out strong brand management signals. When presenting to investors, be aware that they consider the following line-up of questions, and make the answers part of your presentation:

✔ Does the brand convey the same identity, message, and promise when dealing with all its stakeholder groups, from investors to consumers to employees?

✔ Does the brand express itself through an integrated marketing program that projects the same look, tone, message, and promise in advertising, in fulfillment materials, online, and in its bricks-and-mortar establishments?

✔ Does the brand retain its customers — an indication that it delivers well on its brand promise?

✔ Does the brand have coordinated internal management, as evidenced by a brand experience that's without variation whether it's encountered as a prospect, a customer, a job applicant, a supplier, or an investor?

If your organization seeks support from the investment community, first build a branding program that evokes a strong "yes" response to each of the preceding questions.

Then, at the time of brand launch and periodically thereafter, deliver your brand story to the investor and analyst community by

✔ Creating an investor/analyst presentation that features your brand story and success indicators

For examples of brand presentations, enter "investor analyst brand presentation" in your favorite search engine. The results should lead you to corporate sites that allow you to click on investor podcasts, Webcasts, presentations, news releases, and fact sheets.

✔ Taking your presentation directly to major investment partners and hosting centrally located events for the general investor community to attend

✔ Backing your live presentations with Webcasts and podcasts for those who can't attend the event in person

✔ Following presentations with news release recaps to investment firms and financial media

✔ Posting all investor/analyst information in the online pressroom area of your Web site

Treating your best customers to an insiders' preview

The trick to turning customers into brand ambassadors is keeping your brand promise without fail, delivering a consistently compelling brand experience, and making your best customers feel not only valued but also treasured.

Whether you're rebranding, revitalizing your brand, revamping your brand, or introducing a subbrand or brand extension, don't risk upsetting your best and most loyal customers by letting them hear the news through the grapevine. Deliver the news personally, host customer brand preview events, and plan ways to allow old customers to embrace your new brand through a brand introduction program that turns customers into ambassadors for your company. Chapter 14 gives you advice to follow in this area.

Ten, Nine, Eight . . . Writing Your Brand Launch Marketing Plan

Assemble your brand launch plans into a document that will guide your brand introduction. By putting a plan in writing, you force yourself to clarify the objectives you're seeking to achieve, the strategy and tactics you'll follow, the timeline you'll meet, and the budget you'll live within.

You can launch your brand without a plan or with a plan that exists only in your head, but you shouldn't. It's far easier to stick to your timeline, strategy, and budget; to meet your objectives; and to enlist the support of team members when your plan is in writing on a couple sheets of paper that all those who share responsibility for success can review, adopt, and buy into.

Follow these ten steps to compile your brand launch plans into a document that guides your brand introduction. The following sections delve into some of these steps in greater detail.

1. **State your brand introduction message, following the template presented in Figure 9-1.**

2. **Benchmark your pre-launch situation by determining your brand's current levels of awareness, emotional connection, distinction, credibility and trust, and sales.**

3. **Set your market launch objectives by prioritizing what you want your launch to accomplish and by pinning each priority to a measurable outcome, such as a percentage increase in brand awareness, emotional connection, distinction, credibility and trust, and sales.**

4. **Define your target market so that you can direct communications specifically toward this group.**

5. **Define the brand promise and brand character that must be conveyed in all brand communications and experiences.**

6. **Establish your brand introduction strategies, including your product strategy, distribution strategy, pricing strategy, and promotion strategy.**

7. **Detail your marketing tactics, including how you'll use advertising, publicity, promotions, online marketing, sales efforts, packaging, and point-of-sale efforts to introduce your brand.**

8. **Establish your budget.**

9. **Create your action plan and timeline.**

10. **Measure and monitor your success.**

Benchmarking your pre-launch situation

Chapters 3 and 4 include information on assessing your market situation and conducting research to find out more about your brand's awareness, distinction, and preference in your market. Use the form in Figure 9-2 to benchmark your pre-launch situation and to monitor shifts in brand presence and performance during the post-launch period.

Setting your goal and objectives

Your *goal* is what you want your brand launch to achieve; your *objectives* define how you'll achieve your goal. For example:

- ✔ **If your goal is to win awareness for your brand and its distinctions,** your objectives may include gaining name recognition and knowledge of your unique point of difference among a defined percentage of consumers in your target market with in a certain length of time from the conclusion of your brand launch.

- ✔ **If your goal is to enhance credibility and trust,** your objectives may be to achieve awareness of and belief in your point of difference and your brand promise among a defined percentage of consumers in your target market within a certain length of time from the conclusion of your brand launch.

- ✔ **If your goal is to motivate sales,** your objective may be to add at least one new distribution channel and to realize a specified sales increase without sacrificing unit sale price within a certain length of time from the conclusion of your brand launch.

Commit your goals and objectives to writing in order to keep your efforts focused only on marketing strategies and tactics that contribute to your success. Then each time a new marketing opportunity arises, you can put it to this easy litmus test: *Will this opportunity help us meet our goal? Does it support one or more of our objectives?* If the answer is "no," you can quickly decline the offer and turn your attention back to your plan.

MEASURING THE IMPACT OF YOUR BRAND INTRODUCTION				
	Pre-launch benchmark	Situation at launch conclusion	Situation 2–3 months post-launch	Situation 6–12 months post-launch
Sales: Revenue; units sold; other sales indicators				
Market share: Percentage of sales of like-offerings in your market area captured by your brand				
Price: Price per item sold or other pricing indicator				
Awareness: Percentage of market that knows your brand name				
Emotional Connection: Percentage of market that prefers your brand over competitors or that places your brand in the Top 3 or Top 5 in your category				
Distinction: Percentage of market that understands how your offering is uniquely different				
Credibility and Trust: Percentage of market that understands and believes your brand promise				
Purchase Motivation: Percentage of market that intends to purchase, repurchase, or recommend a purchase of your offering				

Figure 9-2:
Benchmark and monitor the impact of your brand introduction by using this worksheet.

Defining your target market

In defining your target market, answer these questions:

- ✔ Are you targeting new customers?

- ✔ Are you targeting existing customers?

- ✔ Are you targeting those in a position to refer customers to your business or to speak on your behalf?

- ✔ Will your introductory efforts be confined geographically to a specific city or region, or will they target broadly dispersed consumers who fit a defined prospect profile?

REMEMBER

Targeting your market puts you in a position to reach prospects effectively with well-chosen media and messages. It also helps you plan staffing and distribution to meet the market demand your communications generate.

TIP

Nearly all successful brand introductions start with narrowly focused target markets for these reasons:

- ✔ **A brand introduction requires intensive communication in order to rapidly achieve a necessary level of awareness.** It's far easier and vastly more affordable to achieve intensive communication when prospects all live in a limited geographic area that can be reached with regional media, or when they share lifestyle or interest similarities that allow you to reach them with special interest media or one-to-one communications.

- ✔ **Most brand introductions come from small businesses that work with relatively small budgets.** Huge corporations either buy and reintroduce existing brands or introduce parent-dominant brands that slide into the market under the strong umbrella identity of the well-known corporate brand. Nearly all other brands start with budget, distribution, and staffing constraints that are best managed by introduction in highly focused target markets.

- ✔ **Even major brands benefit from target marketing at the time of introduction.** By introducing a brand in a single geographic market or through a single distribution channel or even a single retail chain, the brand can achieve a high level of awareness while building a success story that creates publicity, word-of-mouth, and other forms of viral marketing.

Setting your strategies

Most marketing plans include strategies for the *4Ps:* product, pricing, promotion, and place (or distribution channels). When creating the marketing plan for your brand introduction, establish the strategy you'll follow in each of these four areas:

✔ **Product:** Most brand launches revolve around the announcement of an altogether new offering or the announcement of changes to an existing offering. Be aware that new products require a higher level of introduction, explanation, and purchase motivation than are required by product revisions, which are often introduced to an already committed audience.

✔ **Pricing:** If one of your brand introduction priorities is to achieve new sales, particularly from new customers, your pricing strategy is an essential element in your brand introduction. To motivate decisions, consider limited-term introductory pricing or payment options, rebates, trial offers, or other purchase incentives.

✔ **Promotion:** Your promotion strategy describes how you'll get the word out about your brand. Most brand launch promotions involve public relations, advertising, and online communications, each described in detail in Chapters 10, 11, and 12.

✔ **Place or distribution:** Your brand introduction needs to be backed by a distribution strategy that allows consumers to access the product as soon as interest is ignited. To a business-to-business brand marketer, the distribution strategy may take the form of a new location, new Web site, or some other new means of access. To a consumer brand marketer, the distribution strategy must lead to an easy-to-access purchase point.

Often, businesses introduce consumer brands first through a single distribution point or chain. This approach allows the marketer to maximize in-store visibility while minimizing the requirements of distributor discounts and slotting fees that can erode profits to the point of killing a consumer brand before it has time to get off the ground.

Selecting your brand introduction tactics

In order to achieve cost-effective visibility and credibility, most brand launches rely heavily on publicity and public relations rather than on advertising, which often is used as a follow-up to news and personally delivered announcements of the new brand.

As you plan the tactics you'll use to deliver your brand introduction message in your target market, keep the following points in mind:

✔ **Public relations activities are the backbone of most brand introductions.** The field of public relations includes employee or member relations, community relations, industry relations, government relations, and media relations that result in news coverage of your brand introduction message. Events, meetings, newsletters, exhibitions, and publicity all fall under the category of public relations. All spread news and generate understanding without involving paid advertising. Turn to Chapter 10 as you plan your public relations game plan.

✔ **Promotions are marketing activities that aim to trigger a desired consumer action over a short period of time.** Marketers launching consumer brands use promotions to win support from distributors and retailers and to prompt customers to a first-time trial of the new product. See Chapter 11 for guidelines on promotions.

✔ **Advertising creates awareness in audiences reached by newspapers, magazines, radio, and television.** Most consumer brands, as well as most brands being introduced over large market areas, use advertising to convey their brand messages to broadly dispersed markets. Chapter 11 offers advice for scheduling, creating, and placing your ads.

When using advertising as a brand launch tactic, time your ad schedules so that ads break *after* your brand is released via news stories. After your message runs in ad form, editorial contacts may not view it as news, and you forego the chance to gain the credible third-party voice of a reporter or newscaster.

✔ **Direct mail is advertising that's delivered on a one-to-one basis to mail boxes or e-mail in-boxes rather than through mass media.** It's a great way to provide invitations, detailed information, or publicity reinforcement to individuals who are targeted because they precisely match your customer profile. Follow the advice in Chapter 11 on how to create great ads as you create your direct mailers. If you're delivering your mailers via e-mail, turn to Chapter 12 for information on how to create e-mail that gets opened and read.

✔ **Personal presentations and sales efforts are especially important to brand launches that depend on personal relationships, referrals, or support from established contacts and customers.** Most business and service brands include launch events and personal presentations as essential introduction tactics. Chapter 13 covers how to prepare your sales force and how to take your brand story on the road to key audiences.

✔ **Sales materials, packaging, and point-of-sale displays are essential for consumer brands and for brands that involve complex features, high prices, or considerable deliberation prior to the purchase decision.** For all but the smallest local market brands, sales and packaging materials require the design talents of established professionals. Begin by answering the communication planning questions in Chapter 11 and then hire a designer, ad agency, branding, or packaging specialist to create your materials. Chapter 11 can help you through the selection and hiring process.

✔ **Online communications play an increasingly important role in brand introduction tactical plans, as described in Chapter 12.**

Establishing your budget

Based on the brand introduction tactics you select (see the preceding section), you're ready to plan and set your brand launch marketing budget. Use the worksheet in Figure 9-3 to help you estimate costs involved to implement each tactic.

BRAND-LAUNCH BUDGET WORKSHEET		
Tactic	Cost Estimate	Included in existing marketing budget?
Advertising		☐ Yes ☐ No
Public relations **Events and functions** for employees, customers, community groups, industry groups, and other VIP groups		☐ Yes ☐ No
Publicity generation including media kit development, news release generation, and professional assistance		☐ Yes ☐ No
Direct mail including list development/ purchase, mailer production, mailing costs		☐ Yes ☐ No
Marketing materials including brochures, packaging, displays, CD/DVDs, and ad specialties		☐ Yes ☐ No
Online marketing		☐ Yes ☐ No
Web site development		☐ Yes ☐ No
Online ads		☐ Yes ☐ No
Search-related marketing		☐ Yes ☐ No
Other:		☐ Yes ☐ No

Figure 9-3: Estimate costs for each tactic you intend to employ as you prepare your brand launch budget.

Takeoff! Launching Your Brand

Remember that your brand launch needs to happen in two phases: an internal phase and then an external phase. Only after your internal team is on board and every customer touch point is in alignment and ready to deliver on your brand promise are you ready to take your brand outside your organization and to your target market.

Launching internally

Conduct your internal launch in two phases: the first one for senior management and the second one for your full employee team. This sequence is important because you need to ensure that all executives are firmly on board before you start rallying the troops. Otherwise, you risk gaining enthusiasm from employees only to have some vice president (also known as someone's boss) say something like, "I don't know why we're spending so much time and money on this." Just like that, internal support for your branding program can take a giant backslide.

If your company is small to medium in size, your two-phase internal launch can happen over a short time period. If you're dealing with multiple locations or divisions, however, it will take longer. Either way, by involving executives in the brand planning and development phase, you cut down the time needed to bring top-level leaders on board because they're part of the planning team from the beginning.

Starting with the bigwigs: Launching with upper management

Your internal brand launch definitely requires a from-the-top-down approach that starts with top-level executives and moves on to company-wide managers before reaching your full employee corps.

Representatives of the executive group were likely involved in the brand development process, so your management brand launch isn't likely to be an unveiling as much as a chance to bring the whole brand picture into focus. Follow these steps as you launch your brand with your executive team:

1. **Review and win unanimous consent for your brand position, promise, character, definition, and launch message.**

   If some executives have questions or doubts, take time to address them at this phase of the launch so that all leaders are reading from the same page when your brand message moves into your organization.

2. **Gain agreement regarding your brand launch objectives and timing.**

   If some executives see timing conflicts between the brand launch and other company activities, iron out the kinks by altering the schedule, shifting launch responsibilities to other executives, or hiring employees or outside professionals to handle the tasks involved. No matter what, deal with the conflict at this stage of the launch so that it doesn't become a barrier to success as you implement your broader launch.

3. **Preview the materials you'll be presenting at your company-wide brand launch.**

   The tasks covered in the section "Preparing for Your Brand Launch" earlier in this chapter help you prepare your presentation materials. Before using them at your company launch, preview them with your executives to ensure that there won't be any surprises (or resistance) at the time of the company-wide presentation.

4. **Discuss and win agreement regarding how the departments overseen by each senior executive can tangibly integrate the brand promise into every aspect of the organization's products and services.**

   Chapter 14 includes a form for conducting a brand experience audit. Consider asking your executive team to use the form as they assess any brand contact points in need of repair and as they take responsibility for implementing change in their individual management arenas.

Launching company-wide

By taking the time to explain why you're branding, rebranding, or revitalizing your brand and how your efforts link to your business mission and goals, you preempt internal resistance and kick-start the process of creating a team of champions for your brand. (Turn to Chapter 13 for complete information on turning your staff and business partners into your best brand champions.)

The company-wide brand launch should be both an education process and a company rally. For a successful launch, follow these steps:

1. **Make a case about the value of branding.**

   If you can't connect the idea of branding to the company vision, mission, values, and goals, you're setting yourself up to hear murmurs of, "They paid how much for *that?*" Turn to the section "Putting your brand launch into context" earlier in this chapter for advice on announcing your brand in terms that link it to your company's vision, values, and goals.

2. **Present your brand strategy, putting special emphasis on the brand promise and the importance of a brand experience that's reflected through every point of encounter with your business.**

   Refer to the section "Checking your internal readiness" earlier in this chapter as you prepare for this step.

3. **Unveil your brand identity.**

   Show the logo, preview the slogan, and present prototypes of how the brand identity will appear on marketing materials over coming weeks and months.

4. **Give each employee a quality gift — a hat, shirt, pen, or other item — featuring the new logo.**

   The nicer the item, the better the impression, so avoid anything cheap or cheesy unless that's the image you want your employees to take away with them. Instead, accompany your internal brand launch with distribution of quality items that employees will like and want to keep. No click-top pens with flaky metallic imprints up the side, please!

   As you hand out your logo gifts, remind employees of the external launch date and ask them to keep your identity under wraps until that day arrives. If your staff is too large to control, consider holding the distribution of gifts until the external launch occurs.

5. **Ask each member of your team to personally embrace the brand and become an ambassador who delivers the brand experience to customers.**

   We cover this step in more detail in Chapter 13.

Launching externally

Only when your company is ready to walk the talk is it time to take your brand introduction message to the world outside your business. When your brand experience is ready for prime time, amplify the message to your business world by following these steps:

1. **Time your external launch to coincide with public interest in your story.**

   If you serve a particular industry, consider timing your launch to coincide with a major conference or trade show. If you serve a local market, time your launch to coincide with an annual economic development conference, regional business fair, or some other event that brings regional leaders and media together in one place.

2. **Launch a public relations program to carry your brand message into the market.**

3. **Place ads stating your brand and the promise it makes.**

4. **Unveil your brand promise and message on the home page of your Web site.**

As you announce your brand outside your organization, use the information in Chapters 10, 11, and 12 to leverage publicity to launch your brand, advertise to put your stake in the ground, and put the power of the Internet to work to spread your brand message far and wide.

Internal relations involves everything from sharing the story of why you're investing in a branding program to training employees to represent your brand and deliver on your brand message and promise.

Refer to Chapter 9 for help preparing for your internal launch. Then turn to Chapter 13 as you use internal relations on an ongoing basis to turn your employees into a team of champions for your brand.

Any brand introduction that fails to include insiders first is in for trouble. That's why the unveiling of your brand needs to start within your organization. Use meetings, events, communication programs, and information dissemination to build employee awareness and to generate support among the very people who will end up representing your brand image and delivering your brand experience on a daily basis.

Community relations

Creating visibility and understanding for your brand in your home community is especially important if your market is local or if you want to establish your business and brand as forces in your own backyard. To gain community awareness, follow these steps:

1. **Introduce your brand through regional news stories.**

   Follow our advice in the section "Extra! Extra! Making News" later in this chapter for targeting and providing news stories to local media.

2. **Gain awareness among community leaders, business and government leaders, and key customers by previewing your brand at a brand launch event.**

   Consider timing your brand launch to coincide with a major conference or trade show where industry leaders, media representatives, and customers are gathered looking for news stories. Or, if you serve a local market, time your launch to coincide with an annual economic development conference, regional business fair, or some other event that brings regional leaders and media together in one place.

3. **Use the brand launch as the beginning of an ongoing effort to establish your name, message, and brand promise in the minds of community residents and leaders by joining groups, participating in charitable efforts, and contributing time, products, services, or funds to support projects that benefit your home market region.**

   Building a local reputation takes considerably more time than the duration of your brand launch program. However, your launch provides an ideal opportunity to introduce — or to reintroduce in the case of brand revitalization or rebranding — your brand in your home community.

Industry relations

If your brand meets the needs of a *vertical market,* which is a market with specialized interest in a particular industry or area, consider timing your launch to coincide with a major industry event.

Vertical markets span the alphabet from advertising to zoos, and each has its own industry association and annual gathering. By arranging your brand launch to coincide with a major industry conference or trade show, you can introduce your brand to customers, suppliers, industry leaders, and representatives of industry-specific media outlets all in one fell swoop.

If your business (or your budget) is too small to merit major industry event presence, you can still employ industry relations as part of your public relations program. Use the advice in the section "Introducing Your Brand with Publicity" later in this chapter to cultivate industry-specific media relations and resulting publicity. Also, consider joining your industry association and taking a leadership position. If you do, your business benefits in two major ways:

- ✔ You keep your business at the forefront of industry advances.
- ✔ You acquire industry information that you can share with local and business media, making you a valuable news resource and giving your business valuable news exposure at the same time.

Government relations

If your business is regulated or depends on relationships with elected officials, include government relations in your overall public relations program.

Whether your focus is local — on your mayor, city councilors, and county leaders — or whether it goes to the state or national level, take time as part of your brand launch to make a special introduction to your relevant leaders by employing one or several of these approaches:

- ✔ **Distribute information to key government leaders.** The officials may be too busy to sit down for a meeting with you, but they'll take note if you send a mailing, perhaps in the form of a brand launch press kit with a cover letter. In the letter, briefly explain the reasons behind your brand launch and your aspiration to be a positive employer and economic engine in your marketplace. Refer them to the press kit for more information, and add an invitation to count on your business as an industry resource or to offer assistance with relevant projects.
- ✔ **Add government officials to the invitation list for your community brand launch event.**

> ✔ **Keep in contact by sending copies of company news releases, reprints
> of favorable news features or articles, annual reports, and other indi-
> cators of your success.**

Media relations

Publicity delivers your message through news mentions in mass media outlets. A carefully orchestrated and impeccably maintained media relations program results in publicity that benefits your brand in three ways:

> ✔ Publicity is often a cost-effective way to gain media exposure. Sure, it
> costs money to write and distribute news releases and to cultivate
> media relationships. But unlike advertising, publicity isn't purchased.
> You obtain it as a result of editorial contacts and information delivery
> rather than through paid ad placements.

> ✔ Publicity contributes to your credibility for the simple reason that
> people find editorial content more convincing and believable than simi-
> lar information delivered through paid ads.

> ✔ After you obtain publicity, you can reproduce the articles or news seg-
> ments and circulate them as part of your marketing efforts, including
> them on your Web site, in direct mailings, as part of presentations, and
> in press kits.

Successful media relations rely on targeted and established editorial relationships, distribution of newsworthy releases and story ideas, and ongoing
availability as a reliable and trustworthy news resource. The section titled
"Extra! Extra! Making News" later in this chapter gives you advice to follow
for meeting these requirements.

Writing your public relations game plan

A public relations program doesn't just happen. In fact, without a firm commitment to the task and a dedicated plan to follow, it's too easy to turn your
energies toward building sales or putting out management fires and, as a
result, neglect the opportunity to build and develop a favorable image for
your brand among your public audiences or stakeholder groups.

To outline the public relations program you'll use to introduce your brand,
follow these steps:

1. **Define and prioritize your audiences and communication approaches.**

   Go through the list in the preceding section and determine which
   approaches — employee relations, community relations, industry relations, government relations, and media relations — are most important
   to the success of your brand launch.

Nearly all brand launches begin with a focus on employees and internal audiences. From there, depending on the objectives of the introduction, each brand launch follows a different public relations path. If you seek to heighten awareness in general or industry-specific markets, the media is a primary target audience for your brand launch. If you seek to heighten customer loyalty or support, you should focus efforts on current customers. If you're seeking enhanced credibility in your marketplace, your emphasis should be on industry, community, and government leaders.

2. **Select and prioritize your public relations tactics.**

   When you're clear about your target audiences, you're ready to choose which tactics will best deliver your message to those you're trying to reach. Publicity, mailings, hosted events, personal presentations, and participation in community or industry gatherings are among the most frequently used public relations tactics. (If you think your public relations skills could use a brush-up, start by turning to *Public Relations For Dummies,* 2nd Edition by Eric Yaverbaum, Robert W. Bly, and Ilise Benun [Wiley].)

3. **Establish your public relations program budget by allocating the funds necessary to implement each of your scheduled public relations tactics.**

   Chapter 9 includes a budget worksheet. As you complete the public relations portion of the budget, include all the expenses you project for launch events (for employees, customers, investors, business associates, community leaders, and industry or trade gatherings), publicity generation (including media kit development and news release generation and distribution), and direct mailings to stakeholder groups. Also, include costs for professional assistance from designers, publicists, or public relations firms if your program exceeds the capabilities or capacity of those on your staff.

4. **Establish your action plan and timeline.**

   Assign dates by which each tactic must be planned and implemented. Then assign responsibility for getting the task completed on time so that your plan and your brand introduction take advantage of every public relations opportunity.

When your public relations plan is down on paper, insert it into your brand launch marketing plan under the section titled "Promotional Strategy." See Chapter 9 for step-by-step help in writing your overall marketing plan if you haven't yet prepared one.

Introducing Your Brand with Publicity

Your brand launch is an ideal opportunity to generate publicity *if* — and this is a big if — you can turn it into a newsworthy story, which means a story that contains news of interest to the audience of the news outlet in which you hope the story will appear.

In brand launch after brand launch, we've learned this valuable lesson: Unless your brand already enjoys a sky-high level of public awareness and interest, audiences don't really care that you have a new or revitalized brand identity. What they do care about is how your brand announcement matters to them and their lives. They care if you've launched a new business or product that's projected to create 12 new jobs in your market area, or if your new line of services fulfills a demonstrated market desire, or if your expansion into national or international markets will positively impact the local economy.

Ask yourself, "How is our brand announcement important to the audience of the media outlet where we want a story to run or air?" When you have a clear answer, prepare to generate publicity by following these steps:

1. **Decide the target audiences you want to reach via publicity and the nature of the story you want consumers to see, hear, or read about your brand launch.**

   Depending on your objectives, you may want to get your story to the financial world, to those in your industry, to your local community, or specifically to those who are or are likely to become customers of your business.

2. **Target media outlets by researching and selecting publications and broadcast vehicles that reach the audiences you're trying to reach.**

   If your objective is to reach customers but you're not completely certain about your customer profile, flip to Chapter 5 and complete the Customer Profile Worksheet.

3. **Prepare and distribute your news, either via personal calls during which you share story ideas and provide background information or via news releases that you hand-deliver, fax, mail, or e-mail to editorial contacts.**

Matching publicity efforts to your brand launch objectives

As you work on your brand launch, you welcome all good publicity, but you derive the most value from publicity that carries your story to your highest-priority audiences, which are the audiences whose positive opinions are most likely to contribute to your success.

To set your publicity generation efforts off in the right direction, begin by defining who you most want to reach via publicity, the story you want to convey, and the type of media that's most likely to carry your news to your target audiences.

Refer to Table 10-1 as you create your publicity game plan.

Table 10-1	Planning Publicity Objectives and Approaches	
Publicity Objective	*Media Channel*	*Nature of Story*
Heighten awareness among business leaders and the financial industry	Business and financial publications, business sections of daily newspapers, business segments of broadcast outlets, business Web sites	Tie brand introduction to the announcement of a new business, product, or strategic direction, including forecasts for market opportunity, new jobs, and business growth
Heighten awareness in local or regional market area	Local and regional news outlets, including daily and weekly newspapers, radio and TV stations, alternative press, and Web sites distributing local/regional information	Tie brand introduction to the announcement of new products, services, or opportunities of interest to customers, prospective customers, and local/regional residents
Heighten awareness in the national/global market	Network radio and television channels, national and major metro newspapers, news wire services, consumer and lifestyle magazines, major Web sites and news portals	Tie brand introduction to a major announcement of a new product or service, new business direction, or other news of impact and interest to national and international consumers

Publicity Objective	Media Channel	Nature of Story
Heighten awareness within your industry or trade group	Trade, technical, and professional publications and Web sites	Tie brand introduction to the announcement of a new product, service, production, distribution, or marketing campaign of interest to customers, suppliers, wholesalers, and retailers in your industry

Targeting media outlets

The *media list* for your brand launch publicity program may be so short that it includes only the few news outlets in your hometown, or it may be long enough to list all the publications, broadcast outlets, wire services, and Web sites that reach your market locally, regionally, nationally, and globally.

Long or short, your target media list should be limited only to media outlets that reach your target audience and that carry news of the nature you're working to spread. The following sections provide advice to follow, resources to tap, and how-to information for developing your list.

Knowing the right media outlets when you see them

Put media outlets on your list only if they match your needs on the following fronts:

- ✔ Geographically, they serve audiences in the market areas you wish to reach.

- ✔ Their audiences are comprised of people with the lifestyle interests and demographics — age, gender, education level, income level, and so on — of those you're trying to reach.

- ✔ Their editorial focus aligns with the nature of your story.

- ✔ Their audiences are likely to be interested in your news.

News editors confirm that the preceding advice gets ignored on a regular basis. As a result, community newspapers receive releases with no local news slant whatsoever, national outlets get releases regarding local stories with no broad-reaching impact, and special interest media outlets receive news of no significance to the interests they serve. It's no surprise that the misdirected news stories take a direct route from in-box to trash bin. Save your news from this demise by first researching news outlets to be sure they match up with the nature of your news and then crafting the presentation of your news to match up with the needs of the editors and audiences you're seeking to influence.

Tapping into media list resources

As you develop your target media list, turn to the following resources:

- ✔ **dir.yahoo.com/News_and_Media:** This online directory of general and industry-specific news outlets categorizes outlets by news and media formats and subjects.
- ✔ **Bacon's Media Directories:** Available by subscription online (www.bacons.com) and in the reference section of major libraries, these media directories profile U.S. and Canadian newspapers, broadcast outlets, and Internet media.
- ✔ **Standard Rate and Data Service (SRDS) Media Source books:** Available by subscription online (www.srds.com) and in most major libraries, SRDS provides media profiles, advertising data, and contact information for business publications, consumer and trade magazines, newspapers, and interactive media sources.

Creating your list

When you know which media outlets reach those in your target audiences, create your target media list. For each media outlet, record the following:

- ✔ Media outlet name and contact information, including mailing and e-mail addresses, general phone number, and Web site address
- ✔ Media publishing or broadcast frequency, circulation or reach statistics, and deadline information
- ✔ Editorial contact information, including the name or names and contact information for those managing or reporting on the type of news you'll be generating

Prioritizing editorial contacts

Go through your complete target media list and select outlets that most effectively reach your target markets with editorial content that best matches up with the kind of news stories you'll be circulating. For instance, local media may be more interested in stories about how your branding efforts will affect the size and success of your business in the local market area, whereas industry press may be more interested in stories that describe how your branding program will set a new direction in your business arena.

As you put media outlets on your high-priority target media list — the list of outlets that you want to cultivate for in-depth editorial relationships — find out everything you can about the outlet so you can match your stories accordingly. For each media outlet on your high-priority list, obtain the following information:

> ✔ The name and title of the editor or reporter you should contact with information for stories in the sections or programs that cover your area of interest
>
> If contact lists for editors and reporters aren't available on the media Web site, try calling the media outlet's main phone number and asking for the name of the person on the editorial staff to whom you should send business news and story ideas. When you obtain the name, ask for a direct phone number and e-mail address, too. Record this information on your high-priority media contact list.
>
> ✔ The lead time each outlet requires for story pitches and placements
>
> ✔ Story angle and news submission preferences

Although all media outlets on your target media list are valuable and important to your publicity program, your high-priority editorial contacts are the ones to whom you'll give special attention. They're the ones most apt to deliver in-depth coverage that goes straight to your most important audiences.

Pitching your story

Instead of simply crossing your fingers and sending a news release, contact high-priority contacts in advance and pitch your story. Your goal is to provide a heads-up about your upcoming news and to persuade each contact to cover the story. When pitching stories, keep these points in mind:

> ✔ **Do your homework in advance.** Before making contact, know the media outlet's format, deadlines, and audience as well as the editorial contact you want to talk to and the program, section, or column where your news fits.
>
> ✔ **Be newsworthy.** Editorial staff members aren't interested in promotional messages. They want to know that the story you're proposing is of interest to their audiences and that it fits well within their editorial format.
>
> ✔ **Be concise and compelling.** Your contacts are on tight deadlines, so be ready to pitch your story quickly and completely.
>
> ✔ **Be professional in your delivery.** Don't hem and haw, stumble to find words, or sound uncertain about the story you're proposing.
>
> ✔ **Get the information you need to fulfill the interest you generate.** When the reporter shows interest, obtain information about how to deliver your news — in person or by mail, fax, or e-mail — and by what deadline.

When pitching your brand introduction story to high-priority media contacts (either verbally or in writing), you should limit your presentation to 400 words or less. Plan your presentation by compiling these elements, in order:

1. **Introduction: In an attention-getting introduction, describe your proposed story and how it relates to the interests of the media outlet's audience.**

   For example: "After a year of research, development, testing, and approval, our company is unveiling the new identity of ABC Company, including its revolutionary line of all-natural plant-pest control products that will be manufactured here in River City and shipped worldwide to enhance environmentally responsible crop production on an estimated 500 million acres over the upcoming three years."

2. **Story overview: Summarize what makes your announcement newsworthy; how it's relevant to current events, audience interests, and market trends; and any research or supporting material you can provide to the editor.**

3. **Desired coverage: Mention the kind of coverage you seek: a feature story, news coverage, event coverage, interview of an executive or industry official, attendance at media conference, and so on.**

4. **Additional information: Describe how you can assist in story development.**

   You don't have to provide material at the time of the pitch, but explain the kinds of material you're prepared to provide, from artwork to market trends to company history to arrangements for interviews and so on.

5. **Contact information: Provide contact information so the editor can get back to you with a story decision or requests for additional information.**

6. **Follow-up: Offer to provide a short summary of your pitch via e-mail as a follow-up to your conversation and to confirm your contact information.**

Preparing and distributing news releases

News releases are the standard currency in the publicity realm. Whether you're delivering news in person, at a news event, or by hand, mail, or e-mail, the minimum standard is to pass along a news release that summarizes your story and says who to contact for more information.

In the past, nearly all news releases were printed on paper and delivered by hand, mail, or fax to editorial contacts. Today, most news releases are created electronically and delivered via e-mail, with hard-copy versions available for subsequent handout and follow-up. Additionally, a growing number of companies now package news into audio or video form for ready-to-go transmission to broadcast audiences.

The following sections tell you how to proceed with each of these news release approaches.

Hard-copy news releases

Printed news releases generally fit on no more than two double-spaced pages that provide the following information, in the following order:

1. **Whom to contact for more information:** Along the top of the page, type, "For more information:" followed by the name, telephone number and e-mail address of the person who can provide additional facts.

2. **When the news can be released:** Most releases follow the "For more information" section with the announcement that the news is "For Immediate Release." If it's absolutely necessary to hold the news until a certain time, instead of typing, "For Immediate Release," use the space to announce an *embargo,* stating that the news may not be released until a set date or time; for instance, "Embargo until 12:01am January 15, 2007." If you embargo your news, be sure that you have a very good reason why it can't be released earlier and that the reason is made clear in the news release (for instance, "On January 15, Global Enterprises announced its merger with Worldwide Business . . ."). Call editorial contacts in advance to alert them to the time sensitivities, and see that your own organization keeps a lid on the news until the date that you authorize the media to announce it.

3. **A succinct headline:** On no more than two lines, summarize the topic of the news release in a statement that uses active voice as opposed to passive voice. For example, use "New Brand Identity Appeals to Expanded Global Marketplace" instead of "New Logo Unveiled."

4. **The news release dateline:** The body of the release begins with the name of the city and the abbreviation of the state from which the news originates, followed by the date of the release (for example, "PORTLAND, OR, December 1, 2006").

5. **The news:** Present your news in an *inverted pyramid* style that tells who, what, where, when, why, and how right at the beginning of the release so that the most important news remains intact if an editor cuts the release from the bottom up.

6. **Quotes:** Include brief quotes from executives, industry leaders, or other authorities, along with complete attribution.

7. **Boilerplate closing:** End your release with a one-paragraph summary of your company's mission and background, including facts about the size and purpose of your company and your brand promise.

To distribute hard-copy news releases, use one of these approaches:

✔ Handle the task on your own by mailing, faxing, or delivering releases to your target media contact list.

✔ Contract with a public relations professional or public relations agency to write and distribute your news releases.

✔ Use a news distribution service such as PR Newswire (www.prnews wire.com) or Business Wire (www.businesswire.com) to achieve simultaneous distribution of important news to national, international, or business media. (For examples of e-mail news distribution services, visit www.ereleases.com, www.prweb.com, and www.internet newsbureau.com.)

E-mail news releases

Increasingly, journalists prefer to receive news via e-mail. Before assuming that your news is welcomed by online delivery, however, do the following:

1. **Confirm with your target media outlet or editorial contact that your release will be accepted if it's transmitted via e-mail.**

2. **Obtain the correct e-mail address.**

3. **Ask whether to send the release as an e-mail message or e-mail attachment.**

Staff at most media outlets don't open unsolicited attachments, so don't send your release as an attachment unless you're specifically told to do so.

When preparing releases for transmission via e-mail, follow this format:

1. **E-mail address:** Send the e-mail directly to your editorial contact.

2. **Subject line:** In the subject line, enter a benefit-oriented headline in 50 or fewer characters.

3. **Message:** In the message portion of your e-mail, pull the elements of your news release together in this order:

    1. State when the news can be released, usually using the words "For Immediate Release" or, if necessary, by announcing when the news can be released, using a line such as, "Embargo until 12:01 am, January 15, 2007."

2. Double-space and type the release dateline (the city name and state abbreviation where the news originates), followed by the date of the release.

3. Type a dash followed by the body of the news release (single-spaced except between paragraphs). Limit the release to about 500 words.

4. Share information on how to obtain additional information (for example, "To schedule interviews . . ." or, "To obtain photos and artwork . . .").

5. Close with boilerplate information, just as in a hard-copy release (see the preceding section).

6. Add the contact person's name, phone number, and e-mail address; and the company name, contact information, and Web site address.

When e-mailing releases, use plain text rather than HTML or other markup language. Prepare a traditional hard-copy version of the release as well to enclose in media kits, to post within your company, to distribute to clients and key contacts, and to provide as follow-up information to editors.

Audio and video news releases

News releases in audio, video, and multimedia formats present prepackaged news stories to broadcast outlets.

- *Video new releases* (VNR) either package news in the same style as that used in television news reporting or provide video footage for use by broadcast outlets when producing news segments.

- *Audio news releases* (ANR) usually take the form of 60-second news stories tailored for use by radio stations and networks.

- Webcasts allow marketers to present portions of offline events — such as major presentations or announcements — to online audiences.

Audio and video releases require a high level of production capability. Contact advertising agencies and broadcast professionals for assistance, and visit www.prnewswire.com for information.

News release artwork

Today's publications put heavy emphasis on photos and illustrations, so publishers count on those seeking publicity to submit good images to accompany the stories they propose. The better the artwork and photography you submit, the better the chance that you receive publicity. To improve your chances of getting a news release with artwork published, follow these tips:

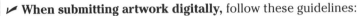

✔ **When hand delivering or mailing artwork,** provide photo prints in a minimum size of 5-x-7 inches, or provide slides, transparencies, or computer files that meet the size, resolution, format, and quality required by the media outlet. Specifications vary widely, so always inquire with your editorial source before submitting anything. When providing hard-copy illustrations, submit first-generation reproductions on bright white paper.

✔ **When submitting artwork digitally,** follow these guidelines:

- **Submit artwork in at least the size you hope it will run or in the size requested by the media outlet.**

- **Prepare your artwork in an acceptable format and with adequate digital resolution.** JPEG files are nearly universally accepted, and most publications can use your material if it arrives with a resolution of 250 to 300 PPI (pixels per inch). To be safe, ask before sending.

- **Transmit your image in RGB (red green blue) color format.** This is the default setting in most photo software and the most common on-screen viewing mode.

- **When sending digital photos, rename photo files from the default name given by the camera.** Bring the image up on your computer monitor and use the "rename file" function to label the photo with a name that identifies the photo or provides a short caption.

✔ **When selecting and submitting artwork,** provide only high-quality images and professionally produced graphics, each accompanied by a caption or cutline. The *caption* titles the photo; the *cutline* describes the image in detail. When writing your cutline, include the names of all identifiable people (from left to right), information about the photo, and the name of the photographer and photo credit request, if any.

Always obtain permission before submitting artwork as an e-mail attachment because most media outlets don't open unsolicited or unexpected attachments.

Creating a media kit

Beyond providing a news release and artwork, many marketers provide editors and reporters with a media kit in the form of a folder full of background information that helps inform writers about the business and the brand so that they can produce better stories. When preparing a media kit for your brand launch, include the following elements:

- Your brand story

- Your company history

- Fact sheets about your products or services and the markets you serve

- High-quality artwork of your new brand identity

- Prototypes of how your brand will be applied over the coming weeks and months

- A company brochure (unless your brochure is a sales piece that contains little or no background information)

- Your most recent annual report or a one-page summary of financial facts

- Contact information including names, phone numbers, and e-mail addresses of those who can be reached for additional information

Building an online pressroom

Journalists increasingly turn to *online pressrooms* to find company contacts, check facts, obtain information, or download images, so before launching your brand, consider adding a pressroom to your Web site. An online pressroom should contain all the information that's in your media kit along with the following additional background and resource materials:

- Company history, product information, and market information

- Executive profiles

- Financial information

- Current and recent news releases

- Recent media coverage as well as a searchable archive of past news stories

- Downloadable photos and graphics

- Scheduled events worthy of media coverage

- Background information, including annual reports, research reports, transcripts of major speeches or presentations, and copies of *white papers* (papers that state your organization's position or philosophy on topics of importance to your business arena in language that most readers can understand).

- Links to useful Web sites

- Contact information for media spokespeople

Extra! Extra! Making News

To turn your brand launch into a newsworthy story that earns publicity exposure, include in your announcement information that's relevant, timely, interesting, and useful to media audiences.

Each brand launch situation differs, but the following examples may spur ideas:

- ✔ A new company that aspires to become a regional economic force announces its brand by bringing in an industry leader to share perspectives on the industry and to describe how the new brand will play an important role.

- ✔ A nonprofit organization announcing a major brand revitalization invites the governor or a key state cabinet member to help unveil the brand and discuss how the organization's new direction supports important statewide agendas.

- ✔ An entrepreneur announces a new brand in tandem with the announcement of partnership agreements with several key distributors, thereby increasing the financial impact of the company's announcement.

- ✔ A developer unveils the brand for a new environmentally sensitive residential development along with the announcement that a percentage of all development profits are dedicated to a regional clean-air fund.

Make your brand announcement newsworthy by including information of genuine news value. The opposite of newsworthy information is information that belongs in sales pitches. The minute your "news" becomes promotional, it's labeled as hype and trashed accordingly.

Good deeds make good news

Here's an easy-to-remember definition of *public relations:* Doing the right thing and then talking about it.

As you work to generate public interest and media coverage for your brand, one surefire way to gain positive attention is to participate in community or humanitarian efforts that better your world and the world of those you're seeking to reach with your brand message.

Consider the headline-making actions of Starbucks. In 2006, the company leveraged its commitment to community, education, and literacy programs by producing and publicizing the movie *Akeelah and the Bee*, which carried the tagline, "Change the world one word at a time."

Your own efforts are likely to be much smaller in scale, but by building ties to your target markets by joining groups; serving on boards; heading up charitable campaigns; and donating time, products, services, or funds to worthwhile causes, you reap the benefit of personal satisfaction while generating news about your altruism.

Staging news conferences

News conferences are far more popular among those seeking publicity than they are among those covering, writing, and producing news. More and more often, journalists shun ribbon cuttings, groundbreakings, and announcements that can just as easily be explained in a news release or phone conversation.

Before you plan a brand launch news conference, consider this advice:

✔ Stage a news conference if your launch includes important news that should be announced simultaneously to all media outlets.

✔ Stage a news conference if you're presenting an important speaker or celebrity.

✔ Stage a news conference if your launch includes displays and presentations that require personal attendance.

If you decide to schedule a news conference, hold it at a time and place convenient to most journalists, start it on time, hold speakers to short time slots, minimize speeches in favor of demonstrations, and have media kits and releases ready for attendees (and ready to be delivered to media outlets not in attendance).

You're on! Shining in media interviews

The whole point of publicity generation efforts is to win the attention of a reporter or news editor. When the request for more information or a media interview comes, don't fumble the call. Prepare yourself for the next step by following these dos and don'ts:

✔ In advance of media calls, do know the main points you want to convey in every brand launch interview. (Turn to Chapter 9 to develop your brand launch introduction message if you haven't yet done so.)

✔ When a media request arrives, do confirm the name of the publication or station, the editorial contact, and the deadline.

✔ During interviews, do begin by asking how much time the reporter has or the length of the broadcast segment, and keep the interview within that timeframe.

✔ Do make your most important points as early in the interview as possible and again later in the interview as appropriate.

✔ Do keep your comments short so that they make good quotes. In broadcast interviews, aim for 20-second sound bites.

✔ Do keep your comments positive and nonpromotional.

✔ Do provide a media kit with reproduction-quality copies of your new brand identity and prototypes of logo usage applications.

✔ Do follow up with your thanks. Follow up within days of the interview, at which time you can offer to provide any additional information that will help the reporter compile the story. Then follow up again right after the story runs or airs, thanking the reporter or editor for the coverage and offering to remain available for any future questions or story ideas.

✔ Don't answer questions if you aren't sure of the answer. Instead, arrange to put the reporter in touch with a more qualified person on the topic.

✔ Don't speak poorly of the competition or argue with the reporter.

✔ Don't try to fill silences with extraneous information that may misdirect the angle of the story.

✔ Don't ask that comments be *off the record.* You're better off simply not saying anything you don't want to see in print or hear on air.

There's No Such Thing as Bad Publicity, Right? Wrong!

Sorry, but sometimes publicity gives a company a black eye. Bad publicity can be the result of bad luck, bad timing, a bad product or service, or a bad mistake made in the process of a media interview, customer encounter, or marketplace mishap.

Chapter 19 tackles the topic of what to do if you run into trouble, but to stay out of trouble in the first place, follow these tips:

✔ **Before meeting with media, be clear about your brand promise and brand character, and stay true to your brand at all times.** Even if the story you're advancing has nothing to do with your brand message, when people read or hear your news, it contributes to the way they experience your brand. If the tone, message, or character you advance is inconsistent with what people expect from your brand, then the resulting publicity is far more harmful than helpful to your company and brand.

✔ **Watch your words.** Don't get flip, don't go off-message or ad-lib, don't try to be funny, and never disparage others. If you attack someone else, the least that can happen is that you erode your brand image. The most that can happen is that you face a libel suit if an untrue statement ends up in print or a slander suit if an untrue statement ends up on air.

Chapter 11

Advertising and Promoting Your Brand

. . . .

In This Chapter

▶ Developing your brand marketing message and communication strategy

▶ Creating ads that work to build your brand

▶ Promoting and packaging your brand

. . . .

*B*rands need awareness like plants need water. If people don't know about your brand, or if they don't have a clear idea about what your brand is and stands for, it will never take root in their minds, which is where brands live and thrive.

Advertising is a primary tool for developing brand awareness for the simple reason that it allows you to tell your story in exactly the terms you want, when you want, and where you want. Unlike publicity-generation efforts (see Chapter 10), which, at best, result in delivery of your message some of the time, advertising is a surefire means to carry your brand message into target market homes, offices, cars, and mailboxes.

Good advertising grabs attention, heightens interest, creates emotional connection, and etches a positive brand image in your target prospect's mind. Good advertising is an investment that pays off by building awareness and, as a result, equity for your brand.

This chapter helps you plan, create, produce, and place advertising that conveys your message, inspires your market, and builds a clear, compelling image for your brand in the minds of your target prospects. We also help you develop the full range of marketing materials that complement your advertising — from sales materials to product packages — so that your ads are part of an integrated marketing program that conveys a single, strong brand image in your marketplace.

Getting Singular with One Brand Message and Tone

When you hear marketers talk about *integrated marketing communications,* they're talking about communications that project a single focused tone and message across all communication channels, whether transmitted via personal presentations, promotions, advertising, direct mail, online marketing, or public relations.

The power of consistency for you and your brand

Great brand marketers all recite the same mantra: Consistency builds brands.

When you deliver the same look, message, and promise across all media channels, in all forms of marketing communication, and through every encounter with consumers, you develop an integrated marketing campaign that conveys one strong, clear image and builds one strong, clear brand.

Brands benefit from integrated marketing communications for a number of reasons, including the following:

- ✔ **Customers gain confidence in brands that convey consistent marketing messages.** If your communications sound or look buttoned-down and professional one day and whimsical or playful the next, customers don't know what to believe and trust about your business. As a result, they're likely to turn to a more reliable product source instead.

- ✔ **Customers count on the tone conveyed in ads and marketing materials to be the voice of the business and brand.** If your business presents one personality in business magazines, another personality in broadcast ads, and yet a third personality online, you confuse customers at the least and cause them to think that your business is inconsistent and unreliable at the worst.

How to present a consistent brand image

To build a consistent brand image, present a consistent tone and the same core marketing message in all communications, regardless of the objective or call to action each communication aims to achieve.

✔ **Your core marketing message** communicates your brand promise to help customers make or save money; improve effectiveness and efficiency; enhance safety, security, or success; or enjoy other valuable benefits. Before settling on your core marketing message, be sure the promise you convey is one you can keep and one that will be reinforced every time a customer encounters your business. For help putting your message to the test, check out Chapter 9.

✔ **The tone of your marketing communications** conveys your brand personality and character. Be sure that the tone you project is compatible with your business's offering and your customers' expectations. For instance, the operators of a preschool may adopt a tone that's caring and playful, two attributes parents seek when choosing a day setting for their children, rather than clinical or professional, qualities people expect from a hospital or bank.

As you put your core marketing message and brand tone into writing, consider this format:

1. **State your brand claim.**

   State the claim you'll make, directly or indirectly, in all communications. For example, "Our brand provides the best solution for ecologically sound, affordable landscape solutions in the Pacific Northwest."

2. **Provide proof.**

   State how you'll back your claim. For example, "We'll prove our claim by presenting before and after examples in our communications as well as on our Web site, where homeowners can complete a do-it-yourself cost estimate and environmental savings form."

3. **Determine the communication tone that you'll incorporate into all your marketing efforts.**

   This statement is used internally to guide the personality presented in your marketing communications. For example, "The tone of our communications is friendly and confident. We want to sound expert but not uppity; casual but not complacent. We want our customers to know through our communications that we're the kind of people they'd like to visit with in their own backyards and that they can count on us for expert, efficient, earth-sensitive landscape service delivery."

A Clear Purpose: Don't Get Creative without One!

Whether you're producing an ad, a trade show display, a brochure, a sales presentation, or any other brand communication, the first step is always the same. You have to start by defining the purpose of your communication so that your job starts and stays on task. Use the following communication planning questions to guide your thinking:

✔ **Who is your target audience?**

In a sentence or two, describe the audience you're aiming to reach with this marketing effort in terms of where they can be reached, who they are in factual terms, and how and why they buy products like the one you're offering.

✔ **What does your target audience currently know or think about your brand, product, or service?**

Define the current mindset before working to achieve change. Does your audience lack knowledge about you, in which case your communication needs to establish awareness? Does your audience hold positive perceptions that you want to reinforce? Does your audience hold inaccurate perceptions that you want to change?

✔ **What do you want your target audience to think — and do?**

Define the outcome you want this marketing effort to achieve. Do you want prospects to call for an appointment, ask for a free estimate, visit a Web site for an online demonstration, attend an event or promotion, make a first-time trial purchase, or simply increase awareness?

✔ **Why should prospects believe you and take the recommended action?**

Summarize the unique benefits that your customers can count on and the reason they should act now.

✔ **What mandatory information do you need to convey in this communication?**

List the things that absolutely must be addressed in the creation of this communication, including brand tone, core marketing message, and graphic standards that ensure the proper presentation of your brand.

✔ **How will you measure success?**

State your desired outcome so that the communication can be designed to accomplish its aim. For example, if you want phone calls or Web site visits, give people a reason and clear instructions for reaching you by phone or online. If you want to schedule a meeting, give the prospect a compelling reason to want to see you and an easy way to make the appointment. If you want heightened awareness, establish a precommunication benchmark against which you can measure changes in attitude.

✔ **What is your timeline and budget?**

To produce your communication on time and on budget, set a timeline and a budget in advance. If you don't, the date will slide and costs will mount.

Gaining Awareness and Getting Some Action

Advertising is how businesses, organizations, and individuals inform and persuade prospects and customers through paid announcements in mass media outlets such as newspapers, magazines, television and radio stations, outdoor boards, Web sites, and other media vehicles.

Most ads fall into one of two categories:

- **When an ad's purpose is to build awareness and interest,** it's considered an *image ad,* which is also called a *brand ad* or an *institutional ad.*

- **When an ad's purpose is to present an offer and prompt a consumer response,** it's considered a *product ad,* which is also called a *promotional ad* or a *call-to-action ad.*

The world's largest brand marketers run big, beautiful, image-building brand ads with no call to action whatsoever. At the other end of the spectrum, the smallest brand marketers run highly promotional call-to-action ads for the simple reason that they need every ad to pull its own weight by delivering measurable results in the form of inquiries, business visits, or sales.

To build your brand *and* gain responses, take a middle road by creating ads that build brand awareness and interest while calling for a specific action. To create ads that build your brand while prompting a measurable consumer action or attitude change, follow these steps:

1. **Develop your brand's core marketing message and brand tone.**

   The section "Getting Singular with One Brand Message and Tone" earlier in this chapter can help with this step. Make sure that every ad or other form of communication, regardless of its call to action, conveys your brand message and tone so that your organization consistently projects a unified brand image that consumers begin to recognize and trust.

2. **For each ad, direct mailer, newsletter, news release, or other communication, answer communication planning questions (see the preceding section) to summarize the unique promotional offer, announcement, or sales message you want to convey.**

3. **Insist that all marketing communications that leave your organization meet the objectives established for the particular piece while also advancing your brand's core marketing message, tone, and image.**

Making an Ad Schedule

Advertising pays its freight when it reaches the people you're aiming to influence with enough frequency to change their perceptions and actions.

The first step toward getting your ad dollars' worth is choosing the right media vehicles. The second step is setting the right ad schedule. The following sections help as you decide which media to use and how to put your ad schedule through the planning hurdles.

Matching media vehicles to your communication needs

Good media schedules include ads placed with media outlets that get your message in front of exactly the audiences you want to reach. For example:

✔ If the objective of your advertising is to reach and influence your prospects and customers, place ads in media with audiences that match your customer profile (turn to Chapter 5 and complete the Customer Profile Worksheet if you're not sure how to define your customer).

For example, if you're branding a private golf club and you know your prospect pool is comprised of affluent golfers, you probably want to place ads in sports sections of newspapers, on golf tournament broadcasts, or in golfing magazines.

✔ If the objective of your advertising is to reach and influence those who influence the success of your brand — through their investments, referrals, or for any other reason — create a definition of the kind of person you're working to reach and then find media outlets that count people who match that profile within their audiences.

For example, if you're branding a senior citizen assisted-living housing community, you may decide that your success depends upon referrals and recommendations from the attorneys, physicians, and adult children of your prospects. Therefore, in addition to advertising in publications that reach adults 75 and older, you also want to announce open houses and offer information packets in media outlets that reach physicians, attorneys, and middle-aged adults in your market area.

You need to know the definition of your target market before you can select the right media outlet for your ad. In most cases, a number of outlets fill the bill in terms of reaching your audience. When that's the case, you can make media selections based on which outlets best reach your market within the cost and timing realities you face. See the sidebar "The media menu" for a quick look the costs, placement considerations, and advantages of various media outlets.

The media menu

Mass media falls into a few widely recognized categories, each offering unique advertising requirements and advantages and each offering a number of media choices — from highly targeted vehicles that reach narrowly defined audiences to widely distributed vehicles that reach diverse audiences. In nearly all cases, you can expect to pay the most to reach the most targeted audiences.

Media Category	Cost Realities	Placement Facts	Advantages
Newspapers, which reach broad cross-sections of local, regional, or national populations	Reasonable cost to reach readers; reasonable ad production	Deadlines allow for quick placement decisions; ads are read immediately upon publication	Good at immediately reaching adults with new product and sale announcements
Magazines, which reach targeted audiences that share unique characteristics and interests	High cost to reach highly targeted audiences; high production costs to create visually competitive ads	Ad commitments are due months before the publication date; ads are read over a long time period from date of issue	Good at establishing credibility and building a competitive reputation over time
Out-of-home media, which reaches audiences in target geographic areas on a repeated basis	Costs are based on ad traffic counts and audience exposure	Prime locations are reserved far in advance billboard ad commitments usually span multimonth periods	Good at building name awareness and conveying single-sentence messages
Radio, which reaches audiences with defined interests, often in concise geographic areas	Costs are low and negotiable except during peak listening times; quality ad production enhances image and impact	Ads must run repeatedly to catch listeners; stations welcome last-minute ads except during peak periods	Good at building immediate interest and prompting responses
Television, which reaches audiences with defined interests via network or local-station ad buys	Costs soar when audience counts are high; quality ad production requires a significant budget	Ads must run repeatedly to catch viewers; ads in prime-time slots are expensive and hard to reserve	Good at building credibility, engaging viewers, and showing or demonstrating products
Online media, which reaches Web users with site ads, directory listings, search engine ads, digital communications, and links to and from related sites	Costs are usually based on ad views or clicks, making online ads among the most measurable ad investments; production costs are low	Ads on major sites book far in advance and at increasingly high prices; pay-per-click ads can be placed on short notice and can be quickly replaced if they aren't drawing results	Good at reaching targeted online users with call-to-action messages that prompt click-through responses to obtain more information

Balancing advertising reach and frequency

Media schedules balance two objectives:

- ✔ **Reach:** The size of the audience that will be exposed to your ad. Print media outlets use subscriber or circulation figures to describe their reach, whereas broadcast outlets base their reach on the number of people who see or hear an ad.

- ✔ **Frequency:** The number of times the average person is exposed to an ad message over a specified time period of usually one month or less.

Most marketers agree that reach creates broad awareness whereas frequency creates recognition, understanding, and responses.

Betting on frequency over reach

Unless your entire objective is to gain widespread awareness, plan your media schedule to limit your reach and to increase your frequency by concentrating ad buys in media that reach a highly targeted audience on a frequent basis.

The opposite of frequency is to try to create a big splash with a showy, one-shot ad — perhaps a full-page ad in newspapers or magazines or a bazillion-dollar airing on a high-ticket television broadcast like the Super Bowl. The problem is that even high-impact ad buys miss a portion of the target audience. Some readers or viewers aren't available when your ad runs or airs, and if you've placed all your bets on a one-time schedule, you don't have the chance to reach them again.

When planning your schedule, factor in these advertising realities:

- ✔ Most media planners say that you need to place your ad nine times to reach your target prospect once for the simple reason that, at any given time, a portion of the potential audience is tuned out, distracted, or just not in the mood or mindset to hear what you're saying.

- ✔ Media schedulers also factor in the fact that you need to reach a prospect as many as three times to achieve attention, interest, desire, and action.

- ✔ Most ads need to run or air up to 27 times to do the job you want them to do.

  There are exceptions, of course. If your ad runs or airs via a publication or program that reaches a highly devoted audience that reads or tunes in almost without fail, you can get away with a schedule that runs your ad fewer times. Be aware, though, that the budget requirement is about the same either way because media outlets charge a premium for ad buys that reach highly targeted and devoted audiences.

Stretching dollars by concentrating on fewer media outlets

To gain frequency within your target market without breaking the bank, limit your media schedule to a few media outlets.

For example, instead of running your ad one time each in six magazines, run it three times in the two that best reach your audience. Or rather than running a light newspaper schedule and a light radio schedule, choose one or the other and run a heavy schedule that achieves the kind of frequency that changes minds and moves markets.

By concentrating your schedule, you gain a number of advantages.

✔ You take advantage of discounted rates offered by media to high-volume advertisers.

✔ You save on production costs by creating ads for fewer media outlets.

✔ You increase visibility in your selected outlets, contributing to a perception of brand strength and clout in the minds of the readers or viewers.

✔ You reach the audiences of your selected outlets on a more frequent basis than would be possible if you were to divide your budget among a longer list of media outlets.

Scheduling your ads

Few advertisers run heavy, continual ad schedules week-in and week-out, 52 weeks a year. Instead, most advertisers vary their ad presence by following one of the scheduling plans shown in Figure 11-1.

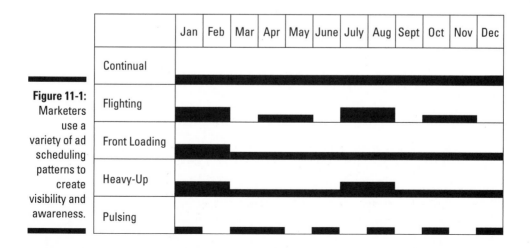

Figure 11-1: Marketers use a variety of ad scheduling patterns to create visibility and awareness.

The types of schedule patterns are

- ✔ **Continual schedules,** which run week-in and week-out for as long as the marketer advertises. They're used to maintain ongoing awareness. Some continual ad schedules involve ongoing placement of big, splashy ads; for example, an ad may appear on the back cover of every issue of a magazine. However, many continual ad schedules are more economical, involving placement of small-space ads that run on a continuous basis in magazines or local newspapers.

- ✔ **Flighting schedules,** which run ads in bursts. They usually start with a heavy ad buy that makes a strong enough market impression to carry the brand through a dormant ad period. After the dormant period, the marketer comes back in with a light ad schedule to renew awareness, followed by another dormant period and then by a heavy schedule that typically coincides with a buying season or marketing opportunity.

- ✔ **Front-loading schedules,** which begin with a heavy ad schedule. They aim to saturate the market with impressions before pulling back to a more economical, maintenance-level schedule that sustains the awareness and interest generated during the schedule launch. Front-loading schedules are a good choice for announcing new brands or business openings, promoting new products, or revitalizing lagging sales.

- ✔ **Heavy-up schedules,** which are similar to front-loading schedules except that they involve several saturation ad periods, also known as *ad blitzes.* They're used to create and keep a high level of market awareness by alternating intense ad schedules with low-level continual schedules in between.

- ✔ **Pulsing schedules,** which run ads on an on-and-off basis. On a sustaining basis, the marketer runs a moderate schedule, goes dormant, runs another moderate schedule, and then goes dormant again. Pulsing schedules are rarely used for launches or to rev up interest, but rather they're used to maintain awareness after it's established.

Creating Ads That Work

Ad creation is where marketing gets fun, so you may be tempted to hurry up and get to this part. Resist this temptation and do something with less flair and more function before you turn on your creative juices.

Start by taking time to figure out what you want your ad to accomplish. Go beyond a vague idea, like "We want to introduce our brand." Instead, get specific with instructions such as, "We want to announce our new brand to our 40-something, predominantly male, regionally based audience with an ad that conveys our brand promise to offer the best private golf experience in the state while extending an invitation to take a club tour and apply for a limited number of memberships."

In other words, get specific about what you want your ad to accomplish and *then* get creative with each type of ad you create.

Print ads

In great print ads, the headline, copy, and design work together to grab attention, inspire interest, promote a brand promise, prompt the desired action, and advance the brand image. That's a lot, but it's not too much to ask. In fact, it's what you need to demand out of every ad you place in a newspaper or magazine.

To achieve success, each print ad must include three powerful components:

✔ **Headline:** Your headline is the equivalent of the ad's stop-em-in-their-tracks introductory statement. Four out of every five print ad readers read *only* the headline, so it had better be capable of targeting the right prospects, grabbing attention, and making people want to read the rest of your story.

You may notice ads without headlines, but take a second look and you either see an amazing photo or illustration that speaks louder than words or a headless wonder that most people look right past. Unless you can afford an amazing graphic element that you're sure has stopping power, use a headline every time.

✔ **Copy:** Good *copy* (which is just a term for the text of your ad) talks directly to the reader, conveying information that tells the reader the benefits of your offering, the promise of your brand, and what to do next to obtain information, take advantage of an offer, or make a purchase.

✔ **Design:** Design is the way your ad looks — how it uses type, art, open space, borders, and placement of elements to create a look that both allows a reader's eyes to move easily through the message and prominently presents the brand identity of the advertiser.

Punching up headline power

Headlines can be long or short. They can sit at the top, in the middle, or at the bottom of the ad. They can feature a single word, a phrase, a sentence, or a question. When it comes to headlines, it isn't the form that matters. It's the function. See the dos and don'ts in Table 11-1 for headline advice to follow and traps to avoid.

Table 11-1	Headline Advice	
Do	**Don't**	**General Advice**
Use your headline to feature your most powerful point.	Feature a clever come-on hoping people will read on to find out what you're talking about. Most people simply won't work that hard.	Use your headline to convey your primary message, and use copy to back up your claim.
Feature benefits rather than features.	List the bells and whistles you offer without telling what they mean to the customer.	"Twice as fast as competing products" is a feature; "You'll get the job done in half the time" is a benefit.
Convey a positive message.	Focus on the problem you solve.	"Get a great night's sleep" conveys a positive solution; "Eliminate insomnia" focuses on a problem.
Use powerful, compelling language.	Use technical terms, blah-language, or words people won't understand.	Among advertising's power words are "free," "new," "save," "better," "how," "now," "easy," "guarantee," "health," "love," "save," "safety," and, most important of all, "you."
Involve the reader.	Talk to yourself.	"Save 20% during our 20th Anniversary Celebration" beats "We're celebrating our 20th anniversary."
Be clear and credible.	Be outrageous or clever to the point of being incoherent.	People give your headline only a few seconds time, so use the time to seize attention, make a compelling point, and advance your brand promise.

Convincing copy

Big, beautiful image ads sometimes contain no copy at all. They rely entirely on the strength of the brand name and logo, along with a captivating photo or other image, to advance the brand and expand market awareness, credibility, and loyalty.

Most advertisers need their ads to ignite action, though, and for that reason, most ads count on copy to play a pretty important role. If you expect your ad to generate consumer response — in the form of changed opinions, enhanced interest, requests for more information, pre-purchase inquiries about price or options, business visits, or other actions that move consumers toward a buying decision — make sure the text of your ad is up to the task.

When writing copy (or when reviewing copy written by ad professionals), keep these points in mind:

- ✔ **Be sure the first sentence is capable of capturing interest and enticing the reader to want to know more.**

- ✔ **Be sure the second sentence lures the reader into the third sentence, with each additional sentence advancing your brand promise and building more credibility and trust.**

- ✔ **Include an invitation to take action.** If you want your ad to deliver results, include a call to action in the form of an invitation or a promotional offer.

- ✔ **Inspire action with an incentive.** Most new brands want to prompt positive changes in consumer opinions or activity. They want to persuade prospects to request more information, view demonstrations, ask for cost estimates, sample the product, or in some other way move toward the buying decision — the sooner the better. Stimulate action by extending limited-time special buying terms, promotional pricing, trial offers, guarantees, or other offers that lower the risk or heighten the ease of taking the desired action.

- ✔ **Call for action.** Don't assume that readers know where to find you, how to reach you, or whether or not you have a Web site, give free estimates, or welcome drop-in business. If you want your ad to generate responses, make responding easy ("Call us toll-free," "Go online to request a free estimate," "Visit our business seven days a week," and so on). Then tell them exactly how to proceed by providing your phone number, directions to your place of business, your Web address, and any other information that makes responding to your ad message easy.

Designing for impact

Professional graphic artists and art directors earn their fees for many reasons, but high on the list is the simplicity of their designs. Flip through the pages of any newspaper or magazine to see the ads that benefit from great design. They're the ones with the fewest elements, the most striking visuals, and the cleanest and most attention-grabbing looks.

If you're investing a significant amount of money in ad buys, seriously consider investing in the creation of professionally designed ads. The section "Hiring professional creative help" later in this chapter guides you through selecting the right resources.

As you create or review ad designs, consider this advice:

✔ **Use art.** Many readers flip through publications at rapid-fire speed, stopping only when a headline or visual grabs their attention. To increase your chance of grabbing interest, include a photograph or an illustration (a drawing, cartoon, or other art) in your ad.

In some ads, the art shows the product being advertised. In other cases, it shows the product in use or represents the benefits the product delivers. In yet other cases, the art relies on what's called *borrowed interest* by featuring a photo or illustration that indirectly relates to the ad message. For example, a company featuring Tuscan vacations may feature a photo of Florence (the product), it may show a photo of people sitting near a villa overlooking a Chianti landscape (the product in use), or it may feature an illustration of wine glasses or grape vines (borrowed interest).

✔ **Keep it simple.** Print media is a cluttered environment packed full of news articles, feature stories, facts and figures, and ads large and small. On a crowded page, the clean, open ad is the one that wins attention for the simple reason that it gives the reader's eyes a place to find a moment's refuge from the visual overwhelm. Streamline your ad design by following these tips:

• **Frame your ad with unfilled space.** Rather than letting your copy or design elements run right up to the edge of your ad space (where they run into the adjacent ad or news story), design your ad so that it isolates itself with white space or a black border.

• **Eliminate unnecessary elements.** When readers view an ad, their eyes sweep across it, usually from upper left to lower right; in a matter of only moments, they note the message, the advertiser logo, and whether they want to pause for a second or move on to the next item on the page. If your ad lacks a clear focal point or fails to convey a message at a glance, it doesn't get a second chance. Help readers grab your message by eliminating all visual distractions. Ads that win awards for their effectiveness are almost always examples of design restraint as opposed to design overload.

✔ **Size your ad to match your message.** If you're promoting a $1.99 offer, an attention-getting, small-space ad may work just fine. But if you're launching a new brand and you want to say, in essence, "Hello, world. We're going to be a big deal, and here's why," make the size of your ad reflect the size of your message. If you have budget restrictions, consider these ideas:

• Rather than run a large ad one time only, create the largest-sized ad that you can afford to run multiple times. Opt for frequency over size.

- Even with a partial-page ad, aim to dominate the page by choosing an attention-getting ad shape. Some publications allow you to run wide, shallow ads that span the entire width of the page or long, narrow ads that run the full length of the page, giving the feeling of a large ad when, in fact, the ad covers as little as a fifth of the page.

✔ **Consistently advance a single ad look and tone for your brand.** Rather than design a new and different ad every time you promote your brand, leverage the impact of your advertising by creating an ad look for your brand and using it consistently every time you advertise. For example, use the same typestyle in all headlines, the same border design, the same style of illustrations, and the same placement of your logo. To establish your guidelines, see Chapter 18.

Broadcast ads

In the same way that print advertisers need to establish a brand look to advance in all ads, broadcast advertisers need to establish a brand sound that consumers can immediately hear and relate to the brand's name. To establish a brand sound

✔ Consider using the same announcer in all broadcast ads.

✔ Establish a broadcast ad style, such as ads consisting of a dialogue between two people, ads that feature testimonials, or ads that consistently convey the same kind of message.

✔ Use music or sound effects consistently so that people can recognize your ad and identify your brand by sound alone.

✔ Seriously consider hiring professional broadcast resources for everything from ad concept development to studio production to talent.

Especially if your brand is competing with big-budget brands, or if your ads will run alongside the ads of major brand advertisers, a professionally produced ad makes you look like able competition; a do-it-yourself ad may well flag your brand — in a few quick seconds — as an also-ran.

Hiring professional creative help

When you're creating a long-lasting marketing piece or ad campaign that involves a major media budget, think seriously about bringing in some pros to help you do the job right. The difference between the look of professionally produced materials and those created in-house by using desktop publishing is usually immediately apparent. The budget is higher on the professionally produced piece, but so is the visual impression. As you produce marketing materials, turn to one of the following resources:

✔ **In-house talent,** providing that you have qualified people who won't be sidetracked from other responsibilities to create your marketing materials.

✔ **Free or almost-free resources,** which are available through media outlets and marketing suppliers such as printers, sign makers, and publishers. If you're simply updating existing materials to drop in a new logo or tagline, free is a great price. But beware: If you want a unique, creative idea or ad look, turn to professionals who can devote the time and talent necessary to do the job, at a price.

✔ **Marketing professionals,** who can include freelance professionals, design or production studios, full-scale agencies, and brand consultants. When considering working with marketing professionals, be sure to do the following:

• **Clarify your needs.** If you're seeking one-time assistance, a freelancer may work fine. If you want to acquire a long-term image development partner, an agency relationship is a better choice.

• **Set your priorities.** If, above all else, you want cutting-edge creative ideas, find an agency that reels in creative awards. If your emphasis is online marketing, head toward a group with proven online experience. If you want help from someone with intimate knowledge of your industry or market sector, or someone with government, business, or even social connections, know that priority before you start interviewing potential resources.

• **Define your budget, and share the financial facts with your top-choice professionals.** If your budget doesn't fit with the professional's client profile, better to know sooner than later.

When you identify the professionals that fit your needs, make your decision by following these steps:

1. **Decide how many professional groups you want to interview.**

   If your project is simple or your budget is spare, start with one top-choice supplier and save yourself and the professionals the drill of a competition that will only eat up the time and money you have for the task.

2. **If you plan to interview multiple groups, follow this process so that you compare apples to apples:**

1. **Share your needs, priorities, budget, and timeline with each firm's CEO, and determine the firm's interest.**

2. **Schedule appointments to find out each firm's capabilities and match them with your needs.**

3. **Review each agency's capabilities and presentations, and then make your selection.**

4. **Get the client-agency agreement in writing.**

   A contract should clarify the services to be provided, the compensation arrangement, the term of the arrangement, how the contract can be terminated, and who will own materials upon payment. Ideally, you want all materials to become property of your company upon payment, but don't make assumptions. Confirm the arrangement, and see that the ownership details are part of the contract you sign.

Measuring Your Ad's Effectiveness

Each time you launch an ad effort, know what you want to accomplish so that you can evaluate whether or not your effort achieves its aim. Chapter 3 contains information on creating your brand's "to-do list," including information that helps you prioritize the objectives of your brand launch effort. Table 11-2 offers examples for measuring how your marketing accomplishes its task.

Table 11-2	Marketing Objectives and Measurement Approaches
Marketing Objective	***Measurement Approach***
Increase awareness	Conduct pre-campaign research to benchmark beginning name awareness ("Have you heard of Café Fantastic?") or top-of-mind awareness ("Can you tell me the names of the top three fine-dining restaurants in our hometown that come into your mind?"). Then repeat the research following your brand launch or campaign.
Increase knowledge of your distinctions	Conduct pre-campaign research to benchmark awareness of how your product differs ("We're conducting research on fine dining in our region. Can you name the restaurant with the best view and setting?"). Then repeat the research following your campaign.

(continued)

Table 11-2 *(continued)*	
Marketing Objective	*Measurement Approach*
Increase sales	Calculate sales revenue or orders for the 3- to 6-month period preceding your campaign. Calculate post-campaign performance, and compare the results to previous performance and to your goal.
Increase interest	Calculate phone, mail, online, or in-person inquiries for the 3- to 6-month period preceding your campaign. Calculate post-campaign inquiries, and compare the results.
Increase satisfaction	Track complaints, concerns, and compliments voiced prior to your campaign, and compare them to similar input received following your campaign.

Packaging Your Product to Convey Your Brand

Product packages are a combination of form and function.

- ✔ The *form* of your package involves design, shape, and a look that captures consumer attention and conveys and reinforces your brand image and promise.

- ✔ The *function* of your package involves usability. In addition to looking good on a shelf, your packaging has to work. It has to be easy to pick up, read, study, use, and carry away.

Even if you don't have a consumer product, you still package your offering, perhaps in a shopping bag, a folder or envelope containing a cost estimate or proposal, or a take-home bag for diners to carry home leftovers.

Regardless of the form your packaging takes, make sure that it accurately reflects the promise and tone of your brand and that it makes an appropriately strong and consistent impression for your business. Chapter 17 includes information on redesigning packaging as part of revitalizing a brand.

Staging Promotions to Build Business and Brand Awareness

Promotions are time-sensitive, attention-generating events that aim to alter customer perception or behavior. Some promotions work to increase purchases from existing customers, some work to attract new customers, some promote new buying patterns, and some work to build business during otherwise slow periods. Most offer price incentives, trial offers, coupons, or rebates.

To advance your brand, be sure that any promotion you stage matches well with your brand character and promise. For example, if yours is the most exclusive brand in your category, a price promotion is out of character, but a series of events featuring celebrities or authorities in your field is compatible with your image.

Also, take care to protect your brand image when entering cross-promotions that tie your brand to another brand. Chapter 16 includes a section on how to cross-promote without diluting the value of your own brand.

Chapter 12

Sending Your Brand into Cyberspace

*I*ncreasingly, the Internet is the primary avenue by which consumers access, evaluate, and consider products and services. Because of the pervasiveness of online searches and online business, organizations large and small put increasing importance on how their brands look and communicate on the Internet. Online, branding is essential for two very different reasons.

> ✔ **If your business relies on the Web as a sales channel, you need to have a strong brand to pave the way for sales success.** Unlike in a bricks-and-mortar outlet, online customers can't touch or try your product, and no one's there to personally explain and reinforce your promise. More than in any other distribution channel, online customers need to arrive confident in your brand's quality and promise. If you rely on online sales, you need your brand to do some pretty significant advance work so that customers arrive at your site confident and ready to make purchase decisions.

> ✔ **If your business relies on the Web to provide information or customer service, you need to make sure that online encounters are a seamless extension of your overall brand experience.** Whether customers meet up with your brand online or offline, they should receive an identical message, tone, look, character, and promise. This consistency leads to a single, consistently reinforced and positive experience regardless of the approach to your organization.

Whether the Internet is a sales channel for your business or simply a key communication vehicle, to a huge number of consumers, it represents the most frequently visited approach to your brand. This chapter helps you create an online experience that meshes perfectly with your total brand experience so that your brand image and promise is reinforced in a lockstep manner whether customers encounter you online or offline before, during, or after the sale.

Creating Your Online ID

In the same way that your brand name is the key that unlocks your brand image in the mind of consumers, your *domain name* — the string of characters Web users type into a browser to reach your site, such as `www.yourbrandsite.com` — is the key that unlocks your brand online.

Ideally, your domain name is comprised of your brand name plus `.com` or `.org`, depending on whether your brand represents a commercial business or a nonprofit organization. When it comes to establishing a domain name, though, the Internet isn't an ideal world. For one thing, it's heavily populated with millions of Web sites accessed by domain names that tie up most of the words in the English dictionary. Beyond that, it's a world where cyber-squatters camp on attractive unclaimed domain names, registering and tying them up until someone pays what feels like a ransom to free them for use.

If you haven't already registered a domain name for your brand, get ready to jump through some hoops. This section can help you get through relatively unscathed.

Naming your site

By a mile, making your brand name the centerpiece of your domain name is the most preferable route to establishing an online identity, and here's why: Internet analysts estimate that 15 percent of Web traffic takes the form of *type-in traffic,* a term that describes users who bypass search engines and simply type the name of the company they're looking for, followed by `.com`, in the address bar of the Web browser. By making your brand name the basis of your domain name, you capture visits from this growing group of experienced Web users. Plus, you reinforce your brand name every time someone searches for you online.

Turn your brand name into your domain name, if you can

The shortcut to establishing an online identity is to start with a brand name that's available for registration as a domain name. By registering both your brand name and your domain name at the same time, you eliminate the grief of settling on a brand name that you later discover isn't available for online use. Plus, you end up with a single name on your physical establishment and on your Web site, a vital first step in creating a single, unified identity for your brand.

Avoid a brand name that's straight out of the dictionary, if you can. Nearly every entry in the English dictionary is already in use in a registered domain name and therefore is unavailable for your online use.

If you haven't already named your brand, preempt a ton of frustration by coining a brand-new word that can be used as both your brand and domain names. Chapter 5 is packed with advice on creating brand names, including how to fabricate syllables or words into great brand and domain names. Microsoft, Cingular, Verizon, DreamWorks, and Firefox are just a few prominent examples.

Devising Plan B domain names

If you're launching a new brand and your top-choice name isn't available as a domain name, return to the brainstorming process until you can find or invent a brand name that you can also use online.

If you're working with an established brand and the domain name you want isn't available, you have to come up with a second-best solution. Try these approaches:

- ✔ **Come up with a tagline or slogan that can become a major part of your brand identity and the basis for your domain name.** For example, if you type in www.wetryharder.com, you're taken to the Avis Web site. Type in www.justdoit.com and you land on the Nike site.

- ✔ **Look into purchasing your top-choice domain name from its current owner.** Be aware that this process can be costly and time-consuming, but if you plan to build a valuable brand, it's probably worth the investment. Many domain name registrars offer assistance with this step; go to www.internic.net/regist.html for a complete list of registrars.

Following are a few things *not* to do when you have to go with a Plan B brand name:

- ✔ If your brand name plus .com is already taken, don't try to beat the system by using your brand name followed by .net. Web users instinctively type .com, so when they type that with your brand name, they'll go straight to someone else's site.

- ✔ If the name you want isn't available, don't try to add hyphens or other unusual additions to your brand name in order to create a domain name that you can register. The result will be a name that's hard to type and remember.

- ✔ If your brand name is too long to make a good domain name, don't invent some abbreviation that will be hard to memorize and recall. For example, the Hawaii Visitors and Convention Bureau can be reached by typing www.hvcb.com, but they don't ask consumers to remember the lineup of initials. Instead, they market the domain name www.gohawaii.com, which offers not only an easy-to-recall address but also a desirable remedy to the mid-winter blues.

Domain name advice

As you plan your domain name, consider the following points:

- ✔ **Keep your domain name short and easy to remember.** Think of the best-known Web addresses as ideal examples: www.aol.com, www.ebay.com, www.google.com, www.yahoo.com, www.amazon.com. Each one is short, memorable, and just about impossible to forget or misspell.

- ✔ **Don't get clever with unique spellings or abbreviations that may make sense to those within your organization but that bewilder strangers to your site.** For instance, a domain name like www.cookeezncream.com may be available, but the chances that most users will type it correctly most of the time are slim.

- ✔ **Think globally.** If your business plan calls for international presence, register your name with various international codes to specify your international offices. For example, www.microsoft.com/uk is the address for information about Microsoft products and services in the United Kingdom.

Registering your name

When you find an available domain name, register it immediately. Enter "domain name registrars" in your search engine to find a near-countless number of registration services, most charging somewhere between $25 and $75 for a three-year period of domain ownership.

When registering your name, consider this advice:

- ✔ The first domain name you need to register is your site name, as in www.yourbrandname.com.

- ✔ If you can, also register your site with the extensions .net, .org, .info, and .biz. By reserving all possible extensions for your site name, you can set the address up to redirect users who type in a wrong extension to your primary address.

- ✔ Also consider registering domain names that users may accidentally type when looking for your Web site. Through a process called *URL redirection*, you can make your Web site available under a number of different URLs or online addresses that are all forwarded to your primary Web address. For example

  - • Register your brand tagline as a domain name so Web users who forget your brand name but remember your slogan can type it in to reach your site.

- Register your brand name with various misspellings. For instance, if you type www.googel.com, you're redirected to the www.google.com Web site. Or if you type www.fordummies.com, you arrive at the www.dummies.com Web site. Establish a similar error-capture program in your own domain name strategy by thinking of ways that users may mistype or misspell your domain name and registering each version.

- Register additional domain names as you discover new user-error tendencies. After your Web site is up and running, regularly check error logs to see what kinds of mistakes people are making when trying to reach your site. And ask those who deal with customers to pass along pronunciation or spelling mistakes that they see or hear so that you can work the errors into your URL-forwarding strategy.

Creating a multiple domain name strategy costs very little. The registration fee on each name is nominal, and you can redirect all traffic to the Web site that carries your primary domain name, incurring no additional site building or hosting fees.

Building a Site That Reinforces Your Brand

If by any slight chance you're wondering if you need a Web site — or a stronger Web site than the one you already have — make a list of brand names you know, and then look online to see if each one has a Web site. We're willing to bet that you won't find a great brand that isn't backed by a great site. That's because in today's wired world, building a great brand and building a great site go hand in hand.

Before building or strengthening the Web site for your business and your brand, give some thought to the kind of people you'll be serving online, the kind of information they'll be seeking, and what you want to achieve through your online presence. Answer the following questions:

- **Who is likely to visit your site?** Will your site be visited primarily by current customers? Or will it be used by job seekers, suppliers, customer prospects, or others seeking information about your business?

- **How will people use your site?** Will people want general information, such as your location, open hours, and product lines? Will they want answers to frequently asked questions about your offering? Will they want to study your organization's background and experience or find out more about your products? Will they want the ability to request quotes or to study customization options? Will they want to buy online? Will job seekers want to apply online? By knowing what people will want from your site, you can design its features and functions accordingly.

✔ **What are your goals for your site?** Every site should advance the brand image. Beyond that, do you want your site to generate leads, capture online sales, provide customer support, or simply deliver information about your business? Your answers in this area help you weigh site development costs against the value you expect your site to deliver.

Settling on the right type of site

Most Web sites fall into one of the following categories:

✔ **Company contact sites:** Easy and economical to build and maintain, these sites are like online business cards, with graphics that advance brand images while delivering the facts that online users seek about businesses. Minimally, a contact site provides your business identity and description, information about your products and services, your open hours, and how to reach you online and at your physical location.

✔ **Brochure sites:** These sites are online cousins to print brochures. This kind of site needs to advance your brand image while delivering clear information about your company background, products, and services.

✔ **Support sites:** These sites reinforce existing customer relationships by providing online service and customer communication, including information about product usage, installation, troubleshooting, updates, and news. They're useful when many customers have similar questions or service needs that can be addressed online by companies prepared to respond immediately to user questions.

✔ **E-commerce sites:** These are sites designed to sell goods online. They invite and allow customers to view products, make choices, place orders, submit payment, and, often, track delivery. Because of the complexity of the functions required, these are the most expensive sites to build and maintain.

Considering content

Content describes electronically delivered information, including text, photos, or graphics. As you plan the content for your brand Web site, keep the following tips in mind:

✔ **Build your site page-by-page.** Don't think of your site as a single unit with many pages. Think in modular terms, with an introductory home page and links to pages that each cover a single topic.

✔ **Think of your home page as the welcome mat to your entire site.** Just as you wouldn't try to tell your whole story on the cover of your brochure, don't try to tell your whole story on your home page. Use your home page to establish your brand image, convey your brand promise, and invite users to click for specific information. For help developing your home page, check out the section "Making your home page your online business lobby" later in this chapter.

✔ **Use keywords to your advantage.** *Keywords* are words or phrases that people enter into search engines when they're seeking information or a particular Web site. As you develop each page on your site, think of the keywords that describe the content of your page. Then use those words in the page headline and several times in the page copy so that, when consumers seek information through keyword searches, your page has a chance of appearing in the search results.

Keyword searches may send users to internal pages of your site rather than to your home page, so be sure that every page identifies your brand and provides an easy link back to your home page.

✔ **Be spare with words and generous with design.** Online, people skim pages, grabbing information from headlines, clicking on easy-to-understand buttons, and stopping only when they see information that seems to meet their needs. To catch the attention of these fast-moving page skimmers, avoid long blocks of text in favor of quotes, testimonials, headlines, graphics, and a design that's clear, clean, and capable of conveying your brand image at a glance.

Mapping out easy navigation

Navigation is how users access information on your site. Most sites use menu bars and colored or underlined text or icons to help users navigate Web pages and know where to click to reach the information they want.

On your home page, present clearly labeled selections so that site visitors know exactly how to proceed to get their questions answered. Look at the "after" version of the home page in Figure 12-1 as an example. Along the bottom of the home page, options invite visitors, customers, or employees to enter site areas designed specifically for their interests. Along the top of the site, people can click to reach general information about the company, its locations, or its services, or they can click to contact the company. Nothing about the site is ambiguous. People don't have to translate terms such as "What people are saying," or "How you can count on us." Each label is clear and easy to understand. Aim for the same clarity when you plan your site's home page.

When you're putting together the content of pages other than your home page, follow this advice:

- ✔ On each page, provide navigation keys so that users can jump from site page to site page with ease.
- ✔ On each page, provide a link back to your home page.
- ✔ Keep navigation choices clear and to a minimum.

Integrating your brand image online and offline

When people arrive in your Web space, your site *is* your business in their minds. If it's slow, cluttered, confusing, or unresponsive, visitors will link those labels to your brand. Likewise, if it's easy to navigate, if it communicates clearly, and if it responds to user requirements with ease, the reputation of your brand will soar as a result.

For an example of a site that establishes a strong brand, visit the Web site of the resort Verana at www.verana.com. Although the resort offers just seven private guesthouses, its Web site clearly establishes it as a first choice for discerning travelers. The site's design mirrors the resort's brand image as a "small yet unforgettable retreat comprised of a cluster of secluded bungalows in a remote and unspoiled location." Were you to arrive at the resort and ask how first-time guests made their choice, you'd hear the words "Web site" repeated like a mantra. The Verana site is both well designed and well produced. It expresses the brand perfectly, and as a result, the success of Verana eclipses its larger and longer-standing competitors. With careful design, your site can and should do the same.

The power of one: Using one look, one message, one tone

As you build your business's Internet presence, take extra care to see that the look, tone, and character you present online is identical to the image you present in your other communications and in your bricks-and-mortar outlet, if you have one.

Your Web site rarely makes the first impression for your business. Almost always, it reinforces an impression that's first made through your advertising and marketing materials, your physical business outlet, or online links to your site. If your Web presence isn't consistent with the brand image customers expect to encounter, they're likely to think they're on the wrong site.

As you design your site, keep in mind that online customers may also see your magazine ads, walk by your front door or display windows, look you up in the phone book, or meet you or your staff at business or social gatherings. For your Web site to work for your brand, it needs to synch with all the other impressions people form about your organization. Online, use the same style of type, the same colors, the same logo presentation, the same slogan, the same design approach, and the same core marketing message that guides all your other marketing communications.

Online customers also expect the same kind of responsiveness they receive at bricks-and-mortar outlets — and then some. In person, you can apologize if something takes a bit longer than usual or if a service mishap occurs. Online, you don't have that luxury. If your site crashes, is slow to load, is confusing to navigate, or doesn't immediately present the desired information, customers are likely bail out, never to return.

Making your home page your online business lobby

In the same way that a physical business space has an entry area where visitors are greeted, oriented, and inspired to enter and consider purchase transactions, your home page needs to provide a similar welcome to your Web space.

In many ways, the Internet is like a giant shopping mall. As people shop, wander, or collect information, they go from one site's home page to the next. At each online stop, they count on the home page to tell them where they are, what they can expect to find, and how to proceed to get more information.

Your home page is the single most important page of your Web site. It's where most traffic arrives and where most consumers form their initial impressions of your online presence. If your home page doesn't do its job, the rest of your site hardly has a chance. To make sure your home page is the best it can be, follow this advice:

- ✔ **Create a home page that makes a strong, clean, clear impression for your brand.** The most frequent mistake that online marketers make is to create a home page with an overload of information in a visually chaotic layout that's easier to ignore than it is to look at.

- ✔ **Assign your home page three functions and three functions only:**

    - • To announce that the user has landed in your brand space

    - • To make a quick and strong impression for your brand by establishing your brand look and promise

    - • To immediately communicate how the user can access additional information

- ✔ **If your home page starts to look like a newsletter for your company, redesign it ASAP.** Great home pages are clean and inviting with obvious buttons to click to quickly access all additional information. See Figure 12-1 for before and after examples of a home page that was redesigned to heighten effectiveness.

Figure 12-1:
A good home page establishes the brand identity, conveys the brand promise, and clearly communicates how the user can click to access more information — without information overload or design clutter.

Courtesy of Western Title & Escrow. Revitalized Web site design by Brand Navigation, LLC.

Getting People to Your Site

Opening your Web site is a lot like opening the doors to a new business location or getting a new toll-free phone number. It only matters if you promote the news, gain interest in the offering, give people a reason to be in touch, and do everything possible to lead people to your site.

Register with search engines

When online users want to find information, most often they visit a search engine or directory, enter a description of the material they're seeking, and wait for the results to appear in the form of a list of Web pages that seem to fit the request.

- ✔ **Search engines** like Google collect information by using a program called a *spider* to read and index Web sites, sending keywords from the sites back to the search engine index. Then each time a Web user searches for keywords, the engine goes to its database, finds sites with words that match the request, and provides a list of results.

- ✔ **Directories** like Yahoo! include lists that are categorized by people who read the sites and index information for access by users.

When your site is ready for prime time, submit your URL or domain name address to leading search engines and directories in order to begin the process of getting your site recognized in Web searches. Minimally, follow these steps:

1. **Register your site at Open Directory (`www.dmoz.org/add.html`).**

   Submit your site address for free, wait three weeks, check to see if your site is in the directory, and resubmit it if it hasn't been picked up. The Open Directory Project is the largest, most comprehensive human-edited directory of the Web. Registration with this site is an essential step because Open Directory powers the core searches of the Web's largest and most popular search engines, including AOL Search, Google, Netscape Search, and hundreds of other sites. When you're on this free directory, you're likely to be listed with the other major search engines as well.

2. **After registering with Open Directory, register your site with individual major search engines and directories as well.**

   To do this, go to Search Engine Watch (`www.searchenginewatch.com`) and click on Search Engine Submission Tips for current information on registering your site with search engines and directories. The arena of search engines and registration fees changes rapidly, and this site can keep you up-to-date.

Help search engines find your site

Google powers the majority of online searches, and the goal of most Web site owners is to achieve good Google presence. An outstanding resource for achieving this victory is *Building Your Business With Google For Dummies* by Brad Hill (Wiley), which includes these tips:

✔ Build pages around core keywords that define each page's topical focus.

✔ Incorporate core keywords into the page's content.

✔ Place core keywords in each page's <META> tags, which are the hidden HTML code commands that search engines scan.

✔ Fill in the <TITLE> tag, using core keywords.

✔ Use <alt> tags, with keywords, on page graphics.

✔ Use text, not graphical buttons, for navigation links.

✔ Register and use domains that describe the site's business.

✔ Avoid *splash pages,* which are entry pages that visitors must click through to get to your home page.

✔ Devote one page to a comprehensive site map.

✔ Keep pages focused, and write new pages for divergent subjects.

✔ Don't use spamming, keyword stuffing, or cloaking. All three techniques aim to trick search engine spiders into heightening a site's ranking in search engine results. They're considered unethical approaches, and when discovered, they prompt search engines to take action ranging from lowering the site's rank to banning it from the index.

✔ Build a network of incoming links from other sites to your site (see the following section of how-to advice).

Building Your Business With Google For Dummies offers other valuable advice, including the suggestion that you test your keywords at www.wordtracker.com. This fee-based service offers a free trial after which you can subscribe for periods ranging from one day to one year. Another free resource is the Google Keyword Sandbox. Go to adwords.google.com/select/ KeywordToolExternal, enter a general keyword or phrase for your business or product, and review the long list of related terms that appears. This tool is intended for use by businesses using the pay-per-click advertising program called Google AdWords, but nonusers can benefit from it as well.

Build incoming links to your site

Nearly all Web search experts agree that the best way to optimize your online presence is to establish a broad network of links that direct traffic to your site. Get started by following these steps:

1. **Submit your site to search engines and directories (see "Register with search engines" earlier in this chapter).**

2. **Establish link exchanges with compatible sites to build visibility for your site and drive incoming traffic.**

   Contact sites that attract visitors with interests similar to your site's visitors, and work out arrangements whereby you each link to the other's site in order to increase traffic to both sites.

3. **Publish articles online to generate publicity and gain links to your site.**

   Also, submit articles to e-zines, newsletters, and magazines that are delivered via e-mail to subscribers. Turn to `www.zinos.com`, `ezine dir.com`, or `www.ezinearticles.com` for article submission advice.

4. **Develop online referrals by getting your link included on the Web sites of manufacturers whose products you carry, professional organizations to which you belong, and organizations with which you do business.**

5. **Develop online affiliations that link your site to sales sites in return for a commission on resulting sales.**

   For information on this type of connection, visit Commission Junction at `www.cj.com`.

Promote, promote, promote

To gain brand visibility online, use every resource available to lead people to your site, beginning with the following approaches:

- ✔ Include your Web site address on all your stationery products, including business cards, letterhead, envelopes, and note cards.

- ✔ Include an invitation (and a reason) to visit your Web site in all your marketing communications, including ads, brochures, news releases, presentations, and displays.

- ✔ Feature your Web site address on your packaging and products.

- ✔ Post your Web address on your business vehicles and signage.

- ✔ Include your Web address (and a reason to visit your site) in your voice-mail recording, on-hold messages, and e-mail signature file.

- ✔ Include your Web address on every page of printed or electronic newsletters or brochures.

- ✔ Add a "Tell a friend" function to your Web site so that visitors can refer others to your site.

Using Blast E-Mail to Reach Your Market

Blast e-mail — also known as *bulk e-mail* — resembles direct mail except that it goes out electronically and is regulated by antispam regulations.

If you have a good list of customers, associates, and business contacts who have given you permission to send them e-mails, an e-mail blast is a great way to announce your brand or to share brand news on an ongoing basis.

All you need for e-mail blasts is a list of people who have opted in to receive your e-mails, e-mail messages that are likely to be opened and read, and a way to manage the program.

Building permission marketing networks

Before sending e-mail blasts, be double sure that the people on your e-mail list will welcome your message by seeing that they match at least one of the following descriptions:

- ✔ They've opted in to your e-mail list by providing your organization with their e-mail addresses. Most well managed e-mail programs include a double opt-in system that accompanies a first e-mailing with a response request so that the recipient either reconfirms interest or opts out of future mailings.

- ✔ They're friends, colleagues, suppliers, customers, or prospects who have requested similar information in the recent past.

- ✔ They were referred to you by a trusted resource.

After you create an opt-in mailing list, manage it well by taking these precautions:

- ✔ Never publish your e-mail list on your Web site, even in a well-meaning way that provides contact information for organization members or clients.

- ✔ Never enter recipient addresses in the "To" section of your blast e-mail. Protect addresses by entering your own address in the "To" area and then entering all recipient addresses as blind carbon copies, using the "BCC" address option in your e-mail program.

✔ Include an Unsubscribe link in all e-mails so that people can opt out of your mailings.

✔ If you haven't used your opt-in e-mail list for three or more months, send a pre-mailing before sending your blast e-mail. In the pre-mailing, briefly announce that you've got a new e-newsletter or brand mailing, and ask recipients to "Click here" to receive your mailing. The pre-mailing helps you determine which e-mail addresses are no longer valid and also helps you steer clear of the spam complaints you're bound to get by sending e-mails to people with whom you haven't been in touch for months on end.

Getting your e-mail opened and read

When you're ready to send a blast e-mail, follow this advice:

✔ **Write a five- to seven-word subject line that your recipients will find familiar.** Include your company name if they know your business. People open e-mails that they believe are relevant to their interests. Avoid the kinds of subject lines that are typical in spam mailings, such as too-good-to-believe come-on lines, titles in all-capital letters, or titles that scream for action with phrases like "limited time offer" or "click now."

✔ **Include your company name in the "From" box.** This step signals that the e-mail is from a familiar source, and it may also help you get past your recipients' spam filters.

✔ **Keep your message brief (ten lines or so) and casual.** To tell a more complete story, link the e-mail recipient to your Web page or invite a subscription to your e-newsletter. Either approach heightens involvement with your brand.

✔ **Expect your e-mail message to be quickly scanned.** Grab interest with an attention-getting opening line, and use a P.S. to inspire further action. Stay away from long paragraphs, double-space every few sentences, and include bullets for easy-to-view lists.

✔ **Use easy-to-open and easy-to-read plain text for news announcements or for quick, special e-mail offers.** If you choose to use HTML, avoid JavaScript, which gets blocked by most e-mail applications.

✔ **Include an e-mail signature file at the end of every message.** Use this area to present your brand name and slogan, physical address, contact information, e-mail confidentiality statement, and a promotional message such as a newsletter subscription invitation. (Go to the help area of your e-mail program if you need instructions for setting up an e-mail signature.)

Spam versus opt-in e-mail

Spam is e-mail that's sent to people who didn't request it, don't want it, and feel that their in-boxes have been invaded by its arrival. *Opt-in e-mail* is e-mail that's been requested. Spam is annoying at best, and illegal at worst. Opt-in e-mail is welcomed and opened. Can you figure out which route you want to follow?

To keep your e-mail out of the dreaded spam category, take time to understand and comply with the CAN SPAM ruling, passed by the U.S. government in 2003. For information on the legislation, visit `www.wilsonweb.com/wmt9/ canspam_comply.htm`.

Blogging and Podcasting

Increasingly, brand builders use online tools to spread their brand messages, to build emotional connections with consumers, and to reach those who influence the brand's success. The two online tools you're bound to hear about most often are *blogs* and *podcasts.*

Blogging basics

Blog, short for *web log,* is the term for online journals that share news, ideas, and — above all — opinions. Blog topics run the gamut, but they almost always have the following features:

- ✔ They're graphically simple and full of short entries, called *posts,* that are updated frequently and arranged so that newest items appear first.

- ✔ They focus on a single point of view or interest area and reflect the opinions of the blog author. Online, they're akin to the newspaper's op-ed page.

- ✔ They're informal in tone.

- ✔ They allow users to search story archives.

- ✔ They use RSS (Rich Site Summary or Really Simple Syndication) or a similar format that allows blog posts to be distributed and shared on other sites with a link back to the originating site.

Gaining visibility

Some brand marketers have their own blogs (for example, check out the Google blog at `www.googleblog.blogspot.com`). Others work to gain mentions in posts on existing blogs.

To gain visibility in the blogosphere:

- ✔ Register your blog with blog directories such as www.blogwise.com, www.blogcatalog.com, and www.bloghub.com.

- ✔ Read and follow blogs that align with the interests of your target audience to gain customer insight and information on market trends. When you find a blog that sounds like a good fit with your own blog, inquire about establishing reciprocal links.

- ✔ When appropriate, post comments on blogs or submit tips or links that match with the blog content.

Starting your own blog

Following are some suggestions for starting your own blog:

- ✔ Be sure you're ready to commit to the upkeep of a blog, which involves keeping content fresh and updated daily or at least weekly.

- ✔ Be clear about the distinct point of view or interest area your blog will advance. If a blog sounds like it's full of corporate lingo, it's basically dead on arrival.

- ✔ Visit www.blogger.com/start for free assistance in getting your blog up and running.

- ✔ Be ready to receive and respond to reader feedback.

- ✔ Promote your blog through ongoing marketing efforts and by registering it with blog directories.

Podcasts

Podcasts are sound files that subscribers can access online and transfer to personal digital audio players in order to listen to them whenever and wherever they want.

Some brand marketers create podcasts to share information about their offerings. Other marketers sponsor podcasts in the same way that advertisers sponsor broadcast shows. For example, in 2005, Lexus announced that it had become a sponsor of California public radio station KCRW's podcasts.

To find out more about podcasting and how to create your own podcasts, start by visiting sites such as www.ipodder.org and www.pod101.com. You can also grab a copy of *Podcasting For Dummies* by Tee Morris, Evo Terra, Dawn Miceli, and Drew Domkus (Wiley).

For some good examples of podcasts, go to www.dummies.com and click on Subscribe to Dummies.com Podcasts. Then choose from any of the podcasts listed on the page.

When you feel you're ready to incorporate podcasts in your publicity program, follow these steps:

1. **Search podcast directories such as www.podcastalley.com or www.podcast.net to find podcasts with content that matches your business arena and listeners that match your customer profile.**

2. **Listen to podcasts to get a feel for their style and content.**

3. **Submit tips, information, news, audio releases, or story or interview ideas to selected podcasts, following the exact same criteria you'd use to gain publicity in traditional media.**

Part IV
The Care and Feeding of Your Brand

In this part . . .

After you build, launch, and gain market awareness of your brand, it's time to kick the brand management process into high gear in order to create the kind of brand experience that results in devoted, passionate customers and true brand value. This part helps you manage a brand that earns its keep — both in the minds of your customers and on the bottom line of your balance sheet.

Count on the upcoming five chapters to help you develop your brand's equity by creating brand champions, consistently delivering on your brand promise, wisely leveraging your brand value, carefully navigating brand extension opportunities, and finally, keeping your brand hale and hearty through brand updates, revitalizations, or out-and-out rebranding if necessary.

Chapter 13

Suiting Up a Team of Brand Champions

. . . .

In This Chapter

▶ Generating organization-wide brand buy-in

▶ Delivering your brand at every customer contact point

▶ Creating brand ambassadors

. . . .

*P*ut simply, people power brands.

Brands are made or broken by human encounters that either advance or erode brand promises because each contact builds brand passion, brand apathy, or brand disdain. The difference between well-launched brands that fizzle and well-managed brands that soar to great value lies in the brand experience, which is the result of customers' everyday encounters with your name, your product, your organization, and your people.

A great brand name, logo, promise, and communication program are essential ingredients for brand success, but to hit a branding home run, you need to staff your branding game plan with a committed team of brand champions. Building an organization full of individuals committed to the brand is the only way to ensure that your brand vision and values are accurately reflected and your brand promise is consistently delivered.

In this chapter, we give you a plan to follow to make sure you have a team of brand champions on your side. We also explain how to get the most out of your sales force and how to target investors and your best customers.

Branding from the Top Down

Great leaders embody great brands. Leading a great brand takes courage and decisiveness. It requires commitment to the brand promise, discipline to build an organization around fulfillment of the promise, and perseverance to keep the promise through all customer contacts and market conditions.

The person whose name sits at the very top of your organizational chart needs to be your brand's evangelist-in-chief.

- ✔ **If that person is you,** be prepared to be your brand's primary champion, your organization's brand coach, the mirror of your brand's promise, and the driving force behind the quality of your customer's brand experience.

- ✔ **If that person is your boss,** gain top-tier involvement before taking another step in the branding process. Without buy-in from the highest rung of your organization's management ladder, your brand will never reach its potential.

Under good leadership, great branding is almost transparent. The brand experience is so all-enveloping that consumers can't tell where branding stops and where business starts because great brands are mirror reflections of great businesses. They represent values and organization-wide commitments that reach all the way to the core of an organization, spanning the entire length and width of the organizational chart.

Writing your branding playbook

To make branding an organization-wide commitment, take three essential steps:

1. **Communicate your organization's mission and vision clearly throughout your company.**

   Your mission defines what you intend to do and the approach you'll follow to achieve your aspirations. Your vision defines why your company does what it does and the ultimate good you aim to achieve through your success. Together your mission and vision orient all who work with your organization to the ultimate aim you're working toward and the route you'll take to get there. For help putting your statements into words, see Chapter 6.

2. **Build organization-wide understanding for your brand identity statement.**

   This statement encapsulates what you do, those you serve, how you differ from all other similar solutions, and the promise you make to all who deal with your organization, so it's essential for your team to be on the same page.

3. **Make your brand promise an organization-wide commitment.**

   Your brand promise is the statement upon which you stake your reputation. It's the essence of your brand and the quality you assure to all who come into contact with your organization. Be sure that your entire team knows the promise they're helping to keep.

Keep in mind, however, that true brand culture stems from the beliefs, personalities, and values those leading the brand. It's so authentic and heartfelt that it's caught, not taught, throughout the organization.

You can't package and impose your brand mission or promise onto employees like a fabricated formula. We've heard about companies that assemble their staffs to recite the mission statement each morning (or worse, to sing it in staff meetings — believe it or not, we've seen this firsthand, much to the embarrassment of the assembled employees). The only way to gain company-wide buy-in is to start with buy-in at the top and to spread it with such enthusiasm that a strong sense of culture naturally follows.

To test how well your promise is known, embraced, and implemented in your organization, answer the questions posed in Figure 13-1.

Becoming your brand's MVP

"Walk the talk" may sound like an overused phrase, but in reality, it's a tenet that could be far better employed in today's business world.

How many times have you entered a business that promises friendly service only to stand around waiting for someone to offer some assistance? How many times have you been assured by a company's communications that "to us, you're a name, not a number" only to place a phone call that burns ten minutes in a voice-mail maze that repeatedly requests your account number, interspersed by blasé background music and an occasional automated voice reminding you that your call is important?

Putting Your Brand Promise to the Test
How do you define your brand promise? State how your offering stands apart from all others in terms of features but more important in terms of consumer benefits. (See Chapter 6 for steps to follow.)
How do those in your organization define your brand promise? Benchmark current awareness of your brand promise by asking individuals at different levels of your organization — from top management to service front lines – to describe how your organization differs from competitors and the unique promise that consumers can count on only from your organization.
How do you communicate your brand promise within your organization? Is your brand promise the basis of your company name or slogan? Is your brand promise explained during employee training sessions? Is your brand promise – and its delivery – discussed during management planning sessions? Do you have programs that recognize and reward employees for actions that exemplify your brand promise?
How have you coordinated the delivery of your brand promised? Have you studied how well your promise is conveyed and kept at each customer encounter point, whether through advertising, online, upon first call or visit, during the purchase transaction, at the point of billing, during delivery and after-purchase transactions, at the point of customer service or concerns, during post-purchase follow-up, through customer loyalty programs, and at all other points where the customer has an experience with your brand?
How well do your customers know your promise? To really test whether your promise is clear, compelling, and well delivered, ask customers how they find your organization different from all competing entities. Ask how they would describe the promise they count on your business to keep. Ask what one attribute they most rely on from you; what one thing they would miss the most if your organization disappeared tomorrow. (Chapter 4 offers advice for conducting research.)

Figure 13-1:
Test your organization's commitment to your brand promise by using questions like these.

To keep your brand promise, build a brand experience that conveys your promise during each and every customer encounter. To do so, you need a team of brand champions who know and believe in the promise, too.

Following are some suggestions to ensure your team is as passionate about your brand as you are:

✔ **Keep the same promise that you make to your customers with your employees.** If you promise customers friendly service, promise your employees a friendly employment setting. If you promise the highest-quality offering, promise your employees the highest-quality work environment, including the highest-quality production resources. If you promise a super-creative product, promise employees super-creative work surroundings. Great brands realize that, to convey a brand promise with true belief, employees need to experience the promise firsthand.

✔ **Make your work environment a mirror image of your brand experience.** If you promise that your business team works together to serve customers, break down the barriers of cubicles and closed doors so that employees actually work in an atmosphere of teamwork. If you promise the most creative solutions, foster a creative work environment (no uniforms, please!). We heard of one ad agency that took its unique creativity promise so far as to say they wouldn't hold company gatherings at an establishment that served its sugar in cubes — a sign of regulated servings and traditional delivery that ran counter to the agency's promise.

✔ **Be sure your brand promise starts at the very top of your organization.** For a good example, the John Deere company Web site features a page with the headline "Our Brand Promise" that contains this statement: "In 1847 John Deere promised, 'I will never put my name on a product that does not have in it the best that I have in me.' For more than 150 years we've remained true to that commitment — building our reputation by building value into every machine that bears our name."

Make an organization-wide commitment to your brand promise, and then make every business decision with the promise in mind, including decisions about how you'll create a work environment, employee training, and employee rewards that help you walk the talk of your brand promise within your organization.

Training Your Team

If you're launching a new brand, before your brand makes its public debut, prepare all players for their roles. Following the step-by-step advice in Chapter 9, which covers training and inspiring your staff.

If you're managing an existing brand, your training needs are twofold: To recruit and train new employees into the brand culture and to enhance and reward commitment to the brand among existing employees. This section addresses these training needs.

Developing brand champions

When training employees to be brand champions, market position, brand promise, and brand character are the three key points you need to be sure to stress.

Emphasizing your brand's unique market position

When presenting your brand's position to staff, use a device such as the positioning matrix (shown in Chapter 5) to illustrate and gain understanding for the unique place your brand holds in its market. The positioning matrix also provides a visual presentation of how your brand offers distinct attributes and a different brand experience from competitive alternatives.

Chapter 5 also offers advice for positioning your brand and mapping your brand's position in your competitive arena.

Promoting your brand promise

Chapter 6 leads you through the steps involved to determine your brand attributes and to write your business promise.

When presenting your promise to your employees, describe how your organization delivers on its promise at every point of your customer's brand experience. Cite a wide range of examples, including how the promise is

- ✔ Upheld upon arrival by phone, in person, or online
- ✔ Echoed in your company's e-mail signature
- ✔ Reflected in your company billings and follow-up statements
- ✔ Conveyed in marketing materials
- ✔ Presented at the point of customer service and even when receiving complaints

Be ready to present examples to help employees understand their own and their associates' roles in upholding your business pledge and your customers' expectations.

Conveying brand character

Your *brand character* is the personality of your brand that's reflected through the look and tone of your brand expressions.

If people have human contact with your brand, your people are the most important representatives of your brand character. For that reason, your staff needs to understand your brand character and ways that they can reflect your company image and promise. Otherwise, if you communicate one brand character and then deliver service through a staff member who reflects a complete different character, you're in line for a credibility train wreck.

The following are ways to train your customers to represent your brand character:

✔ During an initial staff orientation, explain your brand character as a look and tone — a personality — that's based upon your organization's values, vision, and brand promise.

✔ Explain that every employee is a representative of the brand character.

✔ Describe your brand character in a statement such as, "Our brand character is [*a description using words that you'd use to describe the personality of your brand if it were a person or a car; for instance, sophisticated, fashionable, revolutionary, innovative, professional, elegant, or refined*]. We reflect our character through brand expressions that are [*a description of the mood and tone that all your marketing will project; for example, chic and stylish, cutting-edge creative, calm and subdued, high-quality and professional*].

✔ Define how your organization manages its brand character through company dress, customer contact, office décor, correspondence management, background music, aroma, color, and any other way that the personality of your organization is expressed. Create policies where appropriate, but focus on creating a brand promise and culture that runs so deeply through your organization that employees naturally adopt it as their own.

An example of pervasive brand character can be seen when walking through lobby of a W Hotel. The brand describes itself as "W . . . for warm, wonderful, witty, wired. W for welcome." More than words, though, the brand expresses its identity through every presentation point, including employees who, within weeks of joining the hotel team, seem to transform their own looks to become representatives of W's "young, hip" culture.

Gaining team buy-in

To win staff understanding and enthusiasm for your brand, treat brand training as a function worthy of time and effort by doing the following:

✔ **See that each employee takes part in a formal brand training session that presents**

- A snapshot history of your organization

- A description of your market and how you provide the best solution to the market's wants or needs

- Your brand definition

- Your brand's unique position in your competitive arena

- Your brand's distinguishing attributes and how they translate into meaningful customer benefits

- Your brand's character and how it's reflected through employees and at each customer contact point

- How your brand and branding program are keys to your business success

Employees are more likely to buy in if they see how your brand supports your business goals and objectives. For help in this area, check out Chapter 3, which includes a worksheet to help you assess and prioritize the brand strengths that are essential to your success.

✔ **Plan informal brand training sessions that aim to immerse staff members in your brand culture.**

Following a classroom-style introduction to your brand, arrange for new employees to experience your brand as a customer does, beginning with a review of marketing materials and moving through contact with all departments. As a result, each employee will see how various employees uphold the brand promise and the customers' expectations.

✔ **Arrange opportunities that allow employees to watch others make brand presentations so they can see how the brand is described and translated into customer benefits.**

✔ **Make brand training an ongoing effort.**

Periodically ask employees questions such as:

- What attributes do you think customers most appreciate about our brand?

- From your encounters with customers or from your vantage point within our organization, do you think that our customers accurately understand our brand's distinctions and how we differ from competitors?

- If you were one of our primary competitors, how might you describe the greatest weakness of our brand?

- What one customer contact point seems to you to be least effective at conveying our brand promise?

- If you could wave a magic wand and fix one thing that causes our customer frustration or lack of confidence in our brand, what would it be?

✔ **Give employees the authority to go the extra mile to keep brand promises, and reward them for their innovation and responsiveness.**

Nordstrom is a shining example of an empowered team of confident brand champions who are encouraged to use their own good instincts to offer customized solutions, to right wrongs when they see them, and to go overboard to provide the kind of customer experience that fuels the consumer grapevine with positive word-of-mouth. Most amazing, companies like Nordstrom don't tout their service success stories in publicity features or advertising campaigns. Instead, they let the stories reach the outside world via passionate customers who spread the good word with far greater impact than any company-generated communication could achieve.

✔ **On a regular basis, ask yourself and your staff: What kinds of stories are customers telling about our service?**

If you're not totally proud of what you believe is being said about you, turn to Chapter 14 to examine and improve your customer experience.

It's never crowded on the extra mile

The anonymous line that serves as this sidebar title has been used in countless motivational lectures, yet the extra mile remains wide open for those willing to double their service, triple their customer attention, quadruple their commitment to customized solutions, and build brand buzz and brand strength as a result.

To move into the elite group of brands that cruise to success by amazing customers with unfailing and exemplary experiences, follow these four steps:

✔ **Encourage employees to think like brand owners, doing whatever they feel is necessary to provide amazing customer experiences, to anticipate and preempt customer needs, to correct defects, and to create passionate customers — and brand enthusiasts — for life.** For an example of an award-winning service program, visit a page of the Ritz-Carlton Web site, at www.ritzcarlton.com/corporate/

about_us/gold_standards.asp, that shows how the hotel company presents its values, philosophy, promise, and service program.

✔ **Empower employees to customize solutions and service innovations.** Give your staff parameters, including budget guidelines, to provide on-the-spot customer solutions without having to navigate frustrating management layers.

✔ **Recognize and reward outstanding service efforts.** By putting the spotlight on team members who go out of their way to convey your brand promise, you set the bar higher for everyone.

✔ **Live your brand promise inside and outside your business, constantly finding new and better ways to convey your brand message and benefit to employees, customers, and all in your community.**

Prepping Your Sales Force

In most organizations, the salesperson is the active agent in the customer-to-brand relationship chain, which follows this sequence:

1. Marketing communications generate awareness.

2. Inquiry responses inspire interest.

3. Online, phone, or in-person encounters heighten purchase desire.

4. Sales presentations inspire brand trust, reinforce brand promises, address concerns, negotiate terms, and launch the customer relationship.

The best brand marketers view their sales forces as teams of brand ambassadors. They make sure that salespeople are steeped in the brand culture and armed with tools and scripts that help them not only explain the offering but also inspire belief in the desirable benefit of the brand promise.

For example, Victoria's Secret sells underwear, but the salespeople know that what people are really buying when they make a purchase is the idea of sexy romance. Harley-Davidson sells motorcycles, but people are really buying an association with an independent and rebellious spirit. Lance Armstrong's LiveStrong armbands aren't just about supporting research for a cure for cancer; they're also a representation of a belief in living life to the fullest.

Even more than your product, your brand promise inspires your customer's purchase decision. So arm your sales team with scripts for sharing your story, brand testimonials and endorsements, techniques for overcoming objections, and approaches for negotiating terms and closing sales without ever varying from the brand message and promise.

Arming your sales force with testimonials and product endorsements

Branding makes selling easier because it paves the way with trust-building communications that establish credibility, confidence, and understanding of a brand's unique value and benefits.

Still, at the moment of purchase decision, customers need a final bit of inspiration or reinforcement that the brand's offering will deliver as promised. This is true when customers are purchasing in-person, and it's even more important when they're purchasing from Web sites or direct mailers.

To deliver the extra jolt of assurance that a branded product is as good as it's touted to be, provide your sales force with testimonials and endorsements from satisfied customers or authorities.

Personal testimonials

When you share good words from past customers, prospective customers gain confidence that you have a good business track record, that you deliver on your promises, and that you stand by your products and services.

When obtaining and presenting customer testimonials, follow these tips:

- ✔ Wait until purchase transactions are completed before asking a satisfied buyer if he or she would say a few words on behalf of your brand.

- ✔ Encourage customers to provide frank comments. Even if the information isn't suitable for a testimonial, it's valuable as you refine your offering and brand experience.

- ✔ Whether customers speak or write their comments, ask them to focus on the aspect of their buying experience that they found most compelling. Some customers may cite service, some may cite product selection, and some may cite convenience, guarantee, or after-sale service. Specific praise makes the buyer's comments more believable to prospective customers.

- ✔ Ask customers to include details about their experiences. Consider the difference in impact between, "I'm impressed by your willingness to go the extra mile" and "We needed to pick up our new widget late on a Thursday evening in order to fit our travel plans. We still can't believe that you not only worked long past closing hours but that you also made our pick-up unnecessary by delivering the widget to our doorstep. Thanks!" The latter statement obviously gives prospective customers a better idea of the level of service they can expect to receive.

- ✔ When obtaining written permission to use the testimonial get identification information, including at least the customer's first name, hometown, and title or business affiliation if possible and appropriate.

When dealing with customer testimonials, avoid these mistakes:

- ✔ Never offer cash, product, or favors in return for customer testimonials.

- ✔ Don't invent testimonials. They're likely to sound phony (which they are), and the practice is unethical.

- ✔ Don't prompt customers to include marketing messages in their testimonials. Let them speak freely. You want to collect genuine opinions about how customers view the attributes and benefits of your offering and the experience of dealing with your organization.

Celebrity endorsements

Celebrity endorsements link statements of support from well-known individuals with brands that somehow match up with the celebrity's personality and reputation — for a price. Usually celebrity endorsements are purchased with cash, product, stock options, or some other form of compensation.

When considering using celebrities in your brand building program, weigh these points:

- ✔ The most credible endorsements convince consumers that a respected personality uses and benefits from your offering. A perfect example is the pairing of Tiger Woods and Nike.

- ✔ The celebrity you employ to represent your brand must align perfectly with your brand image.

- ✔ The best celebrity representatives actually use and personally support the brands they advance, so you should aim to establish a relationship that goes beyond product endorsement to include product usage and affinity.

- ✔ Celebrity endorsements are worthy of legal contracts that define the relationship, the compensation, and what happens should the celebrity's integrity be damaged by scandal. Don't proceed on a handshake.

Expert endorsements

When experts test, evaluate, and offer positive opinions on products, the endorsements are valuable in developing consumer confidence as long as you follow a few precautions:

- ✔ The expert must have clear and well-recognized qualifications.

- ✔ The expert must conduct a product test that conforms to testing standards in your industry. If the test proves that your offering is superior to a competitor's offering, keep records that support the claim.

- ✔ The expert must have no relationship with your business, or if a relationship exists, you must describe the relationship in all materials that reference the test.

Organization endorsements

An organization endorsement is a seal of approval for a product from a reputable organization. The Good Housekeeping Seal is an example of an organization endorsement. When showing that your offering has met an organization's standards of excellence, turn things up a notch by following this advice:

✔ Feature endorsements from organizations that have credibility and meaning with your customer prospects.

✔ Before featuring an endorsement, comply with the organization's standards and receive a formal acceptance and endorsement.

✔ Present the endorsement by including the organization's name, logo, or seal in your marketing materials and on your packaging.

✔ Feature endorsements *only* from actual, independent organizations, never from organizations created solely for use in your marketing program. Always check with each endorsing organization regarding how you may use the endorsement and what kinds of restrictions apply.

Spreading the good word

When presenting testimonials or endorsements, remember that your top priority is to give credibility to your brand promise. Don't expect the testimonial to make the sale but rather to erase hesitation that tends to precede the buying decision.

To make the most of testimonials from customers, celebrities, experts, or organizations, present them in the following ways:

✔ **Provide testimonials and endorsements in sales presentations.** Share accolades from past customers as well as details on expert test results.

✔ **Include accolades in sales letters and literature.** Intersperse testimonials and endorsements with sales points rather than isolate testimonials to a single page or letter enclosure. The effect will be more conversational and more powerful.

✔ **Feature testimonials on your Web site, where customers have few other ways to gain personal confidence in your brand.** Create a page full of testimonials and endorsements, but also incorporate them throughout your site so that site visitors can see summaries of real-life experiences that encourage them to make a purchase or obtain more information.

Intercepting objections

Objections open the door to brand building opportunities. When customers share concerns or objections with your company's representatives, at the very least, the customers are involved in the sales conversation, and at the most, they provide input that allows your company to clarify misunderstandings and to uncover and address buying obstacles.

Most objections stem from one of three areas of concern.

- ✔ **Lack of trust in your brand:** Here's where testimonials and endorsements can come to the rescue.

- ✔ **Preference for a competing brand:** Arm your sales force with a clear recap of the benefits and value your brand delivers so that they can present a positive response that favorably compares your offering to like products without taking any digs at competitors.

- ✔ **Concern over your offer:** Prepare your sales force to probe the concern and to avoid jumping to the conclusion that price is the issue. Often concerns have as much to do with questions about ease of use, appropriateness of the offering, perceived risk in dealing with a new product or brand, or even lack of authority to make the purchase. For each form of concern, provide sales materials and scripts to address the issue.

  - **Price concerns:** Provide ways to demonstrate worth, present product value, show cost/value ratios, and show money- or time-saving potential. Also provide salespeople with a range of purchase options — from trial offers to bulk discounts to special terms or installment plans — to address price barriers.

  - **Time concerns:** Provide ways that salespeople can demonstrate ease of use, installation, product adoption, training, or other time concerns.

  - **Risk concerns:** Provide demonstrations, trial offers, no-risk guarantees, or service assurances to minimize the risk customers associate with a purchase. Also present testimonials, endorsements, and case studies that replace risk concerns with product assurances.

In addition to dealing positively with concerns, train your salespeople to log concerns and to share them with your organization on a periodic basis. That way, when it's time to revitalize your brand, you know the kinds of issues you're dealing with.

Chapter 14

Getting Customers to Pledge Allegiance to Your Brand

In This Chapter

▶ Creating customer loyalty through brand experiences

▶ Reaching beyond expectations

▶ Igniting customer passion for your brand

*C*reating a brand name, a brand identity, and a brand promise are just the beginning of the branding process. They're like the ante you pay to play in the high-stakes branding arena. They're the down payment required to rise above the noisy floor of me-too offerings and to win a chance at a preferred place in customers' hearts and minds, where great brands live and thrive.

You can't just register a terrific brand name, design an award-winning logo, craft a great brand promise, and then sit back and wait for the magic to happen. Sorry, a great brand framework, of and by itself, isn't enough to build a great brand success story. Even good market awareness and strong consumer purchases aren't enough. Brand success requires one more essential ingredient: customers with brand passion.

This chapter is about moving your brand into the winner's circle by attracting and keeping customers with allegiance, affection, and — the ultimate jackpot — true enthusiasm for your brand.

Kindling Customer Loyalty

Great brands are what they are because of sky-high customer enthusiasm that results in nothing short of brand passion.

For good examples of the power of customer enthusiasm, consider the brands whose logos you see displayed on car windshields or whose labels are worn on the outside of clothes as badges of honor and affection. They're the brands that enjoy both customer pride of ownership and the incalculable value of customer affection, loyalty, word-of-mouth, and brand allegiance.

Passionate employees and passionate customers (in that order) power great brands. You can't put the cart before the horse. You can't create passionate customers without first creating the kind of brand experience that only passionate employees can deliver. For help turning your employees into a team of brand champions, flip back to Chapter 13.

When your organization's ready to deliver awe-inspiring service that fulfills your brand promise at every customer encounter point, you're on your way to developing passionate customers. This section details steps to follow in getting your customers on your side 100 percent.

Turning sales transactions into customer relationships

The first step in developing brand allegiance is sparking a customer relationship. Most customers fit into one of two categories:

- **Transaction customers, who help build your bottom line:** They approach your business seeking a good deal, and their expectations usually are based on low price coupled with outstanding features or convenience. Transaction customers' primary interest is in the deal rather than the relationship. Although they may be happy enough with your business to pass along positive word-of-mouth comments and even to make repeat purchases, in most cases, they leave you in a heartbeat if a deeper discount or better-sounding deal comes along.

    Most transaction customers are transaction customers, period. But sometimes, if you ignite their interest, enthusiasm, and trust, they surprise you (and themselves) by becoming entranced by your brand experience and moving into the *relationship customer* category.

- **Relationship customers, who help build your brand:** They value loyalty, commitment, and trust even more than they value good deals. They prefer to do business with those whose reputations they know and whose promises they believe in.

    When relationship customers choose a brand, they're inclined to stick with it *if* — and this is a big *if* and the whole point of this chapter — you give them the kind of brand experience that turns them into brand zealots and spread-the-word ambassadors.

All customers are important in that they represent revenue and the potential for good or bad word-of-mouth. But relationship customers benefit your brand over and above the dollars they spend by contributing both to your profitability and to your brand perception.

Why customer relationships matter

It costs a lot to win a first-time customer for your business. If that person buys once and heads out the door never to be seen again, your business has seen the only revenue it will ever realize from your customer-attraction investment.

On the other hand, if the customer buys again and again, your marketing investment gets amortized, and the profitability you enjoy from your one-time investment grows higher and higher. Numerous studies show that, by winning repeat business from just 5 percent more customers, a business can improve profitability by 75 to 100 percent.

Unquestionably, your bottom line is one major reason that customer relationships matter. Additionally, relationship customers can develop into so much more.

- ✔ Relationship customers who are treated well and who receive consistently good brand experiences develop into *loyal customers*.

- ✔ Loyal customers who are treated well and who receive consistently good brand experiences make repeat purchases, even when promotions and discounts aren't involved. What's more, loyal customers who are treated like insiders and who gain a feeling of brand ownership turn into *passionate customers*.

- ✔ Passionate customers who are treated well and who receive consistently good brand experiences become *brand ambassadors*.

- ✔ Brand ambassadors who are treated well and who receive consistently good brand experiences spread the word on a brand's behalf, fueling marketplace awareness, positive perceptions, and brand value.

  As proof of the power of brand ambassadors, the 2004 *BusinessWeek*/Interbrand "Best Global Brands" Special Report included this statement: "Companies that are able to instill a sense of ownership in near-fanatical customers showed the biggest gains in our fourth annual ranking of the 100 most valuable global brands."

No doubt you noticed a common theme in the preceding process that turns relationship customers into brand ambassadors. The formula for converting relationship customers into loyal customers, loyal customers into passionate customers, and passionate customers into brand ambassadors is clear: Exceed customer expectations, and deliver a consistently great brand experience.

Delivering a Great Brand Experience

In any competitive arena, brands make similar claims. Each promises to be the friendliest, to have the highest quality, to offer the best pricing, or to deliver countless other distinctions that, on closer inspection, aren't all that different from the claims of other brands that a consumer could choose instead.

Yet when consumers gravitate to one brand over the others, their decisions are rarely based on the words they've heard in marketing messages. Consumers base their brand decisions on their own experiences. They choose and stay with brands that — based on what they've personally seen and sensed — they believe will keep their brand promises.

"Be the brand" isn't just talk, it's the key to branding success. Brand strategy doesn't move markets, but brand experience does.

Jeff Bezos, founder of Amazon.com, is widely quoted for his statement, "A brand is what people say about you when you aren't in the room." Your brand lives in the consumer's mind, and it's based on beliefs that are reinforced every time that person encounters your brand — directly or indirectly, and before, during, or after the sale.

To build the brand you want, create an experience that allows your customers to feel your distinctions and that reaffirms your promise during every single encounter with your brand.

Putting your brand experience to a personal test

The first step in managing your brand experience is to experience your brand, simple as that. How do you do that? Follow these suggestions:

- **Arrive like customers arrive.** Forget your usual insider shortcuts. If customers arrive by car, you should call or go online to obtain driving instructions, and then pull into the lot or circle the block looking for a place to leave your car (and at what price). If your customers reach you online, you should conduct an online search for your business by using both your name and keywords. If customers call your business, you should dial in to see what a phone arrival is like.

- **Shop like they shop.** Go through the buying experience exactly as a customer would, asking to see samples, requesting cost estimates, and comparing various options both within your company and with competitors. Go through the trial or customization process, and experience every other step involved in making the purchase decision.

✔ **Pause where they pause.** Within the buying process, notice where and how you wait. How long does it take to receive an initial greeting? Is the wait time tolerable? Is the greeting appropriate? Do you receive strong brand messages while you wait? Is the wait comfortable? Are you offered refreshments? Does the wait, including its length and its distractions, fit your brand image and promise?

✔ **Use your product just as they use it.** If customers have to sign an estimate or a contract in order to buy your product, notice how the information is presented, whether it's perfectly clear, and what questions, if any, come to mind. If they have to unpackage or assemble your product, go through the steps yourself following the provided instructions to see if it makes sense. Dial your help line to check out your support functions. Then put the product to use to assess the user experience.

Use your findings to smooth the customer experience by

✔ **Creating a map of how customers enter, buy from, and follow up with your business.** This information helps as you conduct your more formal experience audit (see the next section).

✔ **Noting and making plans to eliminate any customer barriers.** Eliminate all barriers, whether they're physical (lack of parking), emotional (undue waits), or product-oriented (packaging is hard to open; instructions are difficult to understand).

✔ **Noting and making plans to address any opportunities for service or product enhancements.** For example, if you find that customers are consistently tailoring your product to suit their particular needs, include customization as a free or low-cost option.

Auditing your brand experience

Brand experiences are the result of brand encounters, and brand encounters are affected by

✔ Your business location

✔ How your signage looks to those passing by your business

✔ The look of the people who shop in your stores

✔ The caliber and cleanliness of your business vehicles

✔ The quality of your advertising

✔ The nature of your publicity

✔ The speed of your Web site

✔ The length of time phone calls are left on hold

✔ The friendliness and experience of customer service staff

✔ The flexibility of your return policies

✔ Whether your walkways are shoveled free of snow in the wintertime

This list barely scratches the surface of the ways that people form impressions about your brand, but you get the idea. A complete customer contact inventory could span the length of this book!

With so many encounter points, it's no wonder that many businesses have trouble maintaining a consistent image. With each lapse, though, no matter how minor, consumers lose confidence in the brand's ability to keep its promise and to maintain its distinctions.

To establish and maintain the quality of your brand experience, take these steps:

1. **Determine every brand impression point that prospects and consumers encounter when dealing with your business, from the pre-purchase stage through the purchase experience and post-purchase.**

2. **Create a brand experience that conveys your brand promise without fail or hesitation through encounters that consistently advance your brand message, your brand tone and look, and your brand character.**

3. **Audit your brand promise on a regular basis to insure against reputation-eroding communication or service lapses.**

Pre-purchase impressions

Pre-purchase impressions usually take the form of advertising, direct mail, displays, publicity, introductory presentations, and positive word-of-mouth comments that aim to establish

✔ Brand awareness

✔ Brand distinctions

✔ Brand position

✔ Positive brand perceptions

✔ Brand relevance to consumer wants and needs

Most pre-purchase communications target prospective, new, or lapsed customers with messages intended to prompt inquiries, product sampling, and, ultimately, purchases.

Purchase experience impressions

During the purchase process, consumers form impressions based on the location of your business, the design of your physical or online setting, the style and attitude of your employees (and even that of other customers), the design of your packaging, the nature of your pricing, and the way they're treated by sales and service staff.

As you define and audit each purchase encounter point, remember that the purpose of contact during the purchase process is to reinforce your brand image and promise and also to

✔ Heighten consumer confidence

✔ Overcome consumer doubts or feelings of risk

✔ Underscore your brand distinctions and competitive advantage

✔ Build trust

✔ Convey your product value and positive price-value relationship

Post-purchase impressions

The strongest post-purchase impression comes from delivery of a branded product that matches or exceeds the customer's quality, use, and performance expectations.

The post-purchase experience also includes your follow-up service, your customer communications, your loyalty programs, your customer events and promotions, how you handle the compliments and concerns that engaged customers will share, and how you encourage customers to become more involved in tailoring the brand experience to their unique wants and needs. (See the section "Recipe for a cult brand" later in this chapter for more information on this point.)

As you define and audit each post-purchase encounter point, be sure that your company's performance underscores your brand promise while also

✔ Demonstrating appreciation

✔ Exceeding customer expectations

✔ Addressing customer needs

✔ Encouraging involvement and brand ownership

Making use of your findings

As you conduct your brand experience audit, use the worksheet in Figure 14-1 as a guide and follow these steps:

1. Identify all brand impression points.

2. Evaluate the strength or weakness of each impression point based on how well your organization currently performs at this point and whether your performance has improved or slipped over the recent past.

3. Identify any gaps between your brand promise and your brand experience.

4. Prioritize the gaps for immediate attention based on the seriousness of the experience lapse and the prominence of the impression point.

5. Set improvement objectives, monitor progress, and reward your staff for performance advances.

Making Sure You're Exceeding Customer Expectations

In today's fast-paced business world, it's hard to meet customer expectations on a consistent basis, let alone exceed them. And yet, market expectations are higher and more important to brand success than ever.

Even customers who value relationships with your brand will defect if their expectations aren't met. In fact, even those whose expectations *are* met will defect if they sense a *quality gap* (an experience that falls short of expectations) or if another brand wows them with an over-the-top brand experience that makes yours pale in comparison.

Protecting your customer base from defection takes work — and a strong brand. When customers believe in your brand promise, and when they consistently receive a clear brand message and a good brand experience, they're more likely to cut you some slack and remain true to your brand even if one encounter falls short once in a rare blue moon.

To measure how well you're doing at delivering an exemplary customer experience, measure your customer satisfaction levels on a frequent basis. Figure 14-2 includes a chart to guide your assessment. As you fill it out, follow your gut instinct and collect input from those who work with customers and manage customer relation departments in your business in order to arrive at your responses. Periodically, you should also conduct customer satisfaction research, following the research advice in Chapter 4.

BRAND EXPERIENCE AUDIT	Rate quality of brand experience at this impression point (1=low, 5=high)			✔ For priority attention
Impression Point	Brand Look/Tone	Brand Promise	Brand Character	
PRE-PURCHASE				
Newspaper ads	1 2 3 4 5	1 2 3 4 5	1 2 3 4 5	☐
Magazine ads	1 2 3 4 5	1 2 3 4 5	1 2 3 4 5	☐
Broadcast ads	1 2 3 4 5	1 2 3 4 5	1 2 3 4 5	☐
Online ads	1 2 3 4 5	1 2 3 4 5	1 2 3 4 5	☐
Phone directory ads	1 2 3 4 5	1 2 3 4 5	1 2 3 4 5	☐
Transit and outdoor ads	1 2 3 4 5	1 2 3 4 5	1 2 3 4 5	☐
Company vehicles	1 2 3 4 5	1 2 3 4 5	1 2 3 4 5	☐
Direct mailers	1 2 3 4 5	1 2 3 4 5	1 2 3 4 5	☐
Product samples	1 2 3 4 5	1 2 3 4 5	1 2 3 4 5	☐
Product literature	1 2 3 4 5	1 2 3 4 5	1 2 3 4 5	☐
Newsletters	1 2 3 4 5	1 2 3 4 5	1 2 3 4 5	☐
Video/DVD/Podcast/Webcast	1 2 3 4 5	1 2 3 4 5	1 2 3 4 5	☐
Web site	1 2 3 4 5	1 2 3 4 5	1 2 3 4 5	☐
Tradeshow/Expo displays	1 2 3 4 5	1 2 3 4 5	1 2 3 4 5	☐
Presentation materials	1 2 3 4 5	1 2 3 4 5	1 2 3 4 5	☐
Word-of-mouth comments	1 2 3 4 5	1 2 3 4 5	1 2 3 4 5	☐
PURCHASE EXPERIENCE				
Building and entry signage	1 2 3 4 5	1 2 3 4 5	1 2 3 4 5	☐
Business environment	1 2 3 4 5	1 2 3 4 5	1 2 3 4 5	☐
Web site environment	1 2 3 4 5	1 2 3 4 5	1 2 3 4 5	☐
Catalogs and sales literature	1 2 3 4 5	1 2 3 4 5	1 2 3 4 5	☐
Reception area and staff	1 2 3 4 5	1 2 3 4 5	1 2 3 4 5	☐
Sales staff	1 2 3 4 5	1 2 3 4 5	1 2 3 4 5	☐
Telephone system and staff	1 2 3 4 5	1 2 3 4 5	1 2 3 4 5	☐
Point-of-purchase displays	1 2 3 4 5	1 2 3 4 5	1 2 3 4 5	☐
Product packaging	1 2 3 4 5	1 2 3 4 5	1 2 3 4 5	☐
Price presentation	1 2 3 4 5	1 2 3 4 5	1 2 3 4 5	☐
Checkout and billing processes and staff	1 2 3 4 5	1 2 3 4 5	1 2 3 4 5	☐
Samples	1 2 3 4 5	1 2 3 4 5	1 2 3 4 5	☐

Figure 14-1a:
Regularly
monitor and
improve
your brand
experience
impression
points.
(continued)

(continued)				
Impression Point	Rate quality of brand experience at this impression point (1=low, 5=high)			✔ For priority attention
	Brand Look/Tone	Brand Promise	Brand Character	
POST-PURCHASE				
Product quality and usage	1 2 3 4 5	1 2 3 4 5	1 2 3 4 5	☐
Use and warranty literature	1 2 3 4 5	1 2 3 4 5	1 2 3 4 5	☐
Invoice and statement process	1 2 3 4 5	1 2 3 4 5	1 2 3 4 5	☐
Customer service staff and policies	1 2 3 4 5	1 2 3 4 5	1 2 3 4 5	☐
Customer surveys	1 2 3 4 5	1 2 3 4 5	1 2 3 4 5	☐
Customer communication	1 2 3 4 5	1 2 3 4 5	1 2 3 4 5	☐
Loyalty programs	1 2 3 4 5	1 2 3 4 5	1 2 3 4 5	☐
Events and promotions	1 2 3 4 5	1 2 3 4 5	1 2 3 4 5	☐
GENERAL				
Correspondence (mail/e-mail)	1 2 3 4 5	1 2 3 4 5	1 2 3 4 5	☐
Publicity (materials/coverage)	1 2 3 4 5	1 2 3 4 5	1 2 3 4 5	☐
Quality of logo item handouts, apparel, and so on	1 2 3 4 5	1 2 3 4 5	1 2 3 4 5	☐
Customer corps (how well customers reflect brand image)	1 2 3 4 5	1 2 3 4 5	1 2 3 4 5	☐

Figure 14-1b:

Igniting Customer Passion

Customers don't fall in love with a brand overnight. First they need a little wooing. Customers need

- ✔ **To meet a brand that interests them.** They need to hear a name, see a logo, and encounter a brand message that somehow makes them think, "Hey, this could be for *me*."

- ✔ **To be presented with a promise that compels them to want to get further involved.**

- ✔ **To have a brand experience that fuels their interest while underscoring their initially formed positive impressions.**

> ✔ **To be overwhelmed by the pride they feel in simply saying that the brand is "theirs."** They need to believe that everything about the brand is so right and that everything about the brand's products, service, promise, people, and clientele is so consistently ideal that the brand is somehow capable of enriching their lives on a personal level.

Only when your brand has achieved awareness, interest, involvement, trust, and pride of ownership can it ignite consumer passion.

Generating buzz

One way to launch the push for passionate customers is to use what's called *buzz marketing,* which is essentially high-powered word-of-mouth that aims to get people telling other people who tell other people about your brand and its products and service.

Buzz marketing is a fairly new term with a long history. For decades marketers have worked to get their brands in use and talked about by those whose opinions influence others. When movie stars stand on the red carpet at the Oscars announcing that they're "wearing Armani," that's buzz marketing. But on a more practical scale, when an online chat room participant touts a new product, that's buzz marketing, too.

What's in a scent?

Want an example of a strong brand experience? Think of Cinnabon. Within a football field's distance of the shopping mall food court, you know whether or not it has a Cinnabon. The company has perfected what's called an *olfactory signature* — more commonly known as a *scent* — that announces the brand's presence and readies customers for what has become a highly predictable brand experience.

Brands are comprised of memories, and according to those who study such things, smell is the sense that most effectively triggers memory. Cinnabon manages its brand around its scent. It distances its stores from outlets that may compromise its aroma, and then it delivers a product and a customer experience that

aligns with the smell that brought people toward the store in the first place.

More and more brands are getting into the scent-as-brand-experience arena. For example, some hotels have started perfuming their lobbies with stress-reducing brand aromas or wafting the smell of the espresso bar toward waiting areas. The latter establishes a brand scent while also supplementing hotel revenues with sales from the coffee bar business. How's that for double-duty!

Not every brand has or needs a brand scent, but at the very least, a pleasant smell leaves a positive lasting impression. So how does your brand smell? Enter your business and inhale to sense the memory that customers carry away.

ASSESSING THE QUALITY OF YOUR CUSTOMER EXPERIENCE

1. Assess current and past performance (1=low; 5=high).
2. Assess competitors' performance.
Areas in which performance has slipped or competitors excel indicate potential expectation quality gaps.

Customer Experience Expectation	Your Performance		Competitors' Performance	
	Current	Previous	#1	#2
COMMUNICATION				
Clear/friendly/courteous/informed	1 2 3 4 5	1 2 3 4 5	1 2 3 4 5	1 2 3 4 5
Error-free	1 2 3 4 5	1 2 3 4 5	1 2 3 4 5	1 2 3 4 5
Prompt	1 2 3 4 5	1 2 3 4 5	1 2 3 4 5	1 2 3 4 5
Open to ideas/concerns/complaints	1 2 3 4 5	1 2 3 4 5	1 2 3 4 5	1 2 3 4 5
RESPONSIVENESS				
Customized solutions	1 2 3 4 5	1 2 3 4 5	1 2 3 4 5	1 2 3 4 5
Flexible, effective responses to requests	1 2 3 4 5	1 2 3 4 5	1 2 3 4 5	1 2 3 4 5
Prompt phone/mail/e-mail follow-up	1 2 3 4 5	1 2 3 4 5	1 2 3 4 5	1 2 3 4 5
Prompt greeting by phone or in person	1 2 3 4 5	1 2 3 4 5	1 2 3 4 5	1 2 3 4 5
Lack of service/management barriers	1 2 3 4 5	1 2 3 4 5	1 2 3 4 5	1 2 3 4 5
COMPETENCE				
Relates to customer wants/needs	1 2 3 4 5	1 2 3 4 5	1 2 3 4 5	1 2 3 4 5
Experienced and informed staff	1 2 3 4 5	1 2 3 4 5	1 2 3 4 5	1 2 3 4 5
CONVENIENCE				
Easy phone/in-person/online access	1 2 3 4 5	1 2 3 4 5	1 2 3 4 5	1 2 3 4 5
Convenient location and parking	1 2 3 4 5	1 2 3 4 5	1 2 3 4 5	1 2 3 4 5
Convenient payment/delivery options	1 2 3 4 5	1 2 3 4 5	1 2 3 4 5	1 2 3 4 5
RELIABILITY				
Keeps/exceeds commitments	1 2 3 4 5	1 2 3 4 5	1 2 3 4 5	1 2 3 4 5
Delivers quality	1 2 3 4 5	1 2 3 4 5	1 2 3 4 5	1 2 3 4 5
Good reputation	1 2 3 4 5	1 2 3 4 5	1 2 3 4 5	1 2 3 4 5

Figure 14-2:
Analyzing the quality of your customer experience.

Consumers helping consumers catch brand spirit

In 2004, when the Mozilla Foundation introduced the open-source Web browser Firefox, it did so with a user-organized viral campaign titled "Spread Firefox" that did exactly as its name implied. Within days of the browser launch, Firefox was generating a million downloads a day. Tens of thousands of brand fans signed up to serve as marketing volunteers on a quest to get Web sites to display Firefox promotional buttons and banners and to get the Firefox word out through blogs, chat rooms, mainstream media, and even a full-page ad in *The New York Times,* paid for with donated dollars.

To get an idea for how a viral marketing campaign is presented and used, visit www.spread firefox.com.

Buzz marketing falls under the category of *viral marketing* because, like a virus, it spreads with a frenzy as soon as it's started, and that's the whole attraction.

To generate buzz marketing, start with product news that people actually want to hear about and talk about. Then spread the word, either on your own or through passionate consumers. Use any of these communication channels:

- ✔ Online, gain visibility in chat rooms and forums where those who fit your customer profile gather and where people discuss products like the one you're offering.

- ✔ Start a company blog (or encourage avid customers to start a brand blog) that's full of information, opinions, and ideas about your brand. As an alternative, provide information to existing blogs that match your brand's image (see Chapter 12 for how-to information on branding online).

- ✔ Use blast e-mails to spread brand news and inspire buzz among your established clientele (see Chapter 12).

- ✔ Get your product in use by passionate consumers who can't say enough about it. Cultivate the kind of fanatics Winston Churchill was talking about when he said "A fanatic is one who can't change his mind and won't change the subject."

Recipe for a cult brand

Cult brands happen when consumers take brand passion to the nth degree. They happen when consumers adopt the brand as "theirs" instead of "yours." When you hear consumers say "my iPod," "my Google news page," "my IKEA," or "myspace.com" (that one's right in the name), they've taken ownership of the brand and its product or service.

For as long as brands have existed, there have been cult brands. But in the past, most cult brands were small, underdog brands that attracted I'd-rather-fight-than-switch customers who stood by their brands with pride even when hardly anyone else even knew the brand name.

Today, even the biggest brands inspire cult brand followings by using all or most of the following strategies:

- ✔ Start with a unique brand identity and promise that consumers truly want to be part of. Then spotlight and stay true to your brand differences and distinctions.

- ✔ Offer products that customers not only *can* customize but that you prefer them to customize in order to adapt the products to their unique consumer preferences, no matter how far-out and unusual.

- ✔ Create a brand experience that's like no other and that never, ever, falls short of the consumer expectation.

- ✔ Emphasize viral marketing, buzz marketing, and good old-fashioned word of mouth over traditional advertising. (See the preceding section for more on viral and buzz marketing.)

- ✔ Create fans both among your employees and among your customers, and support development of brand fan clubs, Web sites, forums, blogs, events, and any other channel that allows those who know and love your brand to share their opinions.

- ✔ Create or at least support the formation of a community of brand fans who personify your brand by displaying it on personalized items, talking about it, and sharing their enthusiasm with others.

Chapter 15

Valuing Your Brand

*I*t seems almost too good to be true that a name, a promise, and a great reputation can be worth thousands, millions, or even billions of dollars, but it's a fact you can bank on when you build and manage a great brand.

Often, when companies are bought and sold, as much as half of the money that trades hands covers the purchase of the brand name and all it means in the marketplace. That means that roughly fifty cents out of every dollar exchanged in many business sales goes not for inventory, buildings, physical items, business contracts, accounts receivable, or other tangible assets but for the purchase of the brand — something no one can actually see or touch, which is why brand equity is called an *intangible asset.*

Brand equity is so important that, in the world's most successful businesses, the most valuable single intangible asset is the brand.

This chapter defines what it takes to build the value of your brand, how to convert brand value to brand equity (and how to protect that equity), how to measure and enhance your brand's worth, and how to leverage the strength of your brand for greater business, financial, and community good.

Great brands are great assets. This chapter helps you get your money's worth.

The Brand Value–Brand Equity Connection

When it comes to the value of a brand, you have two elements to be concerned with:

✔ **How your brand is valued by consumers:** Your brand's value in consumer minds is the result of public perception formed by all the impressions your brand makes in its marketplace. If consumer impressions are positive and consistent, your brand's value is likely to be positive and consistent, too. If impressions are erratic or even negative, brand value is likely to waver and sink on the news.

✔ **How your brand is valued by investors or prospective brand buyers:** Your brand's value as an asset is called *brand equity*. Brand equity is determined by a complex process that weighs your brand's current and future monetary value, based not only on consumer perceptions but also on the ability of your brand to deliver economic advantages to its owner in the future.

Revving up the economic engine

From its invisible post deep in consumers' minds, brand value fuels market activity. When your brand value is high, your brand enjoys a long lineup of economic advantages, including:

✔ **Premium pricing:** When consumers hold your brand's attributes and promise in high esteem, they're willing to pay more for what they perceive is higher value and lower risk than they believe is represented by lesser-known or lesser-valued alternatives. As a result of high brand value, your brand enjoys the benefit of lower price sensitivity and price elasticity. Consumers purchase highly valued brands even when the price fluctuates because their decision is based on the perception of brand quality and not the product price.

✔ **Lower cost of sales:** When consumers value a brand highly, they make repeat purchases and buy with greater purchase frequency — without the need for extensive and costly sales promotions, sales negotiations, and customer retention efforts on your part. As a result, high brand value allows you to reduce sales-acquisition costs by amortizing a one-time sales expense across multiple purchases and a longtime client relationship.

✔ **Lower cost of promotion:** Consumers who value your brand highly become brand ambassadors. They enhance your brand's marketplace visibility by speaking well on your behalf, spreading positive word-of-mouth, and recruiting others into your clientele at no additional promotional cost to your business.

✔ **Higher market share:** When customers stay loyal to your business — and recruit new customers to boot — you enjoy increased *market share,* which is the percentage of market activity captured by each competitor in a market arena. Dominant market share provides a two-pronged economic advantage: It reduces your brand's need for new business development expenses while increasing your brand's immunity from competitive attacks.

✔ **Lower employee turnover:** High brand value almost always exists in the minds of employees before it reaches the minds of consumers. (Chapter 13 is full of tips for instilling a sense of brand value and brand passion in your employee team.) When consumers catch the brand spirit from employees, consumers tend to pass their brand enthusiasm back to employees, making employees' jobs easier and far more enjoyable, thereby reducing employee turnover.

Gaining a competitive advantage

Strong brand value inoculates an organization against competitive threats it may otherwise face. It also provides a number of other competitive advantages, including:

✔ **Consumer recognition:** Brands with high brand value enjoy strong support and loyalty from customers. This loyalty results in long-term relationships that are resistant to overtures from competitors. It also results in higher sales volume, lower cost of sales, and greater return on investments in business development and customer retention.

✔ **Industry recognition:** Brands with high value enjoy stature in their industries that results in advantageous industry leadership roles, industry trade media coverage, favorable relationships with industry suppliers, and profitable industry supplier terms.

✔ **Media recognition:** High brand value results in high market awareness, including awareness among those who cover news stories. When reporters seek comments from industry leaders, they call on the names they know, catapulting high-value brands to even more prominence.

✔ **Financial industry recognition:** The financial world monitors brand value as a strong indicator of the strength of an organization's management and corporate health. Analysts and investors see strong brands as reflections of strong businesses that they reward with higher levels of investment, lower cost of capital, and advantageous financial relationships. (In Chapter 13, you can get help improving your performance in this arena.)

Brands with high value enjoy a protected market position for the simple reason that their market strengths are so hard to tackle that competitors set their sights on different, more open markets or competitors instead.

To assess the current value of your brand, use the worksheet in Figure 15-1.

Estimating Your Brand's Equity

When a customer goes out of his way to buy a pair of sneakers bearing a certain logo, a cup of coffee from a certain outlet, jewelry in a certain pale blue box, a donut made while-you-watch at a certain bakery, or a reference book bound in a certain yellow-and-black cover, he does so because he believes that the product he's buying offers a unique set of benefits. Those benefits translate into what consumers perceive as brand value.

When consumers go out of their way on a repeated basis, when they willingly pay a premium to obtain the set of benefits they attribute to a branded product, and when they encourage others to do the same, they deliver an economic advantage — brand equity — to the brand owner.

As a brand owner, you can estimate your brand's worth by following a few recognized approaches.

Brand equity measuring sticks

To measure brand equity, most brand evaluators assess a brand's ability to achieve premium pricing, lower costs, and business strength and growth.

Sales performance

As a starting point in evaluating the worth of your brand, assess whether your sales are going up and at what rate.

1. **Calculate the percentage of sales growth your brand has experienced for each of the past three years.**

   For example, if two years ago your sales totaled $3 million and last year they grew to $3.25 million, your business experienced one-year growth of 8.3 percent. (Sales were up $250,000, and $250,000 ÷ $3 million = 8.3 percent.)

2. **Calculate your average sales growth over the past three years by totaling the growth (or decline) of sales over each of the past three years and then dividing that number by three.**

ASSESSING CONSUMER PERCEPTION OF BRAND VALUE: WORKSHEET		
Circle responses and add up your score. Totals closest to 100 indicate high brand value.		
Customers are willing to pay a premium to purchase your offering over a similar solution.	Rarely Frequently 1 2 3 4 5 6 7 8 9 10	
Customers typically return for additional purchases without promotional incentives.	Rarely Frequently 1 2 3 4 5 6 7 8 9 10	
Customers arrive at your point of purchase with confidence in your brand and consistently follow through with a product selection and purchase.	Rarely Frequently 1 2 3 4 5 6 7 8 9 10	
Your customers and business associates refer new customers to your business.	Rarely Frequently 1 2 3 4 5 6 7 8 9 10	
Customers change their minds and choose not to purchase upon close consideration at the point of sale.	Frequently Rarely 1 2 3 4 5 6 7 8 9 10	
Customers abandon your business for another in your market area, either due to discontentment or better deals.	Frequently Rarely 1 2 3 4 5 6 7 8 9 10	
Your sales have increased consistently over past years, with equally strong increases in profits.	Definitely Not Definitely 1 2 3 4 5 6 7 8 9 10	
Your brand is presented positively in industry reviews, business coverage, and other publicity.	Rarely Frequently 1 2 3 4 5 6 7 8 9 10	
When you raise prices, purchases by established customers decline.	Frequently Rarely 1 2 3 4 5 6 7 8 9 10	
Your highest-priced or highest-profit offerings are among your best selling items.	Definitely Not Definitely 1 2 3 4 5 6 7 8 9 10	

Figure 15-1: Assess how consumers value your brand.

For example, if you experienced 5 percent sales growth three years ago, 5 percent sales growth two years ago, and 8 percent growth last year, your three-year average growth rate is 6 percent ($[5 + 5 + 8] \div 3 = 6$).

3. **Indicate if extraneous circumstances factored into the growth or decline of any of the past three years.**

   For example, if your business underwent a significant remodel that resulted in fewer customers and lower sales over a one-year period, note that factor and explain how the remodel contributed to brand worth even as it detracted from sales revenue.

4. **Indicate if extraneous circumstances will affect the growth of sales over future years.**

   For example, if your business projects flat sales for the next few years as you complete development of a major new product, explain the development schedule and how the product launch will propel sales and contribute to brand worth in the near future.

Unless you explain that extraneous circumstances affected your sales growth in the past, it's fair for brand evaluators to assume that your average sales growth over the past three years indicates the sales growth rate you'll achieve during the next few years.

Marketing strength

The size, growth rate, and composition of your market arena all affect your brand equity. Obviously, if the size of your market is decreasing, if consumer preferences are turning away from your brand attributes, or if new competitors are grabbing large slices of what used to be your market, the worth of your brand suffers. Measuring brand equity by marketing strength requires you to address the following questions:

✔ **Is your business arena one that attracts growing or declining market interest?** For instance, the home sewing industry, the ski industry, and the tennis industry are three arenas that have seen consumer participation decline over recent years. In contrast, pet ownership, wine consumption, and healthcare usage are all up.

To assess trends in your industry, go to your public or university library reference area and consult the *Lifestyle Market Analyst* published by SRDS and Equifax. The publication presents lifestyle and demographic information for residents of 210 major U.S. market areas. By obtaining your market area statistics for current and past years, you can determine whether your consumer base is growing or declining.

✔ **Is consumer demand for your offering growing or declining?** Consult your own records first. Are your inquiries, your new customer accounts, and your customer purchase rates increasing or decreasing? Then obtain information from publications that serve your business arena. Are their subscription and circulation counts on the increase? Does your business association show increased or decreased activity in your business arena? Together, your findings can help you make a case regarding the strength of consumer demand for your brand's offerings.

✔ **Is your business arena getting more competitive, and is your brand faring better or worse in the competitive field?** List your top competitors for each of the past three years, along with how you ranked in terms of sales against each one. Note whether competitors have entered or left your market arena as well as whether competitors have gained or slipped in market share against your brand. The degree to which you're gaining business from competitors is a good indication of brand strength and resulting worth.

Brand experience

Your *brand experience* is the sum of all encounters with your brand, whether through contacts with you or your staff, your advertising, your Web site, your telephone answering system, your retail environment, your publicity, and even the word-of-mouth that circulates about your brand.

Your brand experience is the means by which customers form impressions about your brand, and as such, it links directly to your brand's success. To assess your brand experience, use the worksheets that appear in Chapter 14. Also consider the following questions:

✔ Are your brand's distinguishing attributes clear and consistently conveyed?

✔ Are the benefits your brand promises ones of increasing value to your consumers?

✔ Does your brand convey and keep its brand promise at every point of contact, whether with employees, suppliers, prospects, consumers, suppliers, investors, shareholders, or any other stakeholder group?

Brand value

To assess your brand value as a contributor to your brand equity, use the worksheet shown earlier in Figure 15-1 and give thought to the following questions. As you arrive at answers, realize that positive responses indicate that your brand value is strong; a mixed-bag set of responses indicates that your brand value is at risk; a lineup of "no" answers indicates that your brand needs serious repair in order to restore its value.

✔ Is your customer base growing?

✔ Is your customer retention rate increasing? (Conversely, is your customer attrition rate rising?)

✔ Is your brand awareness level increasing? When prospective customers are asked to name the top few brands that come to mind in your business arena, how many cite your name, and has that number grown or declined over recent years?

✔ Is your brand's mindshare increasing? When prospective customers are asked to name the *top* brand that comes to mind in your market arena, how many cite your name, and has that number grown or declined over recent years?

✔ Is your average sale price increasing?

The degree to which consumers are willing to pay a premium for your offering is often viewed as a primary indicator of your brand's equity.

Calculating your brand equity

Brands are worth money. As proof, John Stuart, one of the 20th century's great business leaders and a former CEO of the Quaker Oats Company, is widely quoted as saying, "If this business were split up, I would give you the land and bricks and mortar, and I would take the brands and trademarks, and I would fare better than you."

To figure out the equity of your brand so that you know the worth of the asset you're building, protecting, and leveraging *or* so that you understand your brand's possible sale price, use either or both of these two approaches:

✔ Assess the costs involved to establish or replace your brand.

✔ Assess the economic worth of your brand based on its market share advantage, price premium advantage, cost of sale advantages, and reputation.

Figuring out the cost of establishing or replacing your brand

One approach to estimating your brand's worth is to figure out what it would cost if you were to create your brand today or if the organization seeking to purchase your brand were to try to build your brand from scratch.

In assessing your brand from this angle, take the following into account:

✔ **The cost of creating your brand identity,** including:

- Name development and registration

- Logo development and trademarking

- Slogan development and trademarking

- Domain name registration and Web presence

- Development of other brand-identifying elements such as a unique and widely accepted color scheme, an olfactory signature or scent, a musical signature, and any other element that contributes to what your market understands to be the identity of your brand

✔ **The cost to achieve your current level of market awareness,** including what it would cost in advertising, promotion, and publicity to achieve knowledge of your brand name, to establish your brand message and brand promise, and to gain awareness of your brand benefits and distinctions

✔ **The cost to build and retain your current clientele,** including advertising, promotions, relationship development, and implementation of loyalty programs necessary to attract your customer corps and develop the kind of customer retention and passion that leads to your current levels of repeat purchases and positive word-of-mouth

Determining the economic value of your brand's premium market position

When businesses get ready to sell brands, often they begin by calculating the dollars-and-cents economic advantage of the brand. You can assess your own economic advantage by watching two indicators:

✔ **Price elasticity:** When your consumer demand remains high even when your prices go up, your brand enjoys pricing leeway known as *favorable price elasticity.* Price elasticity usually results from high brand value and usually leads to premium pricing.

✔ **Premium pricing:** To assess your brand's pricing advantage, determine how much extra consumers are willing to pay in order to purchase your branded product instead of the offering of a lesser-known or lesser-valued brand. This difference, multiplied by your sales volume, defines the economic value of your premium market position.

In other words, high brand value leads to favorable price elasticity, favorable price elasticity leads to premium pricing, and premium pricing leads to brand equity.

To calculate the worth of your brand's premium pricing position, conduct a calculation following this formula:

1. **Find the price difference between your offering and generic offerings or offerings from lesser-known or less-respected brands.**

   For example, if a six-partner accounting firm sells time for $100 an hour and average rates in the firm's market area are $85, the accountants' price premium equals $15. Or if a bottled water product sells for $2.29 and competing, nonbranded products or products with lesser brands sell for $1.99, the branded water's price premium is $.30.

2. **Multiply the price difference by the number of units sold.**

If the six-partner accounting firm sells a total of 10,000 partner hours a year, its annual price premium equals $150,000 (100,000 hours × $15 price premium). If the bottled water producer sells 600,000 bottles a year, its annual price premium equals $180,000 (600,000 bottles × $.30 price premium).

3. **Adjust your result to account for future brand performance projections.**

These projections include the likelihood that customers will continue to behave in a similar manner in the future; that the brand's current economic reality is transferable to new owners; and that the brand's momentum will continue at its current pace. For example, if a service business commands premium pricing in large part due to the powerful reputation of the owner, and if the owner wants to sell the brand and depart the business, then the value of the price premium would likely be discounted by those considering a purchase of the brand.

When calculating the worth of a brand's premium price position, be aware that the number you arrive at is a valuation starting point, not the finishing line. The effect of future brand-building activities, market growth or retraction trends, actions of competitors, and other market realities need to be weighed on an individual basis to determine whether the value of the price premium should be adjusted upward or downward in assessing the brand's worth.

When you need a pro: Identifying evaluation experts

If you're thinking about selling your brand, a good first step is to follow the advice in the preceding section so that you have a sense of what you believe to be your brand's worth. From there, you may have enough information to begin sale negotiations for a smaller brand, but for larger brands, it's worth it to call on professional assistance.

Evaluating the worth of a brand is both an art and a science. To obtain expert assistance, do the following:

✔ Visit the Web site www.brandchannel.com, which aptly bills itself as "the world's only online exchange about branding, produced by Interbrand." Search the site for "equity evaluation" and you'll find a library rich with case studies, white papers, and brand valuation advice. Go to the About Interbrand section and click Services for information on Interbrand's brand valuation services.

✔ Contact brand development specialists in your market area to see if they're experts at brand valuation or to seek their assistance in directing you to those who are.

✔ Conduct an online search for "brand equity valuation experts." The search results should lead you to thousands of sites offering information and valuation resources.

Getting out what you've put in: Leveraging your brand equity

Leveraging your brand's equity is like boosting your next business opportunity with a loan from your own strong reputation.

When you have a strong brand, you're in a great position to take the credibility you've established over the years and apply it to the launch of a new or related product or business — with instantaneous recognition thanks to the reservoir of good will and trust that resides in your brand name.

Most leveraging opportunities take the form of

✔ **Brand extensions,** which extend the power of an established brand name to a new but related business or product line

✔ **Line extensions,** which add variety to the offerings of an established brand by extending the brand to new but closely related products

✔ **Licensing,** which essentially rents or leases your brand to another company that pays all expenses to produce and market a product that carries the licensed brand identity in return for a licensing fee and royalties on wholesale revenues

✔ **Cobranding,** which capitalizes on the mutual benefits of your brand and the brand of a promotional partner

Regardless of the approach you take, leveraging your brand into new opportunities requires some careful planning and cautious implementation. We dedicate a full chapter to the best advice to embrace and the worst landmines to avoid in this area. Turn to Chapter 16 for leveraging advice.

Protecting Your Brand Equity

For as long as you own your brand, you must consistently protect its value, following the same marketing approach you used to build the brand's equity in the first place.

Chapter 9 includes advice for planning your brand launch marketing plan, including how to set strategies for each of the four Ps in the marketing mix: product, pricing, promotion, and place (or distribution). As you build and protect your brand, regularly update your brand marketing plan, always monitoring these four strategic areas to be sure that all brand marketing decisions are consistent with your brand position, promise, and image.

- ✔ **Product:** If you adopt new product lines or make product adjustments, be sure they match your brand image and market position.

- ✔ **Pricing:** Be sure that all pricing decisions align with your brand's market position and image. Discounting is a popular way to win quick sales in today's cost-conscious market environment, but if your market position is that of the high-end, elite brand, a discounting strategy may be the equivalent of shooting your brand in the foot.

- ✔ **Promotion:** Be sure all promotions are consistent with your brand identity. As brands mature, too often leaders loosen their grip, turning brand management over to those with less passion or understanding. The result is costly, brand-eroding diversion from the brand image and promise.

- ✔ **Place:** As you enhance your distribution — the way you get your product to your market — be sure that you select only those channels that support your brand identity. Too many high-end brands have suffered by cutting distribution deals with warehouse outlets only to later receive the cold shoulder from the boutique retailers with whom they'd built their reputations and clientele.

As if that weren't a long enough to-do list, there's one more "P" to consider, and that's people — the employees who power your brand experience. Turn to Chapter 13 for plenty of advice on how to build brand spirit within your organization and how to achieve brand delivery excellence by developing a team of enthusiastic, knowledgeable, and passionate brand champions.

Chapter 16

Leveraging Brand Value with Brand Extensions and Licensing

*O*f the tens of thousands of new products that enter the retail arena each year, most never become success stories. That's the bad news. The good news is that most of those that "make it" — those that beat the dire product start-up odds — have something in common that, as a brand owner, you can leverage to your advantage.

The common trait shared by most successful new products is that they ride into the market on the magic carpet of a known name. That's why most best-selling new books are by known authors, and most top-selling new music releases are by known artists. Most successful new products either carry the names of known brands or are fueled by the powerful endorsements of known authorities or personalities. By gliding into the market on the current of an established brand, a new product debuts with the advantage of instant credibility, a strength that's basically borrowed from a brand name and reputation that may have taken years, decades, or even longer to build.

Leveraging a brand name is lucrative as long as you avoid a good many danger zones. If your new product doesn't align with your brand message and promise, or if it doesn't build on the emotional connection you've established with your customers, you can actually hurt your brand in the process of trying to help your new product.

Before sharing your trusted reputation with a new offering, use this chapter to help you seize opportunities without damaging the power of your brand name and reputation in the process.

Planning for Product Innovations

Most businesses increase revenue in one of two ways: by selling more of their established products or by introducing and selling new products.

Figure 16-1 illustrates the opportunities you can pursue as you aim to increase purchases by current customers and to attract new customers into your business.

	Current Customers		
Est. Products	Reposition or revitalize your established products to increase purchases by current customers	Launch radically changed or altogether new products to increase purchases by current customers	**New Products**
	Reposition or revitalize your established products to attract purchases by new customers	Launch radically changed or altogether new products to attract purchases by new customers	
	New Customers		

Figure 16-1: Sales growth options.

Product innovations range from minor revisions all the way to brand-new product introductions. Most product announcements fit into one of the following categories:

- ✔ **Brand extension:** When you introduce a new product or product line that supports your core brand message and promise while taking your brand outside its initial category, it's called a *brand extension.* A few examples include Starbucks Coffee Liqueur, Woolite Carpet Cleaner, and Emerilware Cookware and Cutlery.

- ✔ **Line extension:** When you introduce a variation of your existing product or service that features the same characteristics and primary benefit of your established offering but with a new secondary benefit, it's called a *line extension.* A few examples include Diet Coke, Crest Extra Whitening Toothpaste, and Dove Sensitive Skin Body Wash.

- ✔ **Repositioning:** When you present your established product in a way that causes consumers to think of it differently, expanding or altering its potential market as a result, it's called *repositioning.* A few examples include Arm & Hammer Baking Soda as a cleaning and deodorizing solution and St. Joseph Aspirin as a cardiac health treatment.

✔ **Revitalization:** When you make anything from a moderate to a radical product change to address evolving market realities with new packaging, benefits, pricing, or distribution, it's called *revitalizing*. A few examples include Kool-Aid Singles packets for making single servings of Kool-Aid and H&R Block TaxCut Online and Software for do-it-yourself tax preparation. (See Chapter 17 for complete information on revitalizing your brand and offering.)

✔ **Product launch:** Introducing an all-new product is called a *product launch*. Examples are everywhere, including new cars, new software, new restaurants, new sports gear, new grocery items, new music devices, and a near-endless list of other new offerings. Some new products enter the market as new brand launches, following all the brand-building steps in this book. Others take a profitable shortcut by entering the market as brand extensions or line extensions, riding in on the strength of an existing brand name.

As you leverage your brand, realize that you're working with a very valuable asset. In some ways, extending your brand is like taking out a home equity loan to underwrite a new investment. It's a great idea as long as the new venture you're funding doesn't shake the stability of your established asset. Before dipping into the reservoir of goodwill that you've established with your name, look long and hard at the new product opportunity you're considering.

Tiptoeing into the Brand Extension Arena

Most brands loan the value of their names to new offerings in one of two ways:

✔ **Line extensions stretch the brand name to cover a new offering with new and different consumer benefits in the brand's current product category.**

✔ **Brand extensions stretch the brand name to new product categories, usually in one of three ways:**

• By entering a new price or quality category in the same general product arena (such as a car company offering a new brand)

• By entering a new but adjacent product category (such as Crest toothpaste moving into Crest toothbrushes)

• By entering a completely new category (such as Nike introducing sunglasses)

Both forms of leverage — brand extensions and line extensions — come with some common advantages and risks.

✔ **On the plus side:**

- The new offering enjoys faster market acceptance at far lower promotional costs than would be required if the product were to enter the market with a name consumers have never heard of.

- The extension allows the brand to reach current and new customers with a new offering and therefore increases the chance for new sales revenue.

- Announcement of the new product allows the brand to strengthen and renew its brand message and promise in the marketplace.

✔ **On the minus side:**

- If the new product doesn't match up with the brand's position and promise, it can confuse consumers and shake their confidence in the brand.

- If the nature of the new product causes the brand to drift from the brand's core message, the new product can dilute the brand's strength and reduce brand loyalty and passion at the same time.

When extending your brand, the safest bet is to stay in your same product category or to stretch only so far as a complementary category. For example, a window manufacturer may safely extend its brand to screens and awnings.

Extending your name to a distant product category is the equivalent of making a loan to a risky venture, and any good banker will tell you that there's a reason why loan requests for risky ventures are routinely declined. When the profile of the applicant doesn't match the risk of the request, a bank loan officer simply says "no." When it comes to brand extensions, sometimes brand managers need to issue the same response.

If you see an opportunity to extend your brand into an altogether new category, proceed with caution, making certain that your brand promise still makes perfect sense in the new market arena. The section "Putting your extension idea through the hoops" later in this chapter helps you cull good ideas from brand-damaging ones.

Avoiding line extension traps

Of the thousands of new products introduced each year, more than half are line extensions that carry the name and all the characteristics of an established brand while offering a distinct new advantage to the market.

When you extend your line, you seize a number of opportunities.

✔ You capture a greater share of your current customer's billfold by giving that person more reasons to buy from your business.

✔ You attract new customers by offering a new benefit and purchase incentive. For instance, adding a low-fat version of your product suddenly allows you to attract weight-conscious prospects. Or offering single-sized portions allows you to serve one-person households and also gain trial usage by those not willing to make larger-quantity purchases.

✔ In the retail arena, you expand brand presence by creating the need for more shelf space.

✔ Internally, you wring more profitability out of existing marketing and production investments.

Offsetting the upsides of line extensions are some major pitfalls to avoid.

✔ If the new product doesn't live up to brand expectations in terms of quality, market position, consumer preference, or brand promise, it erodes brand confidence in a hurry. Remember New Coke?

✔ If the new product extends your line to a mind-boggling and indistinct assortment, consumers can become confused, which leads to selection dilemmas that result in no purchase at all.

✔ If consumers view the new offering as an improvement of an existing product in your line, they may purchase the new offering at the expense of the established offering (called *product cannibalization*).

✔ If those inside your company aren't clear about the distinct attributes and target market for the new offering, or if they feel the new offering cannibalizes existing offerings, uncertainty and competition may result among the very people who should be championing your products.

Before extending your product line, answer the questions in Figure 16-2.

Often, brands introduce line extensions as reactions to moves by key competitors. For instance, over a short time period, Honda extended its line to include Acura, Toyota extended its line to include Lexus, and Nissan extended its line to include Infiniti. Each worked to protect its share of market by countering an extension move by the other. If your competitive arena prompts a similar extension by your business, don't proceed until you answer the questions in Figure 16-2. Otherwise, you may risk protecting market share at the expense of your brand image or your business strength.

LINE EXTENSION QUESTIONS TO ADDRESS
Why are you introducing a new product? What new benefits will the product offer?
Is the new product clearly related to your other offerings? Will customers quickly and clearly see both the relationship and the distinct differences?
How are the benefits of the new product distinctly different from the benefits of your current product or products?
Are the benefits of the new product ones that are meaningful and needed by current and prospective customers?
Does your business have the financial and human resources necessary to create, produce, introduce, and market the new product without harming the strength of your established products?
Will the new product add enough new sales to offset any decreases in sales from existing products that may occur when customers shift purchases to the new offering?
Does the new product closely match the benefits of a competitor's established offering? If so, how will your product distinguish itself and win the purchase decision from existing and prospective customers?
Will the new product extend your line to the point that it becomes too long or confusing for customers to understand?
Is the new product completely consistent with your brand position (see Chapter 5) and your brand promise and identity (see Chapter 7)?

Figure 16-2:
Before stretching your line, answer these questions.

Look before leaping into brand extensions

Leveraging your brand into new market categories is one of the most valued perks of brand development. It allows you to take the reputation and credibility you've built over time and apply it to new ventures that benefit from instant awareness and competitive advantage.

In many ways, an established brand is like a magic wand for new product introductions. But (there's always a hitch when something seems almost too good to be true) if you haven't done your homework, extending your brand name into a new category can be a dangerous roll of the dice.

To get a feel for what works and what doesn't in brand extensions, visit www.brandchannel.com, enter "top brand extensions" into the search box, and scroll down the results to access the brand paper entitled "Top Brand Extensions." It contains the results of an annual survey of top brand extensions conducted by New York brand consultant TippingSprung, in collaboration with *BrandWeek* magazine. The brand extension winners in 2005 were as follows:

✔ Best overall extension: Iams pet insurance

Iams is a company whose mission is "to enhance the well being of dogs and cats by providing world-class quality foods and pet care products." Moving into the pet insurance category is a logical, believable extension of the promise its customers already trust.

✔ Best in the liquor category: Starbucks coffee liqueur

The Starbucks mission is to be "the premier purveyor of the finest coffee in the world." Extending the Starbucks label to liqueur, in partnership with whisky maker Jim Beam, is a strong cobranding opportunity (there's more on this topic later in the chapter). It's also an innovative way to increase purchases from existing customers, who consume coffee liqueurs at a rate far higher than the general public.

✔ Best in the magazine category: Hardcover books from *O, The Oprah Magazine*

This extension makes double sense. First, it spreads the Oprah commitment to reading from the popular Oprah Book Club to a published line of books. Second, the books are tied to material from *O Magazine*.

✔ Best "overdue" brand extension: Tide to Go stain removal pen

This extension repackages Tide to meet unaddressed consumer needs for a portable stain solution. It also expands the market by moving the use of Tide out of the laundry room and into the office, car, or anywhere else that people on the go find themselves.

✔ Best furniture brand extension: Antiques Roadshow furniture by Pulaski Furniture

This cobranded extension fits well with the attributes, markets, and messages of both brands. The new line features 60 pieces inspired by significant discoveries on the popular PBS program *Antiques Roadshow*.

✔ Best not-for-profit brand extension: National Geographic's partnership with GoogleEarth to offer maps with content from National Geographic

✔ Worst brand extension: Harley-Davidson cake decorating kits. (In the 2004 survey, this award went to Hooters Air airline.)

What works? What doesn't?

Marketing graveyards are filled with brand extension failures. At the same time, business publications are filled with headlines heralding brand extension successes. In all cases, the new products started with good ideas, but from there, the paths went in vastly different directions.

In three steps, here's how you can steer your extension away from disaster and toward success:

1. **Make certain that there's a real market opportunity for your new offering.**

   Turn to Chapter 4 for advice on how to conduct market research. Then turn to Chapter 5 for help finding and seizing a market position for your offering.

2. **Make certain that your business has the staff, production, and financial resources necessary to support the new product without sacrificing the strength of existing offerings.**

3. **Make certain that your brand message and promise both extend to the new offering.**

   If the new offering isn't in complete alignment with the brand image held by those who know your brand, both your new product and your brand will suffer.

The illustration in Figure 16-3 comes courtesy of Prophet, a global brand consultancy specializing in branding and marketing. It shows how market opportunities, organizational capabilities, and brand relevance must converge to create a "sweet spot" for your brand extension.

As you consider brand extensions and look for your brand sweet spot, answer these questions:

✔ **Do you see unaddressed market opportunities that your business is organizationally suited to seize?**

As an example, if a restaurant sees market opportunity based on unmet consumer desire for home-delivered meals and has the staff and transportation capability to address the need, then the business is two-thirds of the way toward capitalizing on a brand extension sweet spot. All that's left is to be absolutely certain that the restaurant's brand and the promise for which it's known will extend to a home-delivered product. If so, all lights are green. If not, the restaurant is better off introducing a new brand to address the market opportunity rather than risking dilution or misdirection of its current brand image.

✔ **Do you see unaddressed market opportunities that fit ideally with your brand image and promise?**

For example, if a restaurant's patrons have an unmet need for home-delivered meals and the restaurant's brand image fits well with a home-delivered product, then the brand is two-thirds of its way to extension — pending determination that the restaurant has the organizational capability to succeed in the home-delivery arena. If the business doesn't have adequate staff or appropriate and available vehicles for transporting meals, then it needs to assess whether the business opportunity is great enough to offset the costs of retooling operationally in order to make the new venture a success.

✔ **Do you see areas where your brand image and organizational capabilities converge to create a new product offering?**

For example, if a restaurant has a fleet of vehicles that it uses to serve business clients with catered meals and a brand image for outstanding meals-to-go, then it has two of the three ingredients necessary for a home-delivery product extension. The missing element is market opportunity. The restaurant needs to determine that there's adequate unmet demand for home-delivered meals. If residents in the market area desire home-delivered meals, if they have the economic means to purchase the offering, and if home-delivery competitors haven't already seized the opportunity, then the restaurant is on its way to a successful brand extension.

Figure 16-3:
The conditions necessary for a feasible brand extension.

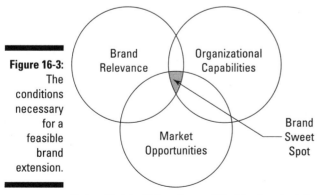

Courtesy of Prophet, a global consultancy specializing in branding and marketing.

How elastic is your brand?

Brand elasticity is a term that describes a brand's capability to stretch into new product arenas without compromising the image or promise of what the brand offers in its market. A good example of a brand that successfully tested its elasticity is Dole, which for years was marketed as a brand for pineapples. Then research showed that consumers linked Dole to the broader concept of sunshine. Aha! Dole revitalized its brand (see Chapter 17) to stand for high-quality fresh fruit, vegetables, and other foods and extended its offerings beyond pineapple to a wide range of products including sorbet, nuts, premium juices, and other offerings.

At the other end of the elasticity spectrum is Disney, which is so thoroughly perceived as a brand that represents family entertainment that it couldn't stretch into movies for mature audiences without creating confusion and conflicts in consumers' minds. That's why you see a second Disney brand — Touchstone Films — on movies that consumers may find too far outside the family entertainment category that they link to the Disney brand.

Don't ask your brand to stretch too far

When brand extensions fail, the downfall rarely stems from a lack of organizational ability or market opportunity. Most businesses stop themselves before stretching the ability of their staffs, production facilities, or management capability. And most businesses make sure that sufficient market potential exists before launching new products.

Most brand extension disasters occur when businesses try to stretch their brand identities into distant product categories where they lack relevance. In doing so, they basically expect the brand's followers to follow the brand via a giant leap of faith. They assume that the consumer's belief in the brand as a preferred solution in product category A will translate into consumer trust in product categories B, C, and even X, Y, and Z.

Expecting your brand to stretch easily from category A to adjacent categories B and C may be reasonable. For example, asking consumers to believe that Oprah's magazine is a good launching pad for a hardcover book series makes sense. Longer stretches, however, get problematic. Remember when high-powered celebrities launched the Planet Hollywood restaurant chain? The effort required consumers to trust that great actors would be great restaurateurs. Shuttered restaurant sites tell the rest of the story.

Putting your extension idea through the hoops

Before proceeding with a brand extension, test the relevance of your brand to the new category by putting it through the process illustrated in Figure 16-4.

Figure 16-4:
Matching
brand
extensions
to your
brand
identity.

| **Your Brand Image** Is it relevant to and enhanced by your new product idea? If yes ──────→ | **Your Product Category** Does it cover or is it complementary to the category of your new product idea? If yes ──────→ | **Your Brand Promise** Does it strengthen and is it strengthened by your new product idea? If yes ──────→ | **Proceed** to write your brand extension marketing plan. (See Chapter 9) |

Submerging subbrands, once and for all

A *subbrand* is a brand that's closely tied to a parent brand but that has its own identity and values in an effort to distinguish it from the attributes of top-level brand. If that definition confuses you, imagine what the concept of a subbrand does to the consumer!

Often a brand introduces a subbrand as a way to offer a lower-priced line without harming the esteem of the top-level brand; Four Points by Sheraton and United Airline's Ted are examples of subbrands.

Coauthor Bill Chiaravalle tells his Brand Navigation clients to consider subbrands a giant marketing taboo.

For one thing, brands (whether top-level brands or subbrands) need esteem to succeed, and you'll never build esteem out of an identity that begins as subordinate to something else. For another thing, subbrands confuse consumers and weaken brand management.

Bill goes so far as to say that there's really no such thing as a subbrand, at least not in the consumer's mind, which is where brands live. To the consumer, a brand is a brand, not a subset of a brand. As a brand manager, you should look at it the same way.

Bill's adamant stance is reinforced by plenty of other brand gurus. James Burgin and Jon Ward, coauthors of *Branding For Profit* (Trump University Press), put it this way: "When it comes to brands, the consumer can only count to one." That doesn't mean the consumer isn't smart, but it makes a point about how the brain works. In today's overloaded marketing environment, the human mind can only take in and remember so much. As a result, the consumer can only handle one brand at a time.

For example, the consumer sees Diet Coke either as its own brand or as a flavor variety of the Coke brand, not as a subbrand of Coke. Likewise, consumers see Jetta and Passat either as their own brands or as flavors of VW.

The consumer keeps it simple, and as a brand manager, you should, too. When developing the branding strategy for a new product, rather than creating some second-cousin-once-removed relationship, ask "Does this product fit best as a flavor or variation of our established brand? Or does it have a unique enough set of attributes, or fit into a unique enough product category, that it should live under its own brand?" In any case, consider "subbrand" the wrong answer.

Cobranding: Brand Value × 2

Cobrands capitalize on the benefits of two compatible brands that present similarly desirable attributes to consumers. In the offing, both brands stand to benefit from a number of advantages that come out of the synergy as long as they manage to avoid a few dangers.

Potential advantages of cobranding are that

- ✔ Both brands benefit from the opportunity to appeal to a greater customer base than either may be able to reach on its own.
- ✔ Each brand stands to enhance its esteem by borrowing on the strength of the partner brand.
- ✔ The brands share marketing costs, resulting in cost savings for each.
- ✔ Each brand benefits from the perceived endorsement of the other.

Potential dangers of cobranding are that

- ✔ Brand management is complicated by the need to integrate the separate operating systems and management approaches of each brand.
- ✔ The cobranded offering can confuse consumers unless the link between the two brands is immediately obvious, sensible, and easy to understand.
- ✔ One brand can be diminished in stature if consumers consider the partner brand to be an incompatible match.

Uniting brands with like visions, values, and budgets

In the most effective cobranding opportunities, the two brands share the following characteristics:

- ✔ Both brands have distinctive and compatible attributes.
- ✔ Both brands share complementary brand images in terms of quality and brand character.
- ✔ Both brands serve markets with similar customer profiles.
- ✔ Both brands share market prominence as well as similar values and beliefs.

Cobranding efforts cover a broad range. They may involve strategic alliances in which two brands unite to reach common goals or cobranded promotions in which two brands team up to achieve short-term sales objectives. Efforts may also involve cobranded product introductions in which two brands bring their production and marketing efforts together to achieve a greater market impact than either could achieve alone.

Recent and prominent examples of cobranded product introductions include the Coach Edition of Lexus, the Eddie Bauer Edition of Ford Explorer, and the Motorola ROKR iPod Phone, to name just a few. In each case, the cobranded products leverage the esteem and attributes of each brand through a partnership that's clearly a good fit in consumers' minds because the brand partners both appeal to similar markets, offer similar quality, and represent similar benefits.

Cobranding checklist

Before joining up with another brand, be sure you can answer a strong "yes" to each of these questions:

- ✔ Are your brands compatible without directly competing with each other?
- ✔ Do your brands appeal to the same or very similar customers?
- ✔ Will both brands enhance their reputations through the cobranding partnership?
- ✔ Do customers, media, investors, and other members of the public equally respect both brands?
- ✔ Are the management and marketing styles of both brand owners compatible?
- ✔ Do you trust each other?
- ✔ Are all the details down on paper and signed by both parties, including the cobranding marketing plan, budget, timeline, and responsibilities?
- ✔ Can you explain the cobranded product or promotion in a sentence that will make sense to your employees, customers, and others? Are both brands explaining it in exactly the same way?

Brand Licensing

Brand licensing is one of the most widely used ways to extend a brand, largely because it allows a brand to achieve new product introductions without gearing up operationally for the task. Instead, the brand licenses its name to a manufacturer that takes on all the production and marketing efforts of the new product.

When you *license* your brand, basically you rent your legally protected brand identity to another business that will manufacture and sell products that carry your name.

To the consumer, licensed products look just like line extensions, brand extensions, or cobranded products. So before you consider a license agreement, be sure that the agreement will result in products that meet all the brand characteristics and that avoid all the brand-damaging landmines detailed in the preceding sections of this chapter.

Understanding licensing lingo

Brand licensing comes with its own language. The terms you hear most include the following:

- ✔ **Licensing:** Leasing a trademarked or copyrighted brand identity, including brand name, logo, tagline, or any other form of brand signature, to another business, usually for use on a product or product line
- ✔ **Licensor:** The owner of the brand and the renter of the rights
- ✔ **Licensee:** The business renting rights to use the brand identity
- ✔ **Contractual agreement:** The formal permission document that defines how the licensee may use the brand and how the licensor will be paid

    The contract should include specific usage purposes, limitations on applications, geographic area, time period, payment schedule, and terms. Rely on an attorney to draw up and review the agreement, and obtain formal signatures. Handshakes are great, but only *after* the ink is dry.

- ✔ **Royalty:** A percentage of the licensee's wholesale revenue (often set at or near 5 percent), which is paid to the licensor in exchange for the rights to use the brand. In most contracts, the licensee agrees to pay the licensor a guaranteed minimum royalty payment plus a royalty on all sales that exceed the minimum payment amount.

Benefits of licensing

In a good licensing agreement, both parties benefit. The licensor gains the benefit of a brand extension and related marketplace presence and sales revenue (via royalties) without any investment in product development, production, or marketing. To the brand owner and licensor, licensing is a no-cost form of brand value leverage.

The licensee gains the benefit of the licensor's brand name, which lends immediate awareness, distinction, and trust to the manufacturer's product rollout. Without the need for any brand development investment, the licensor is able to achieve marketplace dominance and command a premium sales price thanks to the lease of the licensor's brand name.

Licensing steps to follow

Most license agreements result in what looks to the consumer like either a brand produced product or a cobranded product. For instance, Disney licenses its name to Timex, and Timex makes watches featuring Mickey Mouse. The consumer thinks the two teamed up to make the watch possible, and they did, although it was likely through a licensing agreement rather than through a manufacturing and marketing partnership.

How your branded product gets to market is a behind-the-scenes issue that's invisible to consumers. The consumer simply sees the product, links it to your name, and decides whether the product enhances or diminishes your brand image. (The sections "Don't ask your brand to stretch too far" and "Putting your extension idea through the hoops" earlier in this chapter help you evaluate the match between licensing opportunities and your brand image.)

The most important step to follow in brand licensing, therefore, is to give licensed offerings the same level of consideration and scrutiny that you give any other brand or line extension.

Additionally, you should follow these necessary steps:

1. **Build, protect, and manage a strong and highly esteemed brand.**

   Otherwise, few if any licensees will find your name worth the lease price.

2. **Establish licensing guidelines, including how far you'll allow your brand to range — in terms of product categories, price range, and distribution channels — through licensed products.**

3. **License only to well-managed, well-respected, and well-financed companies.**

4. **Limit licensing partners to one or only a few in each product category or geographic area.**

5. **Implement a comprehensive licensee training program to ensure that all licensed products are developed and marketed to your brand standards.**

   Most licensee training programs begin with education that immerses licensees in the brand image and the brand's usage guidelines. They also include presentation of the steps that licensees must take in order to gain approval of marketing communications, packaging, products, and any materials that carry the brand identity.

6. **Monitor and protect the way your brand is presented via licensed products in the same way you protect its usage within your own organization.**

   Be vigilant regarding misuse of your brand identity or infringements on your license. Turn to Chapters 8 and 18 for help.

Chapter 17

Revitalizing Your Brand

. . . .

In This Chapter

▶ Evaluating your need for a brand update

▶ Aligning your brand to current times and market conditions

▶ Launching your revitalized brand

. . . .

*A*s you open to this chapter, the word "rebranding" is probably on your mind, but chances are good that "revitalizing" better explains the brand revision you're looking for.

Rebranding is a catchall term that marketers use when they talk about updating their brand identities and reputations. Especially when business is down or competition is up, the idea of rebranding arises along with hope that a new logo, a new slogan, and maybe even a new name will be the magic pill for an image turnaround.

In fact, few brand owners really need or want a total brand overhaul. Complete rebranding involves basically erasing your current brand identity (along with much of the considerable value that goes with it) and starting the brand development process all over again, following all the steps explained in this book.

Sometimes rebranding is in order (like following a major acquisition, a merger, or a major change in business direction). More often, though, instead of rebranding, marketers need to revitalize their brands by updating their identities to make them more contemporary, more competitive, and a clearer reflection of the businesses they represent.

This chapter helps you to determine what kind of a brand revision you need and how far you want your identity update to go. Then it helps you plan the steps involved to make the changes you have in mind while protecting the brand value you've built to date.

Brands Grow Old, Too

Some brands age gracefully, gaining stature, esteem, and strength in the process. Others show their years in less distinguished ways, becoming out-of-step, a little dowdy, and no longer able to command the interest of those they most need to inspire — whether that means consumers, investors, employees, or other brand supporters.

With attention, many brands come back to life quickly. Some require only cosmetic attention — ranging from a design nip and tuck to a full brand facelift — along with some message and marketing realignment. Others need to be resuscitated with heroic rebranding efforts. Still others need to be put on life support while their owners prepare for their graceful departure from the big, branded world.

As evidenced by the fact that most brands never see their fifth birthdays but others live well into the second century of life, there's no timetable to rely on as you try to plot your brand's growth curve.

What you can count on, however, is that sooner or later your brand will go through all or most of the life-cycle stages illustrated in Figure 17-1.

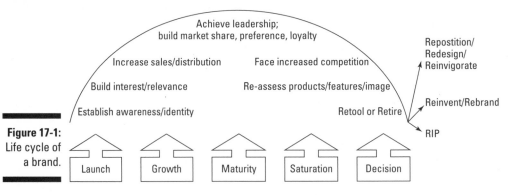

Figure 17-1:
Life cycle of a brand.

Spotting brand aging signs

Times change, businesses change, consumer interests change, culture changes, and sometimes brands need to change, too. To evaluate whether your brand may be in need of an update, ask the questions listed in this section on an annual basis, at the very least.

If you answer "yes" to a number of these questions during your annual brand review, you definitely need to take action and follow the steps detailed in the rest of this chapter.

Has your business changed dramatically?

Most rebranding or brand revitalizing is triggered by internal business changes. When the nature of your business changes, the nature of your brand changes, and realignment becomes necessary. To determine whether your situation merits branding attention, ask these questions:

- ✔ Have ownership or leadership changes led to a new company culture? If so, does your brand identity still accurately reflect your company mission, vision, and values?

- ✔ Has your product line changed, or are you about to add products that will dramatically alter your offerings? If so, does your brand promise still apply to every product and service you offer or plan to offer?

- ✔ Have you changed your distribution channels (how and where you offer your products)? If so, does your brand identity represent you well in all channels, particularly online?

Has your market changed dramatically?

The next most frequent reason for brand realignment is a changing market environment. To assess whether your market is eclipsing your brand strength, ask these questions:

- ✔ Are you facing new or stronger competition? If so, how well do your brand identity, promise, and experience stand up to the challenge?

- ✔ Have new market solutions or customer preferences caused consumers to lose or lessen their interest in your brand attributes or promise? If so, can your brand offerings be realigned to market tastes?

- ✔ Has your brand message and experience become out of synch with current consumer interests and tastes? If so, can you update your experience to make it compelling and competitive?

- ✔ Is your brand identity — your logo, tagline, and other identifying elements — out of step with current design and cultural trends? If so, can you update your identity while retaining the elements that carry the most brand value?

Brand change-of-life warning signals

When your organization (the heart and soul of your brand) undergoes major change, most often your brand identity (the face of your brand) needs to undergo change as well. Otherwise, the core of your organization is out of alignment with the promise you make to your market, and a brand credibility crisis is likely to follow.

Likewise, when your market (the reason for your brand's being) undergoes major change, your brand identity probably needs to change, too. Otherwise your image is out of synch with market needs, tastes, and desires, and a brand relevance crisis follows.

To avoid a brand disaster, frequently scan your business situation for four early warning signs that the strength of your brand may be at risk. The signs are

- Rapid business expansion
- Major product or channel diversification
- A merger or acquisition
- A brand identity that has failed to adapt to your changed business and market

The upcoming sections describe the symptoms of each of these brand health red flags. Scan them, and then complete the questionnaire in Figure 17-2 to assess your brand's vulnerability.

Rapid expansion

Growth is good, but when it happens to your company too quickly, your brand can suffer.

In the race to roll out new products, seize new opportunities, open additional outlets, add new distribution channels, or expand into new market areas, your business can outgrow your brand identity. Suddenly, your core brand message is outdated, you can no longer keep your brand promise, and your brand experience is unpredictable. Even your name and slogan become inappropriate fits with the current realities of your business.

If your organization has experienced dramatic growth in the most recent six-month period, schedule a weekend retreat — and soon — to gather employees to evaluate whether your brand identity still reflects the character, values, and attributes of your evolving business situation. Don't wait until an identity or credibility crisis sets in. Use the questions in Figure 17-2 as your assessment guide.

Major product, channel, or strategic diversification

The marketplace is in constant flux. The Internet has basically rewritten the rules on how businesses communicate, present offerings, and even sell products. At the same time, market territories, even for small businesses, have expanded almost without limits. Self-employed entrepreneurs in home offices now serve market areas that literally span the globe.

Questionaire: Is your brand in need of an update?	
Is your name still an appropriate label for the business you've become, the promise you keep, and the markets you serve?	No = attention needed
Has your organization found it necessary to improvise adaptations of your brand name to make it an appropriate label for some of your offerings?	Yes = attention needed
Has your organization found it necessary to use alternate versions of your brand name, logo, and tagline in certain distribution channels?	Yes = attention needed
If the Internet has become a major distribution channel for your business and you weren't able to seize your business name as your domain name, are you successfully training customers to find you online under a different name?	No = attention needed
Does your staff understand and embrace the business you've become? When asked to describe your brand, do employees all give nearly identical answers?	No = attention needed
Do your customers understand and embrace the business you've become? Have your best customers stayed loyal and enthusiastic as you've grown?	No = attention needed
Has your brand experience begun to get unpredictable? (See Chapter 14 for help evaluating the experience you deliver.)	Yes = attention needed
Does your brand identity look dated, with a typestyle, ink colors, and graphic design that seem stuck in the past?	Yes = attention needed
Does your brand identity match the quality and sophistication of the business you've become?	No = attention needed

Figure 17-2:
Uncovering
brand health
red flags.

Amidst this change, companies are refocusing or changing strategic direction — and brand identities — to adapt to changing business environments. Among the best examples are businesses that have moved their bricks-and-mortar businesses online; businesses that have shifted emphasis to address environmental realities; and companies that have altered their product lines, distribution approaches, and business strategies in order to serve global markets.

UPS is a good case in point. Over the past decade, UPS shifted its emphasis from fleets of delivery trucks to teams of global logistics experts. In the process, the company changed its marketing message, redesigned its logo and Web site, and developed a new tagline to address the company's changed structure and market. As recently as 1993, UPS marketed under the slogan, "The package delivery company more companies count on." Today, in the United States, the company asks, "What can brown do for you?"; globally, UPS declares, "Deliver more." Both taglines eliminate references to packages and shipping, instead opening the consumer's mind to the company's expanded market and capabilities.

BP (British Petroleum) is another good example of a business that restructured strategically and then realigned its brand accordingly. After multiple mergers and acquisitions, BP needed to declare that it had become more than a petroleum company. The company underwent a revolutionary visual update. To accurately reflect BP's transformation from "a local oil company into a global energy group," BP recast its identity to a "green" leader, even changing the meaning of "BP" to stand for "beyond petroleum."

A merger or acquisition

When you hear the word "merger," most often you're hearing a euphemism for the reality that one business has been acquired or taken over by another. On occasion, two businesses participate as 50-50 partners in a merger, but even then one company usually emerges as the dominant force.

Whether companies are acquired or merge, their brands rarely blend into one. Essentially, a brand is an organization's promise, so in merging two promises, merged companies rarely end up with a stronger promise. More often, they end up with a two-pronged promise that confuses consumers and rattles confidence.

In most corporate acquisitions or mergers, the two organizations assess the value of each brand and the equity of each brand's identifying elements before adopting one of the following brand approaches:

- ✔ **The acquiring company keeps its name and emerges as the prevailing brand, sometimes with a revitalized look that reflects the benefits of the business acquisition.** (This is what happens in most cases.)

- ✔ **The seller's name prevails.** For example, when SBC acquired AT&T, it chose to adopt the high-value AT&T name and update the identity to appear more agile and youthful. The changes made included a shift in color and typestyle and a redesign of the brandmark to more closely resemble a globe — the market served by the new entity.

✔ **The two combining companies merge their names.** For example, when FedEx acquired Kinko's, it renamed the Kinko's brand FedEx Kinko's to leverage the strength of both companies. Likewise the merger of Price Waterhouse with Coopers & Lybrand resulted in the new brand name PricewaterhouseCoopers. And then there's the Time Warner and AOL merger that resulted, briefly, in the merged brand name AOL/Time Warner, which confused consumers and investors alike and eventually separated into two independent brand names: AOL and Time Warner.

✔ **An altogether new brand emerges with no visible link to either of the brands represented in the merger or acquisition.**

A dated brand identity

In the low-budget start-up days, many businesses resort to brand identities that are either self-designed or whipped up by an aspiring artist recommended by the friend of a friend of a cousin of a brother-in-law. The result is usually a make-do identity created with all the best intentions in the world at a price that seemed right at the time.

Fast-forward several years, though, and what seemed to work fine in the past no longer fits. Maybe the design was never quite right. Or maybe it was right once, but it no longer represents the culture or sophistication of the organization or fits the nature of the market it serves or the culture in which it survives.

Some typestyles, colors, and graphic approaches are stuck in eras thankfully long past. (Think of the colors and style of the 1960s!) When that's the case, brand revitalization is in order, and it's a process you can't take lightly. Simply designing a great new brandmark isn't enough. At the very least, you need to take the following action:

1. **Assess how much you want or need to change your identity.**

   Brand identity redesigns span the gamut from evolutionary to revolutionary depending on whether they move your current identity forward a little or a lot and whether they result in an altogether new name and logo. See Figure 17-3 for examples.

2. **Determine which brand identity assets contribute the most value to your brand so that you know which aspects to protect and carry over to your revitalized identity.**

   Turn to Chapter 3 for help with this task.

3. **Invest in the counsel and talents of a good brand designer as you weigh your existing brand strengths and consider your options.**

   Chapter 11 provides advice for interviewing creative firms, making selections, and getting design agreements in writing.

4. **Adopt a revitalized brand strategy that can represent your brand vision for at least ten years, which is about the maximum frequency that the look of a brand should undergo major change.**

For a summary of FedEx's revitalization, visit `landor.com/index.cfm?do=cPortfolio.getCase&caseid=25`.

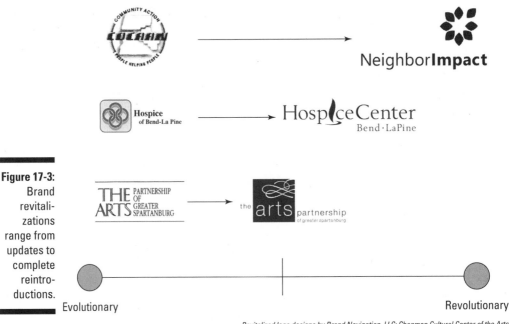

Figure 17-3:
Brand revitalizations range from updates to complete reintroductions.

Revitalized logo designs by Brand Navigation, LLC; Chapman Cultural Center of the Arts Partnership of Greater Spartanburg revitalized logo design by Storyline Studio and Brand Navigation, LLC.

Examining Your Brand's Health

Doctors require X-rays and lists of diagnostic tests before determining health conditions and issuing prescriptive remedies. Why should brands be any different? Before "fixing" your brand, put it through the same kind of checkup.

1. **Start with a brand review, also called a *brand audit*.**

2. **Determine how far you want or need your brand revision to go in terms of changes to your current brand identity.**

3. **Outline your brand revitalization plan by defining your goals, objectives, strategies, tactics, and measuring sticks.**

Revitalizing, because . . .

Revitalizing your brand presents a great opportunity to state anew what your brand stands for.

As brands age, brand messages often get blurry; over time, people within and outside the business become unclear about a brand's identity, what distinguishes it from others, what unique attributes it offers, and what promise it makes.

Revitalizing lets you put a polishing cloth not only to your brand look but also to your brand message. You get the chance to say, "We are revitalizing our brand because . . ."

✔ We've expanded our market territory.

✔ We've added products or enhanced services.

✔ We've changed strategically to better address market realities, needs, and desires.

✔ We've grown through mergers, acquisitions, or meteoric success.

Brand revitalization lets you amplify the good news about what your brand has become. It gives you the chance to reunite everyone in your company and customer corps under a new, clearly stated brand message that gives you something to shout about.

Conducting a brand review

A brand review takes your brand through many of the same steps you took when establishing your brand in the first place. (For an overview of the brand development process, see Chapter 3.)

As you review your brand's situation, give every one of the questions in this section the attention it deserves. Your answers will help you pinpoint where your brand is ailing so you can direct your repair efforts at fixing what's broken rather than overhauling brand attributes that are in good condition. Too often, brands undergo name or logo changes when what they really need to do is improve their brand experiences, starting with the way their products work. Or a company rebrands — basically throwing the baby out with the bathwater — when its old brand actually had good value that could have been revitalized for a whole lot less investment *and* market confusion. By answering each of the following questions, you determine which aspects of your brand are in good condition and which aspects need adjustment in order to truly reflect the business you've become.

What do you want to achieve through your branding program?

Prioritize your goals by selecting from the following brand functions:

✔ Create greater awareness

✔ Enhance emotional connection with consumers and brand stakeholders, including investors, employees, and those who influence brand selection

✔ Clarify or redefine brand distinctions

✔ Build or rebuild credibility and trust

✔ Motivate product preference and purchases

Chapter 3 includes a worksheet that helps you assess how well your branding priorities are supported by your current brand strengths. If your brand is strong in your priority areas, your need for brand revitalization is low. If your brand is weak in the areas that are most important to your future success, however, your brand likely needs assessment, repair, and rejuvenation.

How well does your brand fit in your marketplace?

Sometimes marketplace conditions change in such a way that brands become outdated or even irrelevant. Perhaps the brand's benefits are no longer appealing or the way the brand is presented to consumers no longer fits marketplace trends and patterns. Ask these questions:

✔ How do others — including employees, customers, prospective customers, investors, and suppliers — perceive your brand?

✔ Why do consumers choose your brand? Are their reasons strongly compelling and adequately conveyed in your brand name, logo, tagline, and brand communications?

✔ What attributes do consumers believe distinguish your brand from competing brands? Are those the same attributes that you feel best differentiate your brand and its offerings?

✔ Are the distinguishing characteristics of your brand of increasing or decreasing interest to consumers?

✔ Is your brand well recognized among those you target as customers? When asked to name top contenders in your market category, do all, most, or few prospects cite your brand?

✔ Do your brand name, logo, and slogan appeal to current market and cultural tastes and trends?

See Chapter 4 for advice on how to conduct research to unearth the answers you need in the area of marketplace perception.

Is your brand an accurate reflection of your business?

All great brands share one important attribute: They're mirror images of the companies they represent. To assess how well your brand reflects your business situation, ask these questions:

✔ Does your brand identity mirror your current business mission, vision, and values (see Chapter 6), or have ownership, leadership, or strategic changes made your brand out-of-date?

✔ Does your brand identity accurately reflect the character, personality, and tone of your business? (See Chapter 6 for help arriving at your answer.)

✔ Does the promise you make to consumers convey your strengths and distinctions, and is it believable and consistently reinforced through all brand encounters? (Refer to Chapter 6 as you consider this question.)

✔ Do all products that you've added or that you plan to add fit well under your brand? Do the number of products and the nature of your offerings make sense to consumers? (Chapter 2 addresses brand architecture, and Chapter 16 touches on brand extensions.)

✔ Is your pricing an accurate reflection of your brand message and promise?

✔ Has your brand image been tarnished by events within or outside your control? (See Chapter 19 for help dealing with bad news about your brand.)

Do consumers accurately understand your brand?

Remember, your brand lives in your consumers' minds, so before you begin to revise your image, invest time and effort to discover what those who know your brand currently think of it. Ask these questions:

✔ Does the brand image currently held in consumers' minds reflect the competitive position you aspire to fill in your marketplace? (See Chapter 5 for help staking claim to your market position.)

✔ When consumers rank the top competitors in your field, does the ranking of your brand fit with your market dominance aspirations?

✔ Does your brand attract the clientele you aspire to serve?

✔ Do those who work most closely with your business — including your employees, your business partners, your investors, and your most loyal customers — all describe your brand accurately?

Does your current brand experience reinforce your desired brand image at all contact points?

Consumer opinion about a brand is the result of all contact with the brand, from marketing communications to staff encounters, from the intricacies of the purchase experience to the experience of becoming a brand owner. Determine whether your brand experience contributes to your desired brand image by asking these questions:

✔ Are your brand name, logo, communications, location, and experience consistent with the personality, character, and tone that you want associated with your business?

✔ When consumers encounter your brand, is the experience consistent, compelling, and competitive? (Turn to Chapter 14 for instructions on how to put your brand experience to the test.)

✔ Are your communications — from your ads to your Web site to your phone and mail and in-person contacts — uniformly consistent and competitive in terms of look, tone, character, and brand message?

Does your brand compete well with the brands of dominant competitors in your market area?

As newcomers enter your business arena, their brand offerings can change consumer expectations. Determine whether your brand has remained current by asking these questions:

✔ Is your identity (your name, logo, tagline, and other identifying elements) distinctive and competitive in terms of quality, sophistication, and consistency?

✔ Is your brand promise clear, unique, and appealing when compared to promises extended by your competitors?

✔ Are your services competitive or outstanding compared to those of your competitors?

✔ Is your brand experience competitive and outstanding?

Making the diagnosis: Retool or retire?

After you complete a brand review, the moment of decision arrives: Can your brand be revitalized, or do you need to put it out to pasture? To arrive at an answer, use the results of the brand review to help you answer the following questions:

✔ **Is your brand healthy?** Is it an accurate reflection of your business today? As you look at your plans and hopes for the next ten years, does your brand name, logo, promise, and message extend to cover your aspirations?

If your answers add up to a resounding "yes," give your brand the green light to keep going, along with a double-dose investment of time and money to see that it's well protected and well presented for years to come.

✔ **Is your brand ailing?** Has it lost its fit with your business and market? If so, is the gap between what your business has become and what your brand identity implies vast or minor?

If the alignment between your brand and your business is way off — if your brand is called Main Street Fix-It but you now offer business system reviews and solutions to a global market — you're facing an identity crisis, and complete rebranding may be in order.

On the other hand, if the alignment between your brand and your business is only slightly amiss — if your name is Global Advertising but you now offer global clients strategic planning, branding, and message development services in addition to advertising production and placement — a name adjustment and a brand revitalization may be the extent of your needs.

✔ **Does your brand have high value?** (Chapter 15 can help you make your assessment.) If your answer is "yes," you have strong motivation to revitalize rather than rebrand. By revitalizing — or updating and polishing your current brand — you maintain the high-value identifying elements of your brand, and in so doing you protect the brand value you've built over the years.

When you rebrand, you basically erase previously established value and start over again, building value from scratch. Rebranding is the way to go when the value in your existing brand is so low or in such negative territory that you're better off giving yourself the equivalent of a golf mulligan and taking an altogether new shot. If that's the case in your situation, turn straight back to Chapter 3, heat up your branding iron, and get ready to begin the branding process from square one.

Fixing a Broken Brand

Most brands break not because markets change but because businesses change.

Sometimes, logos go out of style and need updating in order to keep pace with market tastes and cultural trends, but that kind of market-responsive change involves only a cosmetic update, not a brand overhaul.

Brand overhauls become necessary when business overhauls literally change a company's heart and soul. When the core of the business — the base of the brand — changes radically, the face of the brand — the brand's name, logo, and identifying elements — needs to change, too. Otherwise, a disconnect exists between what the brand says it is and what, in fact, the brand is. And *that's* a formula for credibility disaster.

Ten mistakes to avoid when revitalizing

As you audit, update, and realign your brand to address current business and market realities, take a minute to review the most common mistakes brand marketers make so that you can avoid them and sail on toward branding success. The most common mistakes are

- Failure to enlist the head of your organization as the leader of your brand revitalization effort

- Failure to assess whether your product or your brand experience — and not your brand identity — may be hurting your brand's esteem in its marketplace

- Failure to enlist experienced professionals to help with research, name development, logo design, trademark registration, and brand communications

- Failure to inform your staff early on about why you're undertaking a brand revitalization effort

- Failure to understand and protect your current brand assets as you revise your brand for the future

- Failure to maintain a *silent stage,* a time during which brand plans are held close to the vest until they're adopted by management and ready for presentation to your organization's internal team. (Put in familiar terms, loose lips sink ships.)

- Failure to introduce and win support internally before you let your revitalized brand story outside the confines of your organization

- Failure to reach your most loyal customers, investors, and suppliers with news of your revitalized brand before they learn about your brand changes through the grapevine or through mass media

- Failure to establish a brand management plan that ensures continuous and consistent communication of your brand message and promise across all communication channels and at all consumer touch points

- Failure to introduce your revitalized brand with the fanfare it deserves

Protecting your valuables

The most essential step in fixing or updating a brand is determining which of your brand assets carry the highest value in consumers' minds. Brand assets include:

- Your brand name
- Your brand's identifying elements, including your logo, your logotype or script, your tagline or slogan, your color scheme, your packaging, and brand signature items such as a unique scent (think Cinnabon), a musical signature (United Air Lines' background music, for example), or even signature events that consumers link to your name

> ✔ Your brand's core message and promise
>
> ✔ Your brand's dominance in a defined market niche
>
> ✔ Your brand's link to key customer groups

The brand asset analysis worksheet in Chapter 3 can help you determine the value of each of your assets and whether or not the strength of your brand would be reduced if you were to change or eliminate the asset.

For instance, if you discover that your brandmark has low awareness or that its usage has been mismanaged over the years, you may determine that replacing your symbol will serve only to strengthen your image. On the other hand, if you find that consumers have high awareness and regard for your name, you should think long and hard before abandoning it.

Making the change

You can start the revitalization process after you determine which brand assets you should keep and which are dispensable. Take these steps to revitalize your brand:

1. **Get the leadership of your company involved right from the beginning.**

   If possible, the person who leads your company should lead the brand revitalization or rebranding process. Otherwise, you're apt to face an uphill battle when it's time to adopt the new identity.

2. **Determine how you'll refresh, revise, or rebuild your brand promise.**

   In essence, your brand is the promise you make to consumers. The degree to which you alter your promise in large part dictates the degree to which you alter your brand. (Turn to Chapter 6 for help with this step.)

3. **Determine whether you need to alter your name, either slightly or drastically, to fit your business, your market, and your sales channels.**

   In Chapter 7, we help you with your analysis and with the process of renaming your brand, if that's the next step in your brand's life.

4. **Decide whether you need to redesign your logo.**

   Chapter 8 has advice on logo design, but we recommend that you involve an experienced professional in the actual redesign. As part of the redesign process, also rewrite your graphic guidelines and your brand management policies (see Chapter 8).

5. **Refine your brand experience so that every encounter with your revitalized brand reinforces the message and promise you make and the image you want to etch in the consumer's mind.**

6. **Relaunch your brand, starting within your organization and following the advice in Chapter 9.**

   Don't leapfrog over this step. If you fail to gain understanding and buy-in from your internal team, nothing you do externally can save your brand from the ramifications.

7. **When your revitalized brand is known, accepted, and adopted internally (and not a moment before), take your brand public.**

   Begin with a publicity generation effort that shares the story of why you're making the change, how you're building on your brand's heritage while simultaneously embracing your brand's future, and how your new identity and brand strategy focus on a clear, strong, powerful vision. See Chapter 10 for a publicity how-to.

8. **Launch advertising and promotions to amplify your brand's revitalized message (see Chapter 11).**

9. **Invest the time and dollars necessary to build and protect your revitalized brand's value (see Chapter 18).**

Part V
Protecting Your Brand

The 5th Wave   By Rich Tennant

"How about this—'It's not just CRAP, it's Mel's CRAP'? Shoot! That's no good. I <u>hate</u> writing copy for this client."

In this part . . .

This part steers your brand away from trouble. First, we help you take preemptive action against brand attacks by fortifying your brand with necessary legal protections and with an iron-clad set of usage rules.

Then we provide a guide to damage control that we hope you'll never need. But in the unlikely event of brand devaluation, this part can help you stage a brand rescue mission by advising you about which steps to take and actions to consider as you work to recover from natural or other disasters that shake the credibility, relevance, and value of your brand and your business.

Together, the chapters in this part provide an ounce of prevention and a pound of cure, in that order.

Chapter 18

Defending Your Brand

• •

• •

For all their strengths, brands are vulnerable. They're susceptible to infringement by competitors who use disarmingly similar names or logos. Plus they're open to attack by friends and foes alike, who intentionally or innocently mess with your brand's identity and erode your brand strength in the process.

The reasons to protect your brand are many, but none tops the fact that, when brands undergo competitive attack or weak management, marketplace confusion follows. And marketplace confusion is a fatal condition for most brands.

This chapter helps you fortify your brand in two ways. First, it tells you how to take preemptive action by registering your brand identity so that others can't use it — or so that you can take legal action if they do. Second, it lays out a plan for managing the presentation of your brand, beginning with usage guidelines and ending with usage enforcement.

Strong brands thrive under the careful watch of brand owners who never blink and who never turn a blind eye to brand management mishaps or transgressions. The old line "You snooze, you lose" could have been written as advice for brand managers. Vigilance is the prescription for brand strength and the antidote for brand erosion.

Immunizing Your Brand with Government Filings and Trademarks

The extent to which you protect your name legally hinges on the size of your business, the size of your market area, and the vision you hold for your business. If you think that someday your brand will span state or national borders — or if you think that someday you may want to sell it to someone with aspirations of building it into a national or global name — you should put every form of legal protection in place, the sooner the better.

The best and easiest time to protect your brand is right when you name your business because your business name is likely to become your primary brand name. Turn to Chapter 7 for complete advice for choosing a name, screening to see that it isn't already in use, and registering it so it's unavailable to others.

The most common methods of name protection are

 ✔ Filing your business name with local government offices
 ✔ Establishing a trademark

In this section, we provide tips for how to proceed on both fronts.

Filing your name with local government offices

Brand names fit into one of two categories: business names and product names. This section deals with protecting business names.

As you name your business, either you'll choose a name that includes the owners' surnames along with a description of the business or you'll choose what's called a *fictitious* or *assumed name,* which features a name other than your true name. In either case, filing your name with the right local government office is a necessary step. The process is straightforward and relatively easy.

If your business name includes the legal surname of each owner along with a generic description of your business (for instance, Smith, Jones, and Peterson Insurance), follow these steps:

1. **Find out where the database of registered business names is maintained in your state or region.**

Contact the office of your county clerk or your secretary of state for help, or ask your attorney or accountant for instructions. Your banker can also point you in the right direction because financial institutions require name registration information when opening business accounts.

2. **Register your business name by completing a form and paying a fee.**

When you're doing business under your legal name (such as John Johnson Plumbing), a name search and name approval is unnecessary. The exception is if you add a phrase such as "and Sons" or "and Associates" to your name (for example, John Johnson and Sons Plumbing). In that case, the name suggests that other owners are involved, so you need to follow the rules for registering a fictitious or assumed name as described in the following list.

Business names that don't include owners' legal surnames and generic business descriptions are called *fictitious names* or *assumed names.* If your name falls under this category, you need to register the name with a government agency. In most areas, registration takes place though the office of the county clerk, but in some areas the office of the secretary of state handles the task. Your banker or attorney can direct you to the right office. The registration process for these types of names is as follows:

1. **Undertake a name availability search to determine that no competing business has staked a claim to the name you want.**

    To determine name availability, request a search of the assumed names database in all jurisdictions (usually that means counties) in which you want to register your name. Search the jurisdiction where your business is located as well as the jurisdictions that cover each market area you plan to serve. Additionally, consider searching the jurisdictions that cover the heaviest population areas of your state or region because you may choose to expand into those areas in the future.

2. **If your desired name is available, fill out the forms and pay the required fees to register your name in your home region and in each region you plan to do business.**

    Consider also registering your name in the counties that include your state's greatest population counts in order to protect the name from use by most competing businesses in your greater market area.

If a name availability search reveals that your desired brand name is already taken by another business, head back to the drawing board and check out Chapter 7 for naming advice.

Obtaining a trademark

If your business serves only one state, you can inquire with the office of your secretary of state about a state trademark that helps protect your brand identity in your statewide region.

When you obtain a state trademark, you prevent others from using a similar mark in your statewide area. However, the process for obtaining a state trademark includes no search of other state or federal registrations; therefore, your right to use a state mark could be preempted by discovery of prior use by a trademark owner with a federal registration.

A federal trademark provides broader protection than a state trademark and is important if your business serves a far-reaching market area that crosses state or national borders. (A federal trademark is called a *service mark* if it protects the brand of a service rather than a tangible item.)

The process of trademarking is long, tricky, and important for two reasons:

✔ A federal trademark protects your brand identity from use by others.

✔ The process of obtaining a trademark steers you clear of the legal hot water that awaits if you obliviously try to use a name, logo, tagline, or other identifying element that someone else has trademarked.

To obtain a federal trademark, plan to take these steps:

1. **Determine whether the brand identity you want to trademark is blocked by someone else's trademark.**

   To make this determination, you can conduct a preliminary online search of the database maintained by the U.S. Patent and Trademark Office (USPTO). Go to www.uspto.gov, click on Trademarks, click on Search Trademarks, and follow the instructions. (For information on international trademark protection, go to www.uspto.gov/main/profiles/international.htm.)

2. **If your desired brand identity appears to be available, hire an attorney who specializes in trademarks to conduct a more extensive search.**

   Your attorney will determine whether your desired brand identity is available for use without risk of an infringement suit from another trademark holder.

   Don't try to proceed on your own; the trademark process requires professional expertise. (You can find details of the steps and costs involved in this extensive brand identity search in Chapter 7.)

3. **If you get a green light from your attorney, move to secure a trademark as quickly as you can, either through continuous and consistent
   use (see the next section) or through the rigorous process of official
   trademark registration (see the section "Obtaining a registered trademark" later in this chapter).**

Trademarking through common law usage

After you determine that your brand name, logo, tagline, or other identifying
element is available — meaning that it isn't already protected by someone
else's trademark — you can begin to trademark it by using it continuously and
consistently in the course of marketing and selling your branded offering.

When establishing your trademark through common law usage, use the letters
"TM" in superscript (or "SM" if you're establishing a service mark) alongside
the mark you're protecting. In the United States and countries with similar
legal systems, announcing your trademark or service mark claim in this way
lets you begin to accrue trademark rights through common law usage.

In taking the common law approach, be aware of these shortcomings:

- ✔ Common law trademark protection is limited to the geographic areas in
  which your mark has actually been used.

- ✔ You don't have the protection of a federal registration if another party
  were to dispute your claim to your trademark.

- ✔ By using the trademark without undergoing the rigorous search and
  analysis of a formal trademark application, you may be liable for infringing upon someone else's registered mark. Even after your attorney
  screens and conducts a detailed risk analysis for your name, additional
  infringement issues can arise during the trademark application process
  that preclude your usage of the mark, which is why federal registration
  is the ultimate form of trademark protection.

Obtaining a registered trademark

To obtain a federally registered trademark, follow the steps described in the
beginning of this section and in Chapter 7. The federal trademark process is
especially important to undergo to protect your brand if you do or plan to do
business across state or national borders. For information on federally registered trademarks, count on these resources:

- ✔ **For information on U.S. trademarks,** turn to the USPTO Web site at
  www.uspto.gov.

- ✔ **For information on obtaining trademarks in a number of countries
  through a single registration,** visit the World Intellectual Property
  Organization at www.wipo.int or go to the international property section of the USPTO Web site at www.uspto.gov/main/profiles/
  international.htm.

  ✔ **To locate attorneys in your area who specialize in intellectual property including trademarks,** visit the Web site of the American Bar Association at www.abanet.org and click on Lawyer Locator.

Use the trademark designations superscript "TM" or "SM" until your trademark is formally issued by the USPTO, at which time you can begin using the designation ®. Don't jump the gun and use the registered mark before your federal trademark is granted. Doing so is called *false use* and can result in denial of your federal registration.

As soon as you receive your federal trademark, give notice of your trademark in at least one prominent place in every ad, brochure, package, sign, or other medium by

  ✔ Using the symbol ® presented in superscript to the right of the trademarked name or symbol

  ✔ Using "Registered, U.S. Patent and Trademark Office" (or the abbreviation "Reg. U.S. Pat. & Tm. Off.") either in addition to or instead of the ® symbol

Maintaining your trademark registration

Registering your trademark is like jumping through flaming hoops, and the effort doesn't stop when the registration is approved. After you obtain a trademark registration, it's time to kick your trademark protection efforts into high gear. If you don't, your mark and all the work you put into obtaining it can fly right out the window.

Use it or abandon it

We're sure you've heard about cyber-squatters who grab up domain names, register them, and camp on the names with the thought of either using them in the future or selling them to someone else when the time and price is right. Don't try a similar tactic in the world of trademarks. Trademarks are only granted to applicants who are actively engaged or who can prove their intent to be engaged in the fields of commerce covered by the application.

When you apply to register a trademark, the USPTO requires you to list the specific goods and services for which you seek the registration. For each area you list, you must have *use in commerce,* which means that you must be able to provide evidence either that you're currently engaged in commerce in the areas listed or that you have good faith intent to use the mark in the areas listed on your registration application.

Using your mark in commerce means a couple of different things.

> ✔ **For trademarked goods:** The mark is placed on products, labels, packages, displays, or documents associated with the sale of goods that are sold or transported interstate.

> ✔ **For trademarked services:** The mark is used or displayed in marketing and selling services that are provided in more than one state.

Simply putting your mark on stationery products or using it in business presentations isn't enough to prove that it has use in commerce. You have to actually *use* the mark commercially in each of the categories covered by your application, and you have to keep using it. After three years of nonuse in any category, your trademark can be deemed *abandoned* and cancelled as a result.

To protect your trademark, work with and follow the advice of an attorney who specializes in trademark law. Be prepared to periodically assess that your trademark is used in commerce in each of the usage categories for which it's registered. If you aren't using the mark in all its designated categories, take action to amend your registration. Otherwise, you put your entire registration at risk.

Defend it or lose it

By obtaining federal trademark registration, you claim exclusive rights to use a name, symbol, tagline, or other identifying element. With that right, however, comes an obligation to use the mark continuously and consistently and to bar any usage that weakens your exclusive claim to the mark.

As you protect your trademark, rely on information obtained from your trademark attorney and the USPTO. At the very least, follow these suggestions:

> ✔ Don't use your trademarked name as a verb, and don't allow it to be turned into an active word by adding -ing.

> Consider what happened to the trademark Windsurfer. The mark for Windsurfer applied to a wind-propelled, surfboard-like apparatus patented by Californians Jim Drake and Hoyle Schweitzer in 1968. But after the trademarked term was presented as a verb — by using the word "windsurfing" to describe the sport of sailboarding — courts found the mark to be generic and no longer protectable as a trademark.

> ✔ Do use your trademark as an adjective in front of the generic term for your offering, not as a noun that describes your offering. For example, Xerox copier and Macintosh computer are proper uses of trademarks.

> The story of the escalator illustrates what happens if you fail to follow this rule. The name Escalator was once a trademark of the Otis Elevator Company. However, instead of consistently using the mark as a descriptor (as in Escalator brand moving stairs), it was used as a noun (an escalator), and the trademark protection rolled right out of sight.

✔ Do accompany your trademark with the appropriate symbol: superscript "TM" for unregistered trademarks, superscript "SM" for unregistered service marks, and ® for registered trademarks or service marks.

✔ Do present your trademark consistently, with no variation in spelling and no addition of dashes or slashes.

✔ Do separate your trademarked name from surrounding text by underlining it or by presenting it in bold, capital letters, or italics.

If you slack off and use or allow others to use your trademarked term as a verb or a generic label, you dilute your exclusive rights to the term and risk rights to your trademark as a result.

Owners of widely known and cited trademarks go to great and costly lengths to keep their names from being used as common nouns or verbs. As one example, the owners of the Rollerblade mark have spent millions of dollars to educate consumers and competitors about how the mark can and can't be used. The gist of their message is that Rollerblade isn't a generic term for in-line skates, and rollerblading isn't a sport. Rather, Rollerblade is a trademark name of a company that manufactures in-line skates, and it's the brand of equipment you wear when you go in-line skating. Using the term in any other way puts the trademark at risk, and the makers of Rollerblade skates pay dearly to ensure that doesn't happen.

If the world's your market . . .

As you take action to register and protect your name from competitors, think big. In fact, if your products or services will travel the world, think in global terms right from the get-go.

If you intend for your brand to establish international value and strong equity, follow this advice:

✔ As you develop your brand identity, test its relevance and acceptance in other cultures and languages — especially in the cultures of countries where you'll develop clusters of customers as a result of global offices, Internet marketing, or distributor relationships.

✔ If your products or services will travel national borders, obtain international trademark registrations in the very beginning, before others can beat you to the task. If you don't, someday when you seek to protect your brand in distant markets, you just may discover that your name has already been trademarked — but not by your organization.

✔ There's no such thing as a worldwide trademark, but you can file a single international application that allows you to apply for trademark registration in any of the more than 60 countries that participate in what's called the Madrid Protocol. For information, visit the World Intellectual Property Organization at www.wipo.int.

Shielding Your Brand from Misuse

Regardless of the form of legal protection you put in place to protect your brand's identity from misuse outside your company, you need to establish and adopt a set of well-crafted and carefully monitored usage guidelines and standards for use within your company.

Laying down the law with brand usage guidelines

Chapter 8 includes advice for stipulating your logo usage guidelines. Beyond consistent logo usage, well-branded organizations establish style guidelines — "rules" may be a better word — for how their identities may be presented.

As you define how your brand can be presented, be sure to consider and cover all the points in this section.

Logo usage

To ensure that your logo always appears exactly to your specifications, begin by creating digital logo art files that can be scaled larger or smaller only as a single unit. By using these established files, designers and others can't take artistic liberties with logo elements.

Additional ways to protect your logo include:

- Requiring that your logo be reproduced only from approved materials provided digitally or in reproduction-ready form by your organization and never from second-generation versions that risk a loss of quality and clarity
- Providing your logo in horizontal and vertical versions and stipulating that any alternative presentation must be approved prior to usage
- Defining how your logo may be placed in printed materials, including the smallest size in which it can be reproduced and the amount of open space that must surround it in order to protect its presentation
- Explaining allowable color treatments, including whether the logo can be reversed (to appear as a white image in a field of color) and the exact ink colors in which it can appear

Logo usage is covered in more detail in Chapter 8.

Typestyle

A quick way to unify the look of your brand materials is to limit the type-styles or *fonts* that you allow in your ads, brochures, signs, packaging, or other materials. For best results, adopt and limit type usage to one or several fonts for use in headlines and one or several for use in body copy or text.

As you choose typestyles, match how you look in print with the personality and character of your brand (see Chapter 6 for help defining your brand character). For example, if your brand personality is crisp and professional, you won't want to choose a typestyle that's ultra-trendy or playful.

Copy guidelines

To protect your identity, write copy guidelines to define how your name can be presented and what words may and may not be used in association with your brand. Your copy guidelines should

- ✔ Define which parts of your name or slogan must be presented in all capital letters or with an initial capital letter.
- ✔ Define when, if ever, your name may be abbreviated and, if so, what abbreviations are allowable.
- ✔ Prohibit using your brand name as a verb (with -ing) or as a noun. Think of your brand name is an adjective that modifies a generic word that describes your product (for example, JELL-O gelatin).
- ✔ Prohibit using your brand name in plural or possessive form (in other words, don't add an -s or -'s unless your brand is trademarked in that form).
- ✔ Prohibit breaking and hyphenating your brand name at the end of a line.
- ✔ State whether and when your name must be accompanied by a designation such as Inc., Ltd., or LLC.
- ✔ Define which parts of your name or slogan must be accompanied by a trademark, service mark, or registered trademark symbol based on the advice of your trademark attorney.
- ✔ Define whether and how you want your marketing materials to carry a copyright notice (for example, © 2006 Your Brand Name, Inc.). For copyright information, go to www.copyright.gov.

To view the usage guidelines of dozens of established brands, visit www.brandsoftheworld.com/guidelines.

Enforcing the rules

The key to enforcing your brand usage rules is to aggressively monitor how your brand is being presented. Get ready, though, because the task is harder today than it has ever been before thanks to the immediate and far reach of the Internet. It used to take years for a term to make its way into everyday language as a generic descriptor for a product or activity. With the Internet, though, a term can be adopted as everyday language within a matter of months.

The brand name Google is a perfect example. If it weren't for constant brand protection efforts, the name would have long since become a generic label, and the trademark would have been at risk, big time. Instead, Google Technology takes action every time it sees a trademark violation. The infringing party receives correspondence stating that Google is a trademark of Google Technology, Inc. and that use of "Google" must refer to the services of the company and not to Internet searching in general. Along with the letter is a set of instructions on how to use "Google" properly and a request to delete or revise the infringing reference.

What's good policy for the Google brand is good policy for your brand as well. After you establish your brand, take these actions to protect it:

✔ Put the appropriate brand protections in place, from filing your name with local government offices to registering your trademark.

✔ Define your brand usage guidelines.

✔ Name and empower a department or person to monitor and enforce your brand usage guidelines (see the next section).

✔ Train your entire employee team about proper use of your brand and trademarks.

✔ Require all suppliers, copromoters, or licensees to respect your trademark and to follow your brand usage guidelines.

✔ Don't allow any misuse or infringement of your brand and trademarks, either within or outside your organization.

✔ Monitor and manage your trademark registration to be sure you're using your mark properly in all registration categories, and amend or renew your application as necessary to keep it accurate and current.

Naming and empowering a brand cop

Your brand cop, also called a *trademark coordinator,* is the person (or department) that keeps your brand safe from misuse or infringements. Consider assigning the task to your marketing vice president or to a person in your marketing department. The brand cop's job is to enforce brand usage guidelines while continuously monitoring for misuse of your brand from those outside your organization.

Specific tasks include:

✔ Training all employees regarding the use of your trademark and brand identity

Training should take place at the time of hiring and again whenever the brand is updated, extended, or in any way revised. Providing printed or online copies of usage guidelines isn't enough; plan face-to-face meetings and in-person presentations to demonstrate and personally explain correct approaches to your brand presentation.

✔ Reviewing brand materials for consistency with brand usage guidelines

✔ Reviewing (with your attorney) plans for copromotions or license agreements to be sure that they uphold your trademark and brand presentation rules

✔ Monitoring for misuse of your trademark by those within your organization by watching for any of the trademark violations noted in the section "Defend it or lose it" earlier in this chapter

✔ Watching for misuse of your mark by other organizations that may try to use or misuse your mark or to adopt a mark that closely resembles yours and causes marketplace confusion as a result

Scan the Internet for unauthorized usage by entering your trademark name as well as violations of your name — such as your name as a verb — in search engines. Study the search results as well as the ads that appear alongside the results to see if your mark is being used erroneously.

✔ Taking action against trademark abuses

Sometimes the abuse is intentional, but more often it's not. If the violation stems from an employee or supplier mistake or oversight, get it fixed immediately. If it comes from the outside, get legal advice regarding how to proceed to put an end to the misuse.

✔ Keeping records of trademark usage and trademark enforcement

Should your trademark ever be questioned, you want your files to show that, in fact, your trademark was used in commerce in each category covered by the application and that it was aggressively protected and defended, both within and outside your organization.

Chapter 19

Taking Action When Bad Things Happen to Good Brands

*S*ometimes brands make news for the worst reasons. In spite of a million good intentions, brands can run into trouble due to anything from bad management to bad luck. When they do, the situation requires action, *ASAP*. The alternative — waiting around while you try to wish the problem away — is a formula for a public relations disaster.

This chapter is about righting wrongs should they happen. We begin by helping you steer clear of the biggest problems brand owners encounter. Then we prepare you for a major threat to your brand so that you don't get blindsided. Finally, we lay out a plan for kicking a crisis management plan into high gear, when and if the need arises.

If all goes well, you'll never need to implement the advice in this chapter. But follow it anyway, just in case. Your preparation and ability to respond promptly someday may be the key to saving your brand's equity.

Handle with Care: Avoiding Brand Equity Landmines

Most brand-damaging events fall into one of these categories:

✔ **A lapse in social responsibility:** For example, some apparel brands have had their images tainted by news that goods are manufactured in factories where worker mistreatment occurs.

✔ **A lapse in corporate behavior:** For examples, look at the business stories of the early 2000s about companies that cooked the books, violated regulations, and used loopholes to maximize shareholder value, minimizing brand equity in the process.

✔ **A lapse in personal behavior of a high-profile executive, spokesperson, or leading brand representative:** Examples of this kind of situation include the brand damage that Hertz faced after spokesperson O.J. Simpson's double-murder trial, Martha Stewart Living Omnimedia's position after Stewart's stock trading-related trial and conviction, and the state of the Catholic Church following scandals involving abuses by priests. In each case, negative news about the brand's representatives translated to negative news about the brand, risking the brand's reputation and necessitating prompt and extensive implementation of the brand protection measures detailed in this chapter.

✔ **Death or sudden departure of a high-profile corporate leader:** For example, consider the impact of Dr. Robert Atkins's death on Atkins Nutritionals, Inc. Within days of Atkins's untimely death in 2003 from a fall on an icy sidewalk, headlines asked, "Is the Atkins brand toast?" The answer followed in August 2005 when the company filed for Chapter 11 bankruptcy court protection.

✔ **Product failures, malfunctions, or dangers:** Whether real or perceived, these problems may be the result of human errors, inadequate or overlooked quality procedures and controls, violations of procedures, circulation of misinformation, consumer misunderstandings, or out-and-out product sabotage. Examples range from a questionable chemical that endangered the Crayola brand years ago to cyanide-tainted Tylenol Extra Strength capsules that resulted from product tampering and triggered one of the most effective crisis management programs in the history of public relations.

✔ **Crises that result from natural or manmade disasters or accidents:** These events can range from earthquakes or fires to snipers or terrorists.

Before you plan how to handle brand threats, take some time to plan how to avoid them if you can.

The best offense is a good defense. To defend yourself, you need to take two essential steps:

1. **Identify potential threats.**

   Go through the preceding list to identify the kinds of threats that may take a toll on your brand reputation. Then assess the likelihood of those threats actually occurring. For any threat that appears to loom large, work in advance to reduce vulnerability by establishing systems and protective actions that steer your organization away from the potential risks.

2. Prepare a brand crisis management plan.

Prepare a plan complete with assignments for who will lead and serve on the crisis management team, what communication procedures will be followed, and the steps that will get a clear, consistent message out to all affected audiences.

Identifying potential threats

While your business environment is calm, take time to imagine some of the worst-case scenarios your brand may face. Then assess how significantly each threat could affect the strength of your brand, your business, and your reputation. To identify all potential threats, take these steps:

1. Consider potential brand threats that may negatively impact your brand image.

Refer to the preceding list of brand-damaging event categories to prompt your thinking.

2. Rank the likelihood of each brand threat occurring.

For instance, a privately held service business with no shareholders and no production facilities has a low likelihood of encountering a threat from a lapse of corporate behavior. If that same service business is headed by an owner with a high-profile, jet-set lifestyle, however, the likelihood of a real or perceived lapse of personal behavior may be high.

3. Determine which of your brand attributes would be most affected should your brand encounter each potential brand threat.

For example, if your business has to deal with news of a product failure, brand attributes such as safety, precision craftsmanship, or quality would be affected.

4. Rank the impact of each attribute that may be affected on the overall strength of your brand.

For example, if your brand is known primarily for its safety record and suddenly sustains a safety lapse, the impact on brand strength would be high.

Use the chart shown in Figure 19-1 as you assess the likelihood that various potential threats will impact attributes that are important to the strength of your brand image. Wherever you see a likely brand threat to a high-impact brand attribute, take preventive action by fortifying systems and procedures in order to avoid a brand-shaking crisis.

EVALUATING IMPACT OF BRAND THREATS ON BRAND STRENGTH							
In any row that you check "high" in both the Likelihood and Impact columns, the brand threat is both real and potentially highly damaging.							
Potential Brand Threat	✔ Likelihood			Which of your brand attributes would be most affected by the brand threat? (Performance, Design, Prestige, Reliability, Safety, Comfort, Luxury, Expertise, and so on)	✔ Impact of the affected attribute on your brand strength		
	Low	Medium	High		Low	Medium	High
Lapse of social responsibility (due to hiring policies, vendor policies, production processes, and so on)	☐	☐	☐		☐	☐	☐
Lapse in corporate behavior (due to accounting discrepancies; violation of environmental or other regulations; violation of trust of consumers, investors, stockholders, and so on)	☐	☐	☐		☐	☐	☐
Lapse of personal behavior of high-profile owner or leader, spokesperson, or other brand representative (due to legal issues, personal troubles, and so on)	☐	☐	☐		☐	☐	☐
Death or sudden departure of corporate leader	☐	☐	☐		☐	☐	☐
Product failure, malfunction, or danger (whether real or rumored)	☐	☐	☐		☐	☐	☐
Natural or human-caused disaster or accident that affects business access, product delivery, or safety of consumers and employees.	☐	☐	☐		☐	☐	☐

Figure 19-1:
Assessing threats to your strongest brand attributes.

Taking preemptive strikes against brand threats

Complete the chart in Figure 19-1, and scan your results for any rows in which you've checked "medium" or "high" in both the second and fourth columns. These rows indicate areas where your brand faces a strong likelihood of encountering a threat that could shake your reputation to the core.

For each high-risk, high-impact threat, develop both a strategy to reduce the risk and the capability to deal with the threat should it happen. Go so far as to share your preemptive plans with those who have a stake in your brand — from employees to customers to suppliers to investors.

For example, Berkshire Hathaway is a publicly traded company controlled by Warren Buffett, one of the most renowned and richest investors in the world. When it comes to Berkshire Hathaway's brand attributes, the wisdom and wit of Warren Buffett soar right to the top of the list. As a result, the departure of Buffett, who has run the company since 1965, is a valid brand threat. It's also a threat from which the company doesn't run or hide. The 2005 Berkshire Hathaway annual report includes a section titled "Succession Planning" that begins with the paragraph, "As owners, you are naturally concerned about whether I will insist on continuing as CEO after I begin to fade and, if so, how the board will handle that problem. You also want to know what happens if I should die tonight." The rest of the section explains, in detail, how the company is prepared to handle the transition in a way that protects the security of the company and shareholder investments. It ends with the assurance, "We have an outstanding group of directors, and they will always do what's right for shareholders. And while we are on the subject, I feel terrific."

Take a straightforward approach when owning up to and addressing your own brand threats. Follow these steps:

1. **Face facts.**

   Where you know you face a risk, admit it. Trying to wish it away is never a decent strategy. If you're vulnerable because of lax production policies, admit it. If the public places high confidence in your high-profile but aging leader, admit it. Regardless of the threat, if it's real and looming, shed light on it and begin examining how best to minimize the threat.

2. **Gather a team to discuss risks.**

   Form a brand threat management committee to consider potential threats from a number of viewpoints. Involve not just brand management staff but also managers from customer service, production, financial management, and other departments. Discuss what kinds of events may trigger the brand threat and how each can be preempted.

3. Take preventive action.

If the threat is real and the risk is high, address it head-on. Enact new policies. Install new procedures. Establish a succession plan. Create evacuation procedures. Address high-risk behaviors. Take whatever steps are necessary and effective to admit and reduce or erase vulnerabilities that could damage your brand image in the future.

Be Prepared: Reacting to Brand Threats

If the worst happens and your brand reputation is attacked by internal or outside forces, be ready to control the news, tell the story, remedy the problem, and assure the public that it won't happen again.

Public relations professionals talk about a *golden hour* during which you can control the story and move quickly to save your brand image from disaster. Yet too many companies spend the first hour following a brand threat wringing their hands and trying to figure out what steps to take. By the time they're ready to move, the story is out of their hands and being told by others, often with inaccuracies and from perspectives that damage the brand even further.

Commit to developing a brand crisis management plan that includes these components:

- ✔ **Who's who** on your management team, including who will serve as the primary and secondary spokespersons, who will provide legal or technical advice, and who will help staff the plan.

- ✔ **Whom to contact** in the event of a crisis. Prepare a list with home, office, fax, and cell phone numbers; e-mail addresses; and mailing addresses for

  - Emergency and security contacts

  - Top executives and managers

  - Business and financial partners

  - Media contacts

  - Employees

  - Key contacts in your community, industry, and distribution channels

  - Key customers

- ✔ **What to say**, including what happened, what you're doing to make it right, and how it won't happen again — all in terms that describe your concern for the public and not simply your actions to minimize corporate or brand loss. Remember, you can't plan your exact message in advance, but you can plan what your message needs to convey.

> ✔ **What your strategy is,** including plans for releasing the news, establishing and staffing physical and online media centers, handling heightened interest through expanded and even back-up phone and online capacity, and providing ongoing updates regarding how you're working to remedy the problem and prevent it from recurring.

The following sections cover each of these components in more detail.

Compiling a list of who's who

Be ready to activate a crisis management program by knowing in advance exactly who will serve on the management and communication team. Fill the roles explained in each of the following sections.

Primary spokesperson

Each communications crisis needs one calm, knowledgeable person to serve as a spokesperson that presents facts, fields questions, and provides an interface between the media and the brand. In small businesses or organizations, the CEO or the owner often takes on spokesperson responsibilities simply because no one else in the organization has a high enough profile to fill the role. In larger organizations, the person who serves as the communications expert (usually the vice president or director of public relations) assumes the task.

When other qualified candidates are available, many organizations avoid naming the CEO as primary spokesperson. The reasoning isn't that the CEO can't fill the role but rather that, if media representatives are trained to deal with the CEO, they won't settle for statements from a secondary spokesperson. As a result, if the CEO isn't available, media representatives may hold their questions, and potentially damaging information lapses may occur as a result.

As you appoint your spokesperson, be sure he or she is trained in your brand story and message as well as in media relations, including how to conduct and manage interviews and media coverage. Also be sure the spokesperson is

> ✔ Capable of communicating and presenting information well
>
> ✔ Comfortable and experienced in front of cameras and in media interviews
>
> ✔ Knowledgeable about your organization
>
> ✔ Credible, trustworthy, and an empathetic representative to those both within and outside your organization
>
> ✔ Able to inspire confidence and explain issues clearly and without jargon
>
> ✔ Aware of the full scope of the issue and the range of experts who can provide additional information to reporters
>
> ✔ Calm, sincere, and likeable

Name a high-level person within your organization, such as a vice president or your top communication officer, as your primary spokesperson. Avoid naming a lawyer as the primary spokesperson. Doing so indicates that you have legal concerns, which translates to guilt in the minds of consumers.

Secondary spokesperson

Your primary spokesperson can't always be on-call, so name a back-up spokesperson with similar capabilities so that a fully informed person is always available to media and others.

If your primary spokesperson is your CEO, be sure that your secondary spokesperson is a high-level company officer or owner who shares similar clout. Otherwise, media will want to wait to talk with the CEO, potentially costing your brand an opportunity to provide breaking news and facts to the public.

Expert advisors

Depending upon the nature of the brand crisis, you may need to involve representatives from various outside organizations to provide specific information on anything from medical to legal to police activities.

In such cases, ask each outside organization to name its own primary and secondary spokespersons rather than make comments through a long list of different representatives. This arrangement helps you limit the number of people who are explaining the crisis to the public. Otherwise, consumers hear bits and pieces of the story from a mind-boggling number of different representatives, triggering confusion and a lack of confidence in your business and brand.

Your CEO

Regardless of whether your CEO serves as the primary crisis spokesperson, he or she must lead the response to a brand threat, getting involved in the very first moments and signing off on every element of the communication plan so that no second-guessing or finger-pointing occurs along the way of dealing with the problem.

Knowing who to call

In advance of any crisis, prepare a crisis communication contact list that contains full contact information for the following:

- **Internal contacts,** including executives, crisis team members, managers, employees, union representatives, and others
- **Emergency contacts,** including police, security, and government offices

✔ **Media contacts,** including reporters or editors at local, national, international, and trade or industry media that have an interest in news of your organization

✔ **Investor and analyst contacts**, from your local bankers to your shareholders to investors or potential investors

✔ **Community and industry contacts,** from your local chamber of commerce to your industry or trade association to key partners, subcontractors, and competitors

✔ **Business partners,** including customers, suppliers, and distributors

✔ **Special interest contacts,** including environmental, safety, consumer, or other groups that take an interest in your business

List the sequence in which contacts should be made to ensure that those who most need to know are reached most immediately. Also make sure that copies of the contact list are readily available in multiple locations inside and outside your business, including in the offices of your CEO, communications or public relations director, top-level executives, and in a password-protected section of your Web site.

Working out what to do and say

The first priority of every brand manager is to avoid brand crises in the first place. That's why it's important to regularly assess and take proactive steps to defend against the kinds of threats that are likely to attack your brand strength. The chart in Figure 19-1 helps you with this task.

Sometimes, though, in spite of all the best efforts in the world, bad things happen to good brands. If your brand were to undergo a crisis, you need to be ready to launch into defensive action.

A single set of advice applies to *all* crisis situations: Tell the truth, be as complete as possible, issue statements immediately, and aim to restore trust as quickly as possible.

Instead of wasting precious moments debating what to do, take the following actions immediately:

1. **Activate your emergency communication system by contacting those who need to know first about the threatening event.**

2. **Convene your brand crisis communication team.**

   Immediately assess the situation. Determine whether the situation affects your organization legally, financially, administratively, operationally, or in other ways.

3. **Craft the message you'll deliver to explain what happened and what your organization will do to restore safety and confidence.**

   When writing your message, limit it to a few sentences. If you can't explain the situation in seconds, people aren't able to grasp and understand it, and they turn to others for what may be erroneous explanations. Prepare a message that meets these criteria:

   - It has no more than three key points that you use to explain the situation, and each point is summarized in fewer than ten words. For each point, prepare up to three supporting facts that your spokesperson can provide as additional explanation.

   - It includes no industry jargon or words that can't be understood by someone with an eighth grade education.

   - It's relevant and delivered in terms that matter to those who are affected by the situation. This isn't the time to talk about how your organization is affected. This is the time to show that you care about all involved parties and are dealing with the situation on their behalf.

4. **Name who will serve as your primary spokesperson and secondary spokesperson and what additional experts you will need to call on to explain the situation.**

5. **Make a list of a dozen or so of the toughest questions you think your spokesperson will be asked.**

   For each question, prepare and rehearse a short response that includes the name of the person who can provide additional legal, technical, or other specific information.

6. **Have your message and your prepared answers to anticipated questions reviewed and approved by those responsible for the affected functions as well as by your company's CEO and legal team.**

7. **Prepare a news release that explains the situation.**

   Tell who, what, where, when, why, and how you're dealing with the situation, using your approved message and Chapter 10's advice on writing releases.

8. **Make your announcement and distribute your news release as quickly as possible.**

   Notify employees and all organization insiders immediately before or at the same time that you release the story to news media. In addition to circulating your prepared release, deliver a concise statement that summarizes key points and focuses on the steps you're taking to achieve a positive outcome for all affected parties.

Pushing through the pain

One of the most legendary examples of a successfully implemented crisis management plan comes out of the early 1980s, when packages of Tylenol Extra Strength capsules were maliciously filled with cyanide-laced capsules, resealed, and placed on retail shelves in the Chicago area.

Johnson & Johnson, parent company of McNeil Consumer Products Company, the maker of Tylenol, learned of the crisis through the kind of phone call no brand owner ever wants to receive. A Chicago news reporter called to report that people weren't just sick but were dying from poisoned Tylenol product.

Johnson & Johnson wasted no time in launching a crisis response. The company immediately convened a crisis strategy team charged with devising a response to two questions (in this order): How do we protect the people? and How do we save the product?

First, the team used the media to alert consumers nationwide not to consume any form of Tylenol until further notice. They withdrew all Tylenol packages from Chicago-area shelves and stopped all advertising and production. When a tainted product was found outside the Chicago area, they went a step farther and pulled every bottle of Tylenol from every retail shelf nationwide. Simultaneously, Johnson & Johnson offered to exchange all purchased Tylenol capsules with Tylenol tablets, at a potential cost to the company of millions of dollars.

The financial impact on Johnson & Johnson was enormous, but the focus of the company's efforts remained firmly on consumer safety rather than on dollars lost. It established hot lines and issued a constant stream of news updates. Not once did the company spotlight the fact that it had nothing to do with the tainted product. Instead, it put up a $100,000 reward and worked with the police, FBI, and other government agencies to help find those responsible, all the while working internally to devise tamper-proof packaging to protect against such a disaster recurring in the future.

Within months, Tylenol returned to pharmacies and retail shelves, this time wrapped in triple-safety sealed packaging. To bring consumers back to the brand, the company circulated coupons to be applied to new purchases of Tylenol. It launched a new ad campaign, and more than 2,000 salespeople were enlisted to make presentations to members of the medical community to inspire support for the product reintroduction.

Tylenol quickly reclaimed 27 percent of the pain reliever market and today is one of the top-selling over-the-counter drugs in the United States. This fact is a strong testament to the way Johnson & Johnson rapidly responded to the crisis by taking responsibility, putting consumer safety first, working with the media, and, ultimately, recovering from the greatest brand crisis in the pharmaceutical industry.

---

9. **Open a media center where you can meet with reporters in a location that allows them access to the story yet provides adequate distance from the hub of activity so that they don't overhear unplanned comments.**

10. **Activate an emergency Web site, or add designated pages to your online pressroom to present breaking news and background information.**

    See Chapter 10 for assistance in building an online pressroom.

11. **Constantly update and distribute information that provides situation and response updates including steps your organization is taking to ensure the safety of people and products.**

    Remain consistent, forthright, available, and responsive to all who are affected or who have questions or concerns.

12. **When the crisis subsides, assess the impact on your brand and begin work immediately to restore your brand strength by following the steps detailed in Chapter 17.**

Following crisis communications dos and don'ts

Whether you're in the throes of a brand crisis or simply preparing your organization for such a situation, keep this advice in mind:

- ✔ Do be caring and genuinely concerned.
- ✔ Do take responsibility.
- ✔ Do explain the situation immediately in a few sentences that can be widely understood by the general public.
- ✔ Do prepare a concise message and share it within your organization so that everyone is talking from the same page and telling the same truths.
- ✔ Do be prepared to present complete back-up information and explanations upon request, but don't offer more information than requested or you risk confusing the message.
- ✔ Do avoid jargon or language that the general public doesn't understand.
- ✔ Do keep your employees informed of all new developments.
- ✔ Do plan and share remedies for the situation and controls that will prevent it from recurring.
- ✔ Do answer questions in a way that allows you to reiterate the key points of your approved message.
- ✔ Do prepare updated background information and news releases prior to each new announcement or major interview.

✔ Do realize that the spokesperson should provide facts that have been assembled and confirmed by your organization and its expert resources and should stick to the approved points.

✔ Do limit the number of people who explain the crisis to the public. Include only your primary spokesperson, a secondary spokesperson, and a handful of designated expert spokespeople from within or outside your organization who are selected to explain legal, medical, technical, or other aspects of the situation.

✔ Do rehearse presentations and responses to anticipated questions.

✔ Do follow up immediately on all information requests.

✔ Do refer questions requiring technical or legal responses to the designated expert spokespeople.

✔ Do stay calm and positive and demonstrate genuine care and concern.

✔ Don't veer from approved messages.

✔ Don't ask to be "off the record."

✔ Don't respond to negative questions by repeating negative phrases. Instead, address the issue in positive terms.

✔ Don't delay responding to media. If you need additional time, return the call and schedule a return call shortly, by which time you should have the appropriate information to share.

Part VI
The Part of Tens

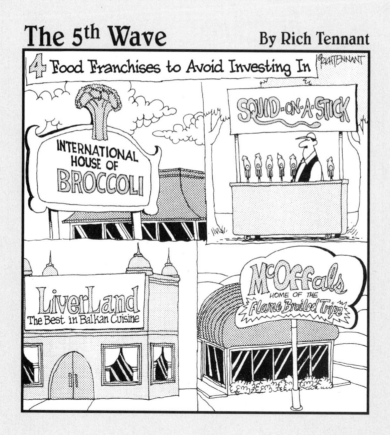

In this part . . .

As you build and burnish your brand, from time to time you'll seek a quick answer or some on-the-spot advice or information. Those are the times when the chapters in this part will come to the rescue.

Each of the upcoming chapters features a concise summary of advice in the famous *For Dummies* ten-item list format.

We share ten branding golden rules and offer advice on how to dodge ten big branding mistakes. Because examples are always helpful, we examine the qualities of the world's most valuable brands.

Chapter 20

Ten Truths about Branding

In This Chapter

▶ Getting to the root of the best brands

▶ Making the human connection

▶ Benefiting from great brand experiences

*T*he best name, logo, ads, and efforts can't compensate for a weak brand. But what's a brand? And how do you build a strong one? The ten truths presented in this chapter offer up answers to these burning questions and summarize the golden rules of great branding.

Branding Starts with Positioning

Your *position* is the birthplace of your brand. It's the unique space in the consumer's mind that only your offering can fill. You need to determine and stake your position before you develop the brand that will live there.

Positioning is the process of finding an unfulfilled want or need in the consumer's mind and addressing it with a distinctively different and ideally suited offering.

Remember these rules about positioning:

✔ **Your position must be open.** Otherwise, you'll need to dislodge an existing brand — and that's big and costly challenge to tackle.

✔ **Your position must be based on a unique point of difference that's believable and truly attractive to consumers.**

✔ **Your point of difference must be one that you can deliver with such consistency that every experience with your brand reminds customers of why they chose and remain loyal to your brand.**

Chapter 4 helps you conduct the research necessary to find an open position you can fill, and Chapter 5 helps you stake claim to the position you find.

A Brand Is a Promise Well Kept

Brands are promises that people believe in. Your brand, in essence, is a promise about who you are and what unique benefits you deliver that gets reinforced every single time people come in contact with any facet of your organization — whether as customers, prospects, investors, employees, suppliers, friends, or neighbors, or through any other dealing.

Your promise is the pledge upon which you stake your brand reputation. It's the expectation that you live up to every time people experience your brand, whether through advertising, promotions, buying experiences, service encounters, or any other contact.

A successful brand strategy results in an accurate reflection of what you are and what you promise to all those who come into contact with your business.

For help defining your promise, flip to Chapter 6.

Branding Happens from the Inside Out

Your brand is a reflection of what you stand for, so it has to align perfectly with the values and purpose of your organization. Otherwise, the identity you present to the world doesn't synch with the identity that resides at the core of your business, and consumers sense the lack of credibility and tune out your marketing efforts as a result.

To arrive at a brand that perfectly reflects the essence of your organization, begin the branding process by writing three essential statements:

- **Your vision statement,** which defines the long-term aspirations of your organization and the ultimate good you want to achieve
- **Your mission statement,** which defines what you do for others and the approach you'll follow to achieve your vision
- **Your brand identity statement,** which covers what you do, those you serve, and the positive difference you promise to make

Chapter 6 includes statement templates and step-by-step advice to follow in writing these statements. Chapter 9 helps you win understanding and buy-in for your brand within your organization before you even think about announcing it to the outside world.

Consistency Builds Brands

After you're clear about what you stand for, you're ready to deliver your product, promise, and brand experience with total consistency. Doing so puts the odds strongly in your favor that you'll win out over brands that shift with the wind, regardless of how beautifully they've polished their identities or their marketing materials.

Create a consistent brand that customers can count on by

- Displaying a consistent look
- Projecting a consistent tone
- Delivering a consistent level of quality, as demonstrated through consistent communications and consistent products and services
- Being consistently true to the heart of your brand

The chapters in Part III help you present your brand with consistency through publicity, advertising, and online efforts, and Chapter 14 provides a blueprint for delivering a great and unfailingly consistent brand experience.

People Power Brands

Brands are made or broken by human encounters that either advance or erode brand promises. Passionate employees and passionate customers — in that order — power great brands. If you develop brand understanding, enthusiasm, and commitment within your organization, customer understanding, enthusiasm, and commitment will follow.

A great brand name, logo, promise, and communication program are essential ingredients for brand success, but you also need brand champions, beginning with the leader of your organization and including every single person who affects the consumer's experience with your offering.

Chapter 13 tells you how to suit up a team of brand champions within your organization. Chapter 14 helps you ignite customer passion.

Brands Live in Consumers' Minds

When people see or hear your name, they automatically conjure up impressions and memories that determine what they believe about you. Their notions may be the result of firsthand encounters with your product or organization. Their notions may be based on communications they've seen or heard — anything from your ads to displays, signs, news articles, even your logo on Little League hats. Their notions may result from secondhand recaps of other customers' experiences that are passed along online or by word-of-mouth.

Regardless of whether the beliefs customers hold about you are many or few, good or bad, or accurate or inaccurate, they comprise the image of your brand in your customer's mind and influence how your customer thinks and buys.

Your brand image lives in your customers' minds whether you intentionally put it there or not. Good branding is the way of making sure that the brand image you have is the brand image you want.

Brand Names Unlock Brand Images

Your brand is a set of memories that's uncovered when people see or hear your name.

The right name establishes your brand from the day it's announced, and it grows with your business and your vision as you reach into new market areas, new geographic regions, and even new product areas.

A great brand name should

- ✔ Reflect the brand character of your business
- ✔ Describe your offering and convey an association to the meaning of your brand
- ✔ Convey or be consistent with your brand promise
- ✔ Be easy and pleasant to say and unique and memorable so that, over time, it appreciates into an asset that you can harvest through premium pricing, licensing, or even a sale to a new owner

Naming your brand is the most challenging, momentous, and necessary phase in the process of branding. Count on Chapter 7 to walk you through the steps involved.

Brand Experiences Trump Brand Messages

In branding, what you say pales in comparison to what you do.

When consumers gravitate to one brand over the others, their decisions are rarely based on reactions to marketing messages alone. Instead, consumers rely on their own experiences. They choose and stay with brands that they believe will keep their promises based on what the customers have personally seen and sensed.

To create a brand experience capable of moving markets and instilling loyalty, convey, reinforce, and amplify your brand promise through every encounter with your organization — from the office of the CEO down and from the first inquiry to the last service call. If one portion of the experience falls short of consumer expectations — from one poorly handled phone call to one erroneous invoice — your brand image suffers.

"Be the brand" isn't just talk, it's the key to branding success. To develop a team of brand champions prepared to deliver a great brand experience and to put your brand experience to the test, turn to Chapters 9 and 13.

Brands Need to Start and Stay Relevant

To win and keep a slot in the consumer's mind, your brand needs to begin and remain credible, competitive, current, and relevant to customer wants, needs, and interests. That means you need to tune in to market conditions, consumer preferences, and cultural trends not only when you first establish your brand but also on a regular basis as your brand ages.

Markets change, and businesses change. When they do, brands that remain stuck in times past pay a high price in terms of credibility and competitiveness.

Follow the advice in Chapter 4 to conduct customer and competitive research before you launch your brand and afterward. Then use Chapter 17 as your guide as you determine what kind of brand update may be in order — from an evolutionary revitalization of your brand logo and look to a revolutionary, full-scale rebranding following a major merger, acquisition, or redirected business strategy.

Either way, the revised brand strategy that you adopt should represent your brand vision for at least ten years, which is about the frequency that brands should undergo major change.

Brands Are Valuable Assets

In the world's most successful businesses, the brand is often the most valuable single asset. When companies with great brands are sold, the value of the brand often accounts for as much as half of the sale price. Plus, brand value translates into everyday economic benefits, including:

- ✔ Premium pricing and reduced price sensitivity
- ✔ Lower costs of sales and promotions
- ✔ Higher market share
- ✔ Reduced threat of competition
- ✔ Greater employee satisfaction
- ✔ Higher recognition by consumers, industry leaders, media, investors, and analysts

Count on the information in Chapter 15 as you assess the value and calculate the equity of your brand. Then check out Chapter 16 to find out how to protect your brand equity as you leverage your brand value into growth opportunities through brand extensions, licensing, and cobranding opportunities.

Chapter 21

Ten Branding Mistakes and How to Avoid Them

In This Chapter
▶ Establishing the right brand in the right way
▶ Doing what it takes to maintain your brand

Some brands get off to great starts. Some are wobbly from the get-go. Others start well and then lose their way through lack of focus, discipline, and follow-through on brand strategies, brand promises, and reliably consistent brand experiences.

This chapter describes ten branding mistakes to steer clear of and provides tips to keep your brand moving continuously in the right direction, constantly gaining esteem and equity as a result.

Thinking of Branding as a Quick Fix

The mistake: When business is down, when consumer interest ebbs, or when competition surges, the idea of branding pops up as some miracle cure for transforming product perceptions and jump-starting success. In the heat of the moment, otherwise cool-headed professionals begin to believe that a new logo — and maybe even a new name, a new tagline, or a new marketing message — will serve as a remedy for all that ails the bottom line.

Those who look at branding as a marketing quick fix make the mistake of thinking that a brand is just a cosmetic application. They think that a new and improved brand identity will be the formula for a new and improved brand image. It doesn't work that way, though, because a successful brand has to go all the way to the core of an organization.

The remedy: Before you create or alter the face of your brand, be sure you're creating an accurate reflection of what's at the base of your brand. The part of your brand that rises into public view — your name, logo, and marketing materials — must mirror the mission, vision, values, culture, leadership, and management that lies at the heart and soul of your organization. Otherwise, a credibility crisis looms large.

Chapter 6 helps you define the essence of your organization and how it operates and then guides your thinking as you put your brand promise, brand character, and brand identity into words. Then, and only then, are you ready to name your brand, design your logo, and create marketing materials and a brand experience to convey your brand accurately and successfully in your world. The process isn't quick, but it's worth it!

Starting with a Weak Identity

The mistake: Weak identities reveal themselves on first sight. They appear in the form of names that limit the scope and success of the brands they represent. Or they're displayed as logos that, at-a-glance, convey that they were created on shoestring budgets by organizations with little chance of competing with big, established businesses.

As long as the businesses represented by weak names and logos are satisfied to remain in the confines that their identities dictate, all's well. But if they want to expand into new product lines, new market arenas, or new competitive spheres, their weak identities are heavy anchors dragging down their success.

The remedy: Invest the time and money required to develop a strong name and logo when you first establish your brand. Remember these points:

- ✔ **In most cases, your name will live as long as your business does, so choose, register, and protect a name that you can grow with over years and decades.** Great brand names travel through time, trends, markets, and even strategic redirections. Settle on a name that conveys your brand promise, supports your brand image, and that's unique, pleasant to say, and easy to recall — all without confining your brand to a specific product or market area. (Chapter 7 has naming advice.)

- ✔ **Your logo will become the immediately identifiable face of your brand, so make it a strong, simple, unique design that reproduces well in all forms of communication and scales up and down in size to look good on anything from business cards to giant signs.** Chapter 8 provides a guide to logo design along with the strong recommendation that you seek professional design assistance. When the time's right to update your look, turn to Chapter 17 for tips on how to revitalize your logo so that it remains a contemporary representation of your brand.

Forgetting the Rule of One

The mistake: Businesses that barely have the budgets and marketing staff required to build one brand try to build two or three or more. In doing so, they dilute the expertise and funding they can devote to any one and build brand strength for none.

The remedy: Unless you're sure that you have the marketing budget and expertise required to build and support multiple brands, stick to the Rule of One: Build one brand for your business rather than a business full of many brands. Apply the Rule of One by following this advice:

- Build a single brand that can preside over all your offerings.

- Introduce each new product or service as an offering under your one-and-only brand. This strategy allows each new product to capitalize upon the credibility of your brand while boosting the strength of your brand through the success of each new offering.

- Wipe the term *subbrand* from your branding vocabulary. Turn to Chapter 16 for information on how subbrands confuse customers and weaken brand management.

Chapter 2 has tips on how to manage a number of products under your one brand, and Chapter 7 can help you develop a family of names under a single brand umbrella. Chapter 16 branches out with tips on how to extend your brand to new products, cobranded offerings, and licensing opportunities.

If you decide to create separate brands for individual products or services, build a separate business unit for each new brand. Separate business units allow each offering to stand on its own, drawing on its own resources and building independent value that you can spin off or sell in the future.

Failing to Differentiate

The mistake: If you can't tell customers what you do best, they have no reason to choose your offering. If you don't give them a clear reason to choose your product, they opt for a different, more distinct solution. And if they think that all available offerings deliver the same value and quality, they simply buy whatever's available at the lowest price.

The remedy: Find a distinguishing characteristic that causes your offering to excel over available alternatives, and build your brand around that point of difference. To differentiate your brand

> ✔ Determine unique aspects of your offering that address genuine market interests or needs.
>
> ✔ Develop a brand identity and brand message to achieve awareness of the unique values consumers receive only when they work with your business or buy your product.
>
> ✔ Reinforce your point of difference every time consumers come into contact with your name, your product, your staff, or your brand experience.

Chapter 5 can help you find your brand's unique position in the marketplace, and Chapter 14 covers delivering your point of difference at every consumer contact point.

Failing to Launch

The mistake: Even business owners that love groundbreakings, ribbon cuttings, grand openings, and lavish celebrations underestimate the importance of staging a brand launch. Either they simply start using a new brand identity and call it a launch, or they invest in a formal marketplace launch of the brand before they take the time to gain brand understanding and buy-in within their own organizations.

If you fail to launch your brand, you lose a great one-time opportunity to make news with your brand identity, point of difference, promise, and message.

If you fail to launch internally first, you lose the chance to unite your team behind the brand. As a result, you almost certainly set your organization up for lapses in delivery of a great and consistent brand experience simply because a good many of your employees don't understand what in the world your brand's all about.

The remedy: Launch your brand from the inside out, bringing every aspect of your business into alignment with your brand promise, personality, and character before you raise the curtain and introduce your brand in your marketplace (see Chapter 9). Chapters 10, 11, and 12 are full of information on how to take your brand public via publicity, advertising, and online communications.

Failing to Protect and Defend

The mistake: Brand owners get complacent. They think that ironclad protective measures aren't necessary to protect their brands from infringement or misuse, so they fail to obtain or defend trademarks, lock up domain names, write brand usage guidelines, or enforce their own brand usage rules when they're broken. Before long, brand names are in jeopardy, brand consistency is at risk, and brand value plummets.

The remedy: Protect your brand in three important ways:

1. **File your name with appropriate government offices, and obtain brand trademarks if your sphere of business crosses state or national boundaries.**

2. **Establish, adopt, and enforce usage guidelines so that those within or outside your organization don't tamper with your brand identity.**

3. **Enforce your rules by following up on every brand usage infraction, without fail.**

   If you don't follow up on infractions, the least that can happen is erosion of the strength of your brand presentation. The worst that can happen is loss of your trademarks due to your own abandonment or complacency.

Check out Chapter 18 for step-by-step advice to follow in order to defend your brand.

Believing That What You Say Is More Important Than What You Do

The mistake: Even with the best name and logo, the most awesome brand launch, and brand marketing materials that win best-of-show in all creative competitions, brands suffer if they don't live up to their promises and deliver the kind of products and service that create loyal and passionate consumers.

The remedy: Realize that your brand is either made or broken not by what you say but by what you do. Consumers base their brand impressions upon the caliber and consistency of their experiences with the brand. To establish and maintain the kind of brand experience that builds passion, loyalty, and brand value, follow the advice in Chapter 14 and take these steps:

1. **Identify every possible point of contact between your brand and your consumer, from pre-purchase encounters through the purchase experience and product usage, to post-purchase communications and customer service.**

2. **Evaluate each point of contact to see that you present your brand message, promise, look, and tone without fail and with total consistency.**

3. **Identify and correct any points of contact where the brand experience falls even slightly short of your brand promise.**

4. **Regularly audit your brand experience to insure against brand-eroding communication or service lapses.**

Underestimating the Value of Consistency

The mistake: Brand owners get bored. They get tired of their looks and messages, so they start improvising. They fiddle with their identities, putting some additional color here or there, adding a new tagline, maybe even embellishing their names or revising their logo designs. They try out new personalities in their marketing messages, sampling humorous approaches when they've always been staid and serious in the past, or trying to look or sound hip instead of keeping their usual conventional tone.

Just like that, consistency goes out the window along with the ability to convey the brand's identity and promise with the kind of clarity that inspires confidence in everyone from employees to consumers to investors and others.

The remedy: To build and maintain a strong brand, you have to be consistent, and to be consistent, you have to

- ✔ Insist that your logo appear exactly the same every single time it's reproduced, with no exceptions in typestyle, color, design, placement of the tagline, or presentation of every other element that contributes to the brand identity consumers know and count on (see Chapter 8).

- ✔ Put your brand promise into words (see Chapter 6) and then make sure it's kept at every point of encounter with your brand, whether with customers, employees, suppliers, associates, or prospects. Only by staying true to your word and consistently upholding your promise can you build trust and loyalty.

- ✔ Define and stay true to your brand character, which is the look and tone that conveys the personality of your organization.

- ✔ Create a set of brand usage guidelines to be followed by everyone who produces marketing materials for your business, and then name a brand cop to keep everyone's efforts in line (see Chapter 19).

If your brand needs updating, don't do it in a haphazard or ad hoc fashion. Take formal action, following the brand revitalization process outlined in Chapter 17.

Asking Your Brand to Stretch Too Far

The mistake: When a good brand extends its name to an iffy product or to a product that contradicts the brand message and promise or that erodes the emotional connection that the brand enjoys with consumers, the brand ends up hurting itself in the process of trying to help the launch of the new offering.

The remedy: Leveraging a brand name is a smart, lucrative action as long as the new offering is consistent with your brand message and promise and capable of deepening the emotional connection you've established with your customers.

When extending your brand, stay within your established product category or only move into categories that are very compatible with your established offering. Extend your brand only to new products that match up with consumer expectations of your brand in terms of quality, market position, and brand promise.

Be careful that your new offering isn't so similar to an existing offering that it confuses consumers, causing them to buy your new product instead of your established product (called *cannibalization*) or leading to selection dilemmas that result in no purchase at all.

Leveraging your brand into new product or market categories is one of the most valued perks of brand development. It allows you capitalize on the reputation you've built over time and apply it to new ventures that benefit from instant awareness and competitive advantage. Chapter 16 provides a good overview for how to seize brand extension opportunities without stretching your name to the breaking point.

Ignoring Brand Aging Signs

The mistake: Some brands get stuck in times past, and the brand owners are the last ones to notice. They're so busy fending off competitors and working to attract and keep business that they fail to notice when their brand identities no longer reflect the essence of their businesses, when their brand identities become out of step with current tastes and trends, or when their brand experiences become outdated, erratic, or otherwise unable to compete well in the contemporary environment.

The remedy: On a regular basis, a great brand undergoes the equivalent of a physical to see if it's experiencing any early warning signs that its age is starting to affect its health. Chapter 17 outlines all the symptoms to watch for in giving your brand a checkup, including:

- Major ownership or leadership changes that affect your mission, vision, values, or strategic direction
- Major changes to your product line or distribution channels
- Major changes to your market situation, including significantly increased competition or major shifts in consumer preferences and behaviors

✔ A merger or acquisition

✔ A brand that no longer reflects your changed business and market

✔ A brand message, experience, or identity that's become dated and out of synch with cultural trends and consumer interests and tastes

Some brand situations benefit from minor cosmetic repair and message realignment, whereas others require more significant revitalization or even total rebranding. Turn to Chapter 17 for help as you conduct a brand assessment and plan what kind of a brand revision, if any, is in order.

Chapter 22

Ten Traits of the World's Most Valuable Brands

*E*ach year, Interbrand, a global branding consultancy, and *BusinessWeek* magazine publish a ranking of the best global brands by value. The study is widely considered the most significant and influential brand and marketing survey. The 2006 report concluded that the following brands are the most valuable in the world:

#1 Coca-Cola	#11 Citi
#2 Microsoft	#12 Marlboro
#3 IBM	#13 Hewlett-Packard
#4 GE	#14 American Express
#5 Intel	#15 BMW
#6 Nokia	#16 Gillette
#7 Toyota	#17 Louis Vuitton
#8 Disney	#18 Cisco
#9 McDonald's	#19 Honda
#10 Mercedes-Benz	#20 Samsung

The traits that the Interbrand/*BusinessWeek* report found common to every brand on this list are summarized in this chapter.

As you dive into the branding process, prepare yourself to encounter the same conversation over and over. People will ask what you're doing, and when you say that you're developing a brand or managing a branding program, they'll give you a blank stare and ask (we know, we've heard it for years), "A brand? You mean like on a horse or cow?" Here's what to say: "No. A brand like on the products that you know and trust more than all others."

Then reel off the names of any of the brands in the preceding list. People will immediately recognize the names and begin to understand why you're devoting your efforts to build even a fraction of the awareness, credibility, and reputations these companies enjoy.

Instilling your brand with the ten traits in this chapter will put you well on your way.

Simple, Powerful Differentiation

A great brand holds a unique place in the minds of those who buy from, work for, or invest in the brand, whether financially or emotionally.

Great brands differentiate themselves in a way that's clear, easy to explain, and meaningful to consumers and all other stakeholders. They hold a unique position in the market because they provide benefits that no competitors can match.

To find and fill your position in the market and in your consumers' minds, turn to Chapters 4 and 5.

A Clear and Compelling Vision

Brands are built from the inside out. That means they originate in companies with clearly established mission, vision, and values statements that drive all organization and branding decisions. Then they express their beliefs in everything they say and do, from the products and services they offer to the staff they attract to the advertising and communications they send into the marketplace.

As you develop or dust off the mission, vision, and values that steer your organization, turn to Chapter 6.

A Promise Consumers Want and Believe

People get emotionally attached to brands that fill unmet or unaddressed wants and needs consistently and without fail. The greatest brands symbolize solutions that consumers want, need, understand, and believe in.

To write your brand promise, turn to Chapter 6.

Distinctive, Reliable, Superior Products and Services

Great brands deliver great products. They excel in product design, production, and packaging; they're known for superb communications; and they're heralded for excellent service before and after the sale.

To see that your product and service is consistent with the vision of your organization and the promise you make to consumers, turn to Chapter 4 for help conducting research.

A Strong, Memorable Brand Identity

Look at the list of great brands at the beginning of this chapter. Just seeing the names should unlock images in your mind of each brand's logo and possibly tagline, musical signature, and ad look as well. That's because each great brand puts forth a brand identity that's simple, strong, memorable, and presented without variation on every product, in every market, through every communication, and at every consumer contact point.

Chapters 7 and 8 offer advice on developing a great identity for your brand.

A Single, Consistently Presented Brand Message

A distinct and compelling brand message is at the heart of all great brand communications, regardless of the communication format or medium. Whether you encounter a great brand through its product or packaging, its print or broadcast ads, its online presence, or in person through a business experience, the character of the brand is always consistent, and the core brand message never varies.

Chapter 6 offers advice for putting your brand character and definition into words, and the chapters in Part III are full of tips for sending a consistent message into the marketplace, whether via public relations, advertising, promotions, or online communications.

An Amazing Brand Experience

So what's an amazing brand experience? It's an experience that positively reinforces the brand message and promise at every single point of consumer encounter. Great brand experiences start at the very first impression and continue without fail through the purchase deliberation, the buying process, and after the sale when awesome service generates the kind of customer brand passion that cements customer-brand relationships for life.

Turn to Chapter 14 for help putting your brand experience to the test.

Brand Allegiance from the Top Down

Great brands are built from the top down and from the inside out. Find a great brand (the list in this chapter puts 20 right in front of your eyes), and you'll find a business that's headed by a brand champion and staffed by a team of brand fans.

To develop high allegiance and commitment to your brand, start with those in the highest leadership and ownership positions and continue through to every staff person who has an impact on your product, promise, and brand experience. See Chapter 13 for advice.

Adaptability to Changing Times

Strong brands remain strong even as they migrate to new geographic areas, into new consumer groups, and through changing economic times and market conditions. In spite of changes in the competitive arena, economic conditions, consumer interests, or market trends, they stay relevant to consumer needs, interests, and tastes.

See Chapter 4 for help researching your brand's relevance, and flip to Chapter 17 for help revitalizing your brand if an update is in order.

Focus, Passion, and Persistence

The final common trait of those who build great brands: They have discipline, persistence, and long-term commitments to their brands. Those who get bored with their brands and start sampling with new marketplace positions, new points of distinction, new looks, and new variations on their brand promises never reach the league of great and valuable brands. The prize of sky-high brand equity goes only to those who stick to their brand messages and propositions with unwavering loyalty. Repetition may be boring, but it builds brands, and brands build value.

Appendix

Resources for Brand Managers

. . . .

*B*randing is a never-ending process that requires constant attention and up-to-date information in order to build and maintain a brand that's relevant, current, consistently presented, well protected, and strongly defended.

Branding For Dummies tells you what you need to know about each step in the branding process, and wherever possible, we direct you to additional resources to make your job easier and more successful.

As you begin to heighten the value and equity of your brand, though, you'll want to see and read more about what other great brand builders are up to. The following resources, most of which link you to hundreds of additional sources of information, are a gold mine.

Browsing Great Branding Web Sites

The Internet is an essential piece of the branding puzzle, so it comes as no surprise that it's also a source of so much useful, up-to-the-minute information. Start with the sites listed in this section.

Allaboutbranding.com

This site is run by DNA Design, one of New Zealand's leading design communications companies. Visit it to read a long list of branding articles, to see book recommendations and reviews, to browse brand definitions and brand quotes, and to put your own brand through a free self-test.

Brandchannel.com

Self-proclaimed as "the world's only online exchange about branding," this Web site is produced by Interbrand, a leading brand consultancy serving clients worldwide.

Brandchannel is an online magazine that provides a global perspective on branding. Sign on to read articles and papers, view lists of branding service providers, and get summaries of books on the topic of branding. You can also sign up for free weekly branding updates.

The site also includes a great glossary of branding terms and definitions at www.brandchannel.com/education_glossary.asp.

MarketingProfs.com

In its own words, this site "provides the know-how, analysis, and perspective of both professors who teach, research, and consult based on state-of-the-art marketing ideas *and* professionals who work in the trenches of marketing."

From the site's home page, click on Topics to access a wealth of information on branding as well as a long list of other topics ranging from advertising to customer service to search engine marketing and more.

Basic membership in MarketingProfs is free. Just click on Become a Member on the home page. Upon joining, you automatically start receiving the MarketingProfs newsletter, or you can subscribe only to receive the newsletter by following the key in the menu on the left-hand side of the screen.

To receive access to more in-depth marketing information, reports, virtual seminars, and a list of other benefits, sign up for a premium membership. Options include one-month, annual individual, or annual corporate memberships with varying dues.

Rebrand.com

Especially if you're getting ready to revitalize a brand, you'll find this site a great resource. It's full of branding case studies and advice on brand repositioning, revitalizing, and redesign. It also features a showcase of success stories from around the world.

Adding to Your Branding Library

If you're looking to dive deeper into various aspects of brand development and management, check out these books:

- *Designing Brand Identity,* 2nd Edition, by Alina Wheeler (Wiley)
- *Positioning: The Battle For Your Mind* by Al Reis and Jack Trout (McGraw-Hill)

> ✔ *The 22 Immutable Laws of Branding: How to Build a Product or Service into a World-Class Brand* by Al Ries and Laura Ries (HarperCollins)
>
> ✔ *Married to the Brand: Why Consumers Bond With Some Brands For Life* by William J. McEwen (Gallup Press)
>
> ✔ *A New Brand World: Eight Principles for Achieving Brand Leadership in the Twenty-First Century* by Scott Bedbury with Stephen Fenichell (Viking Adult Press)

Flipping through Branding Magazines

The magazine rack in any bookstore or library presents an almost unlimited display of brand messages delivered via ads in publications targeting tots to seniors with lifestyle interests ranging from archeology to zoology and everything in between. Pick up any publication for creative inspiration. For specific brand development advice, give special attention to the following magazines.

Brandweek

Brandweek publishes print and online magazines as well as newsletters, special reports, and directories aimed at helping large and small brand developers and managers.

To read the publication online, go to www.brandweek.com. On the site, you can click to begin receiving Brandweek's free newsletters. You can also enroll for a combination print and online subscription to Brandweek that allows access to subscriber-only content.

BusinessWeek/Interbrand Annual Global Brand Report

This report shows the annual rankings of companies that have built the most valuable global brands. To be considered, each company must have a value of at least $1 billion, earn at least one-third of earnings outside its home country, and have publicly available marketing and financial data. Only a small fraction of all brands play in the league of the best global brands, but all brand managers can gain insight into how the best and the biggest built their images and stayed in the branding forefront.

The issue hits magazine racks annually in July. To read the most recent report online, go to www.businessweek.com, click on BW Magazine, then pull down the menu item labeled Innovation and click on Brand Equity.

Checking Out a Trademark Information Center

When it comes time to protect your brand, visit registeringatrademark.com for a good information overview. The site has links to the U.S. Patent and Trademark Office and other resources as well as answers to frequently asked questions about trademarks, copyrights, and incorporation issues.

Index

culture/cultural trends *(continued)*
  golden rule of branding for, 331–332
  international markets and, 40–41
  keeping brands close to, 75–76
  logo design and, 133
customer profiling
  behavioral patterns in, 64, 82–83
  demographics in, 63
  geographics in, 63
  identifying the ideal customer by, 65–67
  market research and, 61–62
  marketing sourcebooks for, 75
  product positioning and, 82–83
  tracking inquiries by, 66
customer research. *See also* focus groups;
      interviews; market research; surveys
  brand experience and, 62, 66–67
  brand name selection and, 113–114
  identifying noncustomers, 76
  Internet resources for, 74
  library resources for, 74–75
  listening to your customer as, 68–69
  observing behaviors as, 70–71, 83
  previewing a brand story with, 152–153
  self-assessment as, 67–68
  using outside resources for, 73–74
customer satisfaction
  avoiding mistakes in, 337
  brand awareness and, 11–12
  brand experience as, 19, 23, 77, 242–243, 331
  brand experience assessment, 151–153, 162,
      243–246
  brand value and, 343–344
  complaints as input to, 69
  emotion plays role in, 50–51
  expectations, 246–248
  firsthand experience and, 86
  logo as expression of, 27
  point of difference and, 81
customer service
  assessing your, 67–68, 243–244
  brand promises and, 9–10, 23, 102,
      228–230, 337
  empowering employee for, 233
  market research and, 68–69
  product marketing and, 25
  service cycle and, 152
  web-based, 205
customers. *See also* consumers
  brand value impact on, 259–260
  defined, 2
  geodemographics, 63

golden rule of branding for, 329, 331
identifying the ideal, 65–66
identifying wants and values of, 64–65
inquiries are prospective, 66
listening to, 68–73
market research and, 32–33, 61–62
service cycle, 152
wish list, 68–69
Cystic Fibrosis Foundation, 92

• D •

Deere and Company, 98, 132, 229
demographics
  customer profiling and, 63, 83
  Internet resources for, 74
  marketing sourcebooks for, 75
  targeting media outlets from, 173–174
demonstrations, differentiation by, 81
Designing Brand Identity (Wheeler), 346
DieHard batteries (Sears), 106
differentiation. *See also* point of difference
      (point of distinction)
  avoiding mistakes in, 335–336
  as brand strategy, 51
  brand value in, 342
  branding and, 23
  budgeting and product, 55
  commodity substitution and, 12, 24–26
  market positioning and, 33
  market research determines, 32–33
  personal brands establish, 28
  unique selling position and, 80–82
direct mail, 159
disasters, natural or man-made. *See* crisis
      management
Disney. *See* Walt Disney Studios
Disney, Walt, 75. *See also* Walt Disney Studios
distinction. *See also* point of difference (point of
      distinction)
  advertising creates, 201
  benchmarking brand, 154–156
  commodity-to-brand differentiation, 12–14
  competition requires, 242–245
  differentiation and, 51–52, 252
  identifying, 20, 30, 47, 232, 289–291
  licensing creates, 279
  logos as source of, 128–129
  positioning for, 81, 86–88
  as purchasing motivation, 53
  taglines as source of, 140–142

• R •

BUSINESS, CAREERS & PERSONAL FINANCE

0-7645-5307-0 (Grant Writing For Dummies)

0-7645-5331-3 *† (Home Buying For Dummies)

Also available:
- Accounting For Dummies †
  0-7645-5314-3
- Business Plans Kit For Dummies †
  0-7645-5365-8
- Cover Letters For Dummies
  0-7645-5224-4
- Frugal Living For Dummies
  0-7645-5403-4
- Leadership For Dummies
  0-7645-5176-0
- Managing For Dummies
  0-7645-1771-6

- Marketing For Dummies
  0-7645-5600-2
- Personal Finance For Dummies *
  0-7645-2590-5
- Project Management For Dummies
  0-7645-5283-X
- Resumes For Dummies †
  0-7645-5471-9
- Selling For Dummies
  0-7645-5363-1
- Small Business Kit For Dummies *†
  0-7645-5093-4

HOME & BUSINESS COMPUTER BASICS

0-7645-4074-2 (Windows XP For Dummies)

0-7645-3758-X (Excel 2003 All-in-One Desk Reference For Dummies)

Also available:
- ACT! 6 For Dummies
  0-7645-2645-6
- iLife '04 All-in-One Desk Reference
  For Dummies
  0-7645-7347-0
- iPAQ For Dummies
  0-7645-6769-1
- Mac OS X Panther Timesaving
  Techniques For Dummies
  0-7645-5812-9
- Macs For Dummies
  0-7645-5656-8

- Microsoft Money 2004 For Dummies
  0-7645-4195-1
- Office 2003 All-in-One Desk Reference
  For Dummies
  0-7645-3883-7
- Outlook 2003 For Dummies
  0-7645-3759-8
- PCs For Dummies
  0-7645-4074-2
- TiVo For Dummies
  0-7645-6923-6
- Upgrading and Fixing PCs For Dummies
  0-7645-1665-5
- Windows XP Timesaving Techniques
  For Dummies
  0-7645-3748-2

FOOD, HOME, GARDEN, HOBBIES, MUSIC & PETS

0-7645-5295-3 (Feng Shui For Dummies)

0-7645-5232-5 (Poker For Dummies)

Also available:
- Bass Guitar For Dummies
  0-7645-2487-9
- Diabetes Cookbook For Dummies
  0-7645-5230-9
- Gardening For Dummies *
  0-7645-5130-2
- Guitar For Dummies
  0-7645-5106-X
- Holiday Decorating For Dummies
  0-7645-2570-0
- Home Improvement All-in-One
  For Dummies
  0-7645-5680-0

- Knitting For Dummies
  0-7645-5395-X
- Piano For Dummies
  0-7645-5105-1
- Puppies For Dummies
  0-7645-5255-4
- Scrapbooking For Dummies
  0-7645-7208-3
- Senior Dogs For Dummies
  0-7645-5818-8
- Singing For Dummies
  0-7645-2475-5
- 30-Minute Meals For Dummies
  0-7645-2589-1

INTERNET & DIGITAL MEDIA

0-7645-1664-7 (Digital Photography For Dummies)

0-7645-6924-4 (Starting an eBay Business For Dummies)

Also available:
- 2005 Online Shopping Directory
  For Dummies
  0-7645-7495-7
- CD & DVD Recording For Dummies
  0-7645-5956-7
- eBay For Dummies
  0-7645-5654-1
- Fighting Spam For Dummies
  0-7645-5965-6
- Genealogy Online For Dummies
  0-7645-5964-8
- Google For Dummies
  0-7645-4420-9

- Home Recording For Musicians
  For Dummies
  0-7645-1634-5
- The Internet For Dummies
  0-7645-4173-0
- iPod & iTunes For Dummies
  0-7645-7772-7
- Preventing Identity Theft For Dummies
  0-7645-7336-5
- Pro Tools All-in-One Desk Reference
  For Dummies
  0-7645-5714-9
- Roxio Easy Media Creator For Dummies
  0-7645-7131-1

* Separate Canadian edition also available
† Separate U.K. edition also available

Available wherever books are sold. For more information or to order direct: U.S. customers visit www.dummies.com or call 1-877-762-2974.
U.K. customers visit www.wileyeurope.com or call 0800 243407. Canadian customers visit www.wiley.ca or call 1-800-567-4797.

WILEY

RTS, FITNESS, PARENTING, RELIGION & SPIRITUALITY

0-7645-5146-9

0-7645-5418-2

Also available:
- Adoption For Dummies
  0-7645-5488-3
- Basketball For Dummies
  0-7645-5248-1
- The Bible For Dummies
  0-7645-5296-1
- Buddhism For Dummies
  0-7645-5359-3
- Catholicism For Dummies
  0-7645-5391-7
- Hockey For Dummies
  0-7645-5228-7

- Judaism For Dummies
  0-7645-5299-6
- Martial Arts For Dummies
  0-7645-5358-5
- Pilates For Dummies
  0-7645-5397-6
- Religion For Dummies
  0-7645-5264-3
- Teaching Kids to Read For Dummies
  0-7645-4043-2
- Weight Training For Dummies
  0-7645-5168-X
- Yoga For Dummies
  0-7645-5117-5

TRAVEL

0-7645-5438-7

0-7645-5453-0

Also available:
- Alaska For Dummies
  0-7645-1761-9
- Arizona For Dummies
  0-7645-6938-4
- Cancún and the Yucatán For Dummies
  0-7645-2437-2
- Cruise Vacations For Dummies
  0-7645-6941-4
- Europe For Dummies
  0-7645-5456-5
- Ireland For Dummies
  0-7645-5455-7

- Las Vegas For Dummies
  0-7645-5448-4
- London For Dummies
  0-7645-4277-X
- New York City For Dummies
  0-7645-6945-7
- Paris For Dummies
  0-7645-5494-8
- RV Vacations For Dummies
  0-7645-5443-3
- Walt Disney World & Orlando For Dummies
  0-7645-6943-0

GRAPHICS, DESIGN & WEB DEVELOPMENT

0-7645-4345-8

0-7645-5589-8

Also available:
- Adobe Acrobat 6 PDF For Dummies
  0-7645-3760-1
- Building a Web Site For Dummies
  0-7645-7144-3
- Dreamweaver MX 2004 For Dummies
  0-7645-4342-3
- FrontPage 2003 For Dummies
  0-7645-3882-9
- HTML 4 For Dummies
  0-7645-1995-6
- Illustrator CS For Dummies
  0-7645-4084-X

- Macromedia Flash MX 2004 For Dummies
  0-7645-4358-X
- Photoshop 7 All-in-One Desk Reference For Dummies
  0-7645-1667-1
- Photoshop CS Timesaving Techniques For Dummies
  0-7645-6782-9
- PHP 5 For Dummies
  0-7645-4166-8
- PowerPoint 2003 For Dummies
  0-7645-3908-6
- QuarkXPress 6 For Dummies
  0-7645-2593-X

NETWORKING, SECURITY, PROGRAMMING & DATABASES

0-7645-6852-3

0-7645-5784-X

Also available:
- A+ Certification For Dummies
  0-7645-4187-0
- Access 2003 All-in-One Desk Reference For Dummies
  0-7645-3988-4
- Beginning Programming For Dummies
  0-7645-4997-9
- C For Dummies
  0-7645-7068-4
- Firewalls For Dummies
  0-7645-4048-3
- Home Networking For Dummies
  0-7645-4279-6

- Network Security For Dummies
  0-7645-1679-5
- Networking For Dummies
  0-7645-1677-9
- TCP/IP For Dummies
  0-7645-1760-0
- VBA For Dummies
  0-7645-3989-2
- Wireless All-in-One Desk Reference For Dummies
  0-7645-7496-5
- Wireless Home Networking For Dummies
  0-7645-3910-8